Paths Towards a New World

Neolithic Sweden

Mats Larsson

with

Geoffrey Lemdahl and Kerstin Lidén

Oxbow Books

Oxford & Philadelphia

Published in the United Kingdom in 2014 by
OXBOW BOOKS
10 Hythe Bridge Street, Oxford OX1 2EW

and in the United States by
OXBOW BOOKS
908 Darby Road, Havertown, PA 19083

Paperback Edition: ISBN 978-1-78297-257-0
Digital Edition: ISBN 978-1-78297-258-7

A CIP record for this book is available from the British Library

Printed in the United Kingdom by Hobbs the Printers, Totton, Hampshire

For a complete list of Oxbow titles, please contact:

UNITED KINGDOM
Oxbow Books
Telephone (01865) 241249, Fax (01865) 794449
Email: oxbow@oxbowbooks.com
www.oxbowbooks.com

UNITED STATES OF AMERICA
Oxbow Books
Telephone (800) 791-9354, Fax (610) 853-9146
Email: queries@casemateacademic.com
www.casemateacademic.com/oxbow

Oxbow Books is part of the Casemate group

Front cover: Long dolmen at Skegrie in Scania (photograph: M. Larsson).
Back cover: *Döserygg*. Re-creation of what the site may have looked like 5,500 years ago (source: Andersson and Nilsson 2009).

Contents

Preface

One year of writing and reflecting has now come to an end and it is now up to the reader to judge the results. Is this the book that I began writing in 2010? Both yes and no is the cryptic answer. Yes, since I managed to limit the amount of text to a somewhat reasonable size, and that I was also able to include the material that I originally intended. No, as I have surely forgotten or neglected places and material that perhaps should have been included. In this case, the fault is my own.

I would like to take the opportunity to thank both individuals and institutions that have helped me in putting this book together. First, I'd like to express a great big thank-you to my dear wife Ylva who has supported me throughout my entire archaeological career, from my dissertation in 1984 up until this book. Thank you!

I would also like to thank the rest of my family – Per, Malin and Stefan, and especially my grandchildren Maja and Måns, who sometimes enticed me to forget all about archaeology.

Thanks also to Professor Roland Hallgren for his support and friendship, as well as the proofreading he performed with such a sharp eye. A big thank-you should also go to Professor Lars Larsson, for many jolly laughs throughout the years, as well as his constructive criticism on the manuscript.

The contributions written by Professors Geoffrey Lemdahl and Kerstin Lidén raise the quality of the book, and without these contributions, I would have been badly off. Thanks!

In addition, I would also like to thank all of my present as well as former colleagues and my friends for many stimulating discussions and meetings over the years. If I don't name any names, then I won't forget anyone! A special thanks goes to those who have generously allowed me to use pictures and illustrations – N. H. Andersen, P. O. Nielsen, M. Andersson, F. Hallgren, K. Jennbert, E. Rudebeck, N. Björck, K. Brink, C. Tilley and H. Browall.

Linköping, February 2012
Mats Larsson

Introduction

Mats Larsson

The idea for this book came to me during one of my many drives commuting between Linköping and Kalmar. Why not write a book about the younger Stone Age in Sweden, a period to which I have dedicated so many years? The target audience would be archaeology students and archaeologists in general, as well as other interested readers. I also began pondering over what I would include in the book. Sweden is a large country with very diverse conditions and research traditions. In this case, I am referring to the natural conditions necessary for early agriculture, for example, as well as how different research traditions emerged. The extensive number of studies during recent years and the abundance of significant new results also meant that the choices were not very easy or self-evident. It is impossible to describe in detail or discuss the quite extensive archaeological material we have today from the younger Stone Age; therefore, I have chosen to discuss fundamental research perspectives concerning the period. I have chosen the sites with this in mind. The selection is my own and reflects my own research interest. Thus, it is not a coincidence that I focus on southern and middle Sweden, though the country's northern regions are in no way forgotten.

The in many ways problematic concept of culture is, and has been, much discussed, especially within research concerning the younger Stone Age, and this is something one should be aware of. However, for the sake of both simplicity and clarity, I have chosen to retain and use the established culture designations such as the Ertebølle Culture, the Funnel Beaker Culture, the Pitted Ware Culture and the Battle Axe Culture. We will look at what these represent in the following chapters.

The quotation from Verner von Heidenstam found below can be seen as a contribution to a long archaeological debate that is still relevant today. Within modern archaeological research, we are still discussing, for example, certain Neolithic cultures' eastern or southern origins and contacts. We should however be wary of trying to see Stone Age people as 'indigenous peoples' who were homogenous throughout the geographical region we today call Sweden. Channels of contact, travel and exchange of goods and ideas changed the relationships between people, but also led development in different parts of the country to diverge.

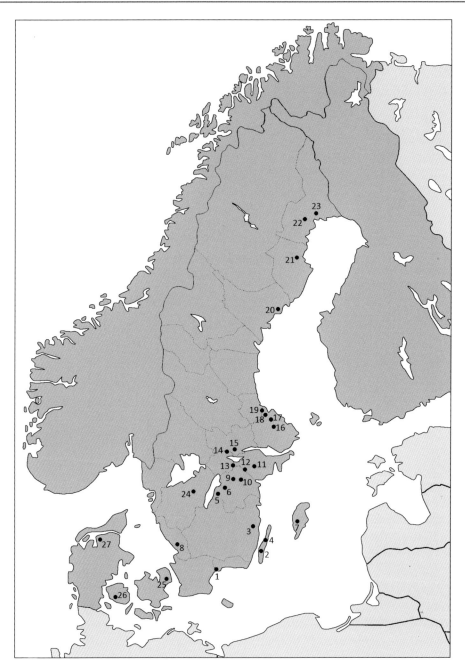

I.1. *Map of Sweden with some of the sites mentioned in the text.*
1. *Siretorp; 2. Resmo; 3. Lilla Mark; 4. Köpingsvik; 5. Alvastra; 6. The Linköping region; 7. Ajvide; 8. Hästhagen,
Slottsmöllan; 9. Åby; 10. Fagervik; 11. Mogetorp; 12. Östra Vrå; 13. Pärlängsberget; 14. Skogsmossen; 15. Fågelbacken;
16. Kyrsta; 17. Bällinge Bog; 18. Högmossen; 19. Fräkenrönningen; 20. Bjästamon; 21. Bjurselet; 22. Voullerim;
23. Lillberget; 24. Rössberga (the Falbygden region); 25. Vedbæk; 26. Sarup; 27. Ertebølle.*

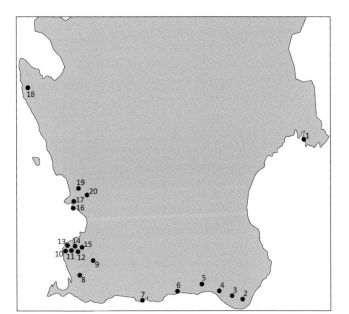

I.2. *Scania, Sweden, showing selected sites.*
1. *Siretorp; 2. Hagestad region;*
3. *Carlshögen; 4. Kabusa;*
5. *Piledal; 6. Mossby; 7. Skateholm;*
8. *Döserygg; 9. Svenstorp; 10. Hyllie;*
11. *Kastanjegården; 12. Fosie IV;*
13. *Hindby Bog; 14. Almhov;*
15. *Soldattorpet; 16. Löddesborg;*
17. *Gillhög; 18. Jonstorp; 19. Dösjebro;*
20. *Stävie.*

Period	Chronology
Late Mesolithic	4600–4000 BC
Primary Early Neolithic	3950–3650 BC
Secondary Early Neolithic	3650–3300 BC
MN A (Funnel Beaker Culture, Pitted Ware Culture)	3300–2700 BC
MN B (Battle Axe Culture)	2700–2350 BC
Late Neolithic	2350–1800 BC

Chronology of the periods discussed in the volume.

"From where have we come?", asked Karilas and motioned questioningly with his hand, first towards the south and then towards the east. "Poets, who of you can answer Ura-Kaipa? Who can solve this mystery? Long have we lived here, and in time we learned to make our weapons shining like gold. I only know, poets, that none of your old local legends tell about such a bright and lovely summer night, and here we will make ourselves a country for people."

(Heidenstam 1915)

In order to make it easier for the reader, the book is chronologically structured and the individual chapters are thematically organized. The journey begins in the Late Mesolithic and ends with the transition to the Bronze Age many thousands of years later. I hope that the book will provide an introduction to the long and interesting period of the early Stone Age, and that it will encourage the reader to pursue further studies in the subject.

Before we begin our journey, I would like to point out that at the end of each chapter you will find a list of books and articles that should be seen as further in-depth readings. At the end of the book, you will find a bibliography of the literature on which my story is based.

1 Environmental History

Geoffrey Lemdahl

Palaeoecological research deals with reconstructing prehistoric environments, ecosystems and landscapes and how these have been affected by different disturbances such as climate change, fire or human actions. Palaeoecology is primarily the study of geological archives. Archaeology also works with geological archives; that is to say, archaeologists dig through the subsoil searching for discoveries that can tell us about earlier human activities. Instead of looking for the remains of objects made by human hands, palaeoecologists look for biological remains, such as remnants of plants and animals. Chemical or physical analyses of soil samples may also be used. The combination of archaeological and palaeoecological investigations is often very useful in solving certain specific problems concerning how humans have shaped previously natural environments or how natural conditions have affected the development of cultures.

Geological archives

Remains from plants and animals are best preserved in oxygen deficient environments, often meaning that the preservation environment was damp or wet when the remains were deposited in the soil. Natural environments that meet this requirement are riverbeds and lake bottoms, fens and bogs. The smallest plant residues such as pollen and spores from land plants are usually dispersed in the air in quite large amounts, which then fall down onto water or land areas mixing with soil sediments and sod. Larger plant remnants such as seeds, fruits, nuts, leaves, twigs and bits of wood will also be deposited in the soil layers. Remains from animals are generally rarer than those from plants; skeletal parts and shells are what are primarily preserved. Taking samples from natural sediment and peat layers is best accomplished using some type of coring equipment that can extract undisturbed core samples through the layers; alternatively, samples can be obtained in open sections by removing samples directly from the walls.

At archaeological excavations, especially those at settlement sites, there are good chances of finding biological remains if there are damp or wet areas at or near the excavation site. Examples of opportune locations for sampling are wells, draining ditches, rubbish dumps and latrines.

Methods of analysis

Pollen analysis

The Swedish geologist Lennart von Post was the first researcher who, at the beginning of the 1920s, began analysing pollen grains in soil samples in order to reconstruct what the flora was like during different periods. Pollen grains, spores and charcoal particles can be identified and counted using a microscope (100–1000 times magnification). In order to concentrate the pollen, samples measuring one cubic centimetre are treated in various chemical stages. The advantage of analysing pollen is that plants produce large amounts of pollen or spores, which are well preserved in moist soil samples. The disadvantage is that determination of species is not possible for many kinds of pollen and they therefore can only be identified to genus or family. The amount of pollen produced varies greatly between different species of plants. Insect-pollinated plants for example are under represented when compared with wind-pollinated plants. The size of the lake or peat bog surfaces regulates what the results represent. A large area (>100 m in diameter) provides a picture of the vegetation in a larger region, while a smaller area (<50 m in diameter) provides a picture of the local vegetation (about one kilometre around the sampling point). Using new calibration methods, the pollen composition in samples can be translated into actual vegetation. Pollen analysis is currently the palaeoecological method most often used, even in archaeological contexts.

Plant macrofossil analysis

Macroscopic plant remains, *i.e.*, plant remains visible to the naked eye, have been systematically studied *in situ* in peat-cuttings as early as during the latter half of the 19th century. Plant remnants, in addition to most macroscopic remains, are normally best preserved in moist environments; however, charred material can also be preserved in deposits that are more arid. Soil samples with a volume of one decilitre are wet sieved after being dissolved in a weak solution of sodium hydroxide (*c.* 10 %). The fine-grained material is 'washed' out of the dissolved soil sample through a sieve with a mesh size of between 0.25–0.50 mm and what is left are discernible plant and animal remnants. Next, the seeds, fruits, nuts, leaf residues and sometimes buds, twigs and pieces of wood are sorted out with the aid of a binocular microscope so that they can be identified. It is often possible to identify the species of relatively intact seeds, fruits, nuts and leaves. By examining the cell structure in a thin section of wood, the species of tree or bush from which the wood came can be identified. Analysis of plant macrofossils is usually the most appropriate method for examining samples taken at settlements and from other structures. The results of the analysis provide information about the local vegetation and, for example, the kinds of useful plants that were grown and utilized. The same samples can be analysed for animal remains.

Analysis of bone and shell remains

Bones and teeth from vertebrates and shells from molluscs are preserved in calcareous, alkaline environments. They can also be preserved in dry environments. In acidic environments, the material is often quickly broken down. Bones, teeth and horns/antlers from larger animals are uncovered directly during excavation, while for smaller animals it is more appropriate to use the same method used for plant macrofossil analysis, wet sieving. In addition to information about species composition, skeletal material can also tell us about the age, size and sex of the animals as well as whether they had been injured or had diseases. Fish bones, fish scales and mollusc shells provide information about the utilization of aquatic resources. Shell-findings can provide an estimate of the openness of the site.

Insect analysis

Insects and crustaceans usually have a robust exoskeleton primarily composed of chitin. Remains of chitin are often common in both lake sediments and peat and can be preserved even under more acidic conditions; however, chitin is susceptible to desiccation. Methods similar to those used for plant macrofossils are used here and the analyses can therefore be advantageously performed at the same time. Without comparison, insects make up our most species-rich group of animals. Insects have adapted to a number of different environments, kinds of climate and food choices. Terrestrial insects often dominate the insect remains. Insect finds can for example provide information about the openness of the landscape (ground-dwelling insects), the presence of grazing animals (dung beetles), materials used in building construction (wood-living insects), the occurrence of running or still water (water-living insects) and vermin in different kinds of food products. This is information that is unique and cannot be interpreted using other methods.

Dating

The most common absolute dating methods used in archaeology are radiocarbon dating and dendrochronology. W. Libby discovered and introduced the radiocarbon method at the end of the 1940s. The radioactive carbon isotope forms in the atmosphere and is absorbed by the photosynthetic system of plants, where it is chemically bound to the organic matter. This is when the radioactive clock starts. After 5,730 years, half of the Carbon 14 (^{14}C) remains in the material (half-life), after another period of 5,730 years, one fourth of the original amount remains, *etc*. Previously, radioactivity was measured in a test that could take several days (the conventional method). Now, the amount of ^{14}C is 'weighed' using accelerator mass spectrometry, taking only a few minutes for each sample. All samples that contain carbon in any form, *i.e.*, organic material, can be dated. In an international research collaboration during the 1980s, through the dating of tree-rings it was discovered that the ^{14}C levels in the atmosphere have varied in different periods and that a ^{14}C-year is therefore not the same as a normal calendar year. Thus, the ^{14}C age obtained must be calibrated by projecting time scales to calendar years, something easily done with computer programs that continuously update the process. Today, ^{14}C laboratories conduct the calibrations as a matter of routine. However, one should be aware that dating results in older publications (up until the 1990s) may refer to ^{14}C-years.

Dendrochronological dating is based on counting annual rings in pieces of wood. More or less clear annual rings can be seen in several different kinds of trees, but not all. An annual ring is created when the summer growth of the tree produces a lighter layer of larger wood cells that are delineated from the winter layer, which is darker due to the cells being smaller and denser. The relative variation in thickness of annual rings within the same tree species in a region is determined by the temperature and precipitation conditions during the year. As these conditions change, the thickness of the annual rings differs from year to year. Only annual rings within the same tree species and the same region can be compared. By overlapping tree-ring series, beginning with living trees and through to the lumber in buildings, and then through the overlapping of logs found in peat bogs for example, one can construct so-called dendrochronological reference curves. In southern Sweden, the reference curve is based on annual rings from oak, while reference curves in central and northern Sweden are based on annual rings from pine. In southern Sweden, the reference curve goes back to over 2,000 years ago, while the curve for Lapland goes back 7,500 years. Thus, comparing the series of annual rings with variable thickness with the data from the reference curve can provide the date for a piece of wood. This requires that the piece of wood comes from the same region as the reference curve and that the wood comes from the same kind of tree. Dating reliability is dependent on how many annual rings the piece of wood contains. Dendrochronological dating can be used even farther back in time than for the period the reference curve covers. One application is to analyse pieces of wood from a structure or settlement in order to find out how long it was in use. Building material from the Alvastra pile dwelling in this way could provide valuable information about how long the structures had been used. No absolute dates for the pieces of wood are obtained; however, a so-called floating chronology is determined, which can also be quite valuable.

Examples of palaeoecological applications

Today, environmental history analyses are conducted almost as a matter of routine in conjunction with archaeological excavations; however, often only a few analytical methods are utilized, for example analyses of charcoal, bones and pollen, and the results are often separated from each other. A better concept for gaining a more relevant and detailed picture of the historical landscape and settlement environments is to combine as many palaeoecological analyses as possible and allow the experts to cooperate in sampling, analysing and the final interpretation of results. Each method provides its piece of the puzzle to create a general picture of the environmental history. There are several examples of such successful collaborative projects regarding Mesolithic and Neolithic sites. Following are a few examples from Sweden, which have in common that the sites were located at or near wetlands where conditions for preservation were optimal.

In conjunction with the site excavations at the Ageröd V settlement at Ringsjön in Scania, pollen, macroscopic plant remains including wood and charcoal, bones from mammals, birds and fish, as well as insect remains were all analysed. Based on the results of the analyses of plant and insect remains, a relatively detailed picture can be given of the local environment of that time around the settlement. This points towards an environment with great biological diversity, which would have been optimal for a hunter-gatherer culture. This rich environment is reflected in a very concrete manner in the identified bone material, where animals hunted included chiefly red deer, European elk, wild boar and roe deer, as well as important fur-bearing animals such as marten, polecat, otter and possibly brown bear. Hunting was supplemented with snared birds and fish from wetland areas, which during this period was largely made up of a lake.

At the excavation at Alvastra spring fen (pile dwelling) in Östergötland, several different palaeoecological studies were also undertaken. These excavations were a very important part of reconstructing the building technology, determining how long the structure was in use, what the local environment was like and what activities took place at this Middle Neolithic pile dwelling. In addition to determining the kinds of trees used for the platform, the wood analyses show that wood from younger trees, probably from coppice forest, was also used. The analyses also show that the structure was utilized during a relatively short time and was primarily used as a cult centre for what were probably brief ceremonies. However, results from the analyses of macroscopic plant remains, remains from animal droppings as well as insect remains provide a different picture. These results indicate that animals have been stabled on the platform and been fed there. In particular, the earliest find in Scandinavia of a housefly provides definite evidence of farmyard manure. For comparison, we can mention a Central European project based on the excavation of a pile dwelling settlement on the shore of Lake Constance, Arbon Bleich 3. In addition to very meticulous archaeological studies, a large international research team has also conducted palaeoecological studies. Based on these results, a quite detailed picture of the daily life at the settlement could be reconstructed, as well as information regarding living conditions, economy and the local environment.

At Stavsåkra, north of Växjö and Lake Helgasjön, grave structures and isolated finds indicate continuous settlement, at least from the Neolithic period. One of the questions addressed was how open the landscape was during the Neolithic and Bronze Ages, and how the grave structures were exposed. After detailed fieldwork in a small forest bog adjacent to the site, a continuous sequence of lake sediment and peat deposits was discovered stretching from the end of the last ice age to the present, *i.e.*, about the past 12,000 years. From the same sequence pollen, macroscopic plant remains, charcoal and insect remains were analysed. The results of the studies provided a unique picture of the area's local forest and landscape history during the past 10,600 years. The results from all of the analyses indicate that about 4,400 years before our present time, the landscape became more open, mostly due to slash-and-burn agriculture and grazing. About 2,800 years before present, grasslands began to be transformed into heath land dominated by heather due to increasingly more intensive grazing on relatively nutrient-poor tills. After the planting of coniferous trees and the discontinuation of grazing and meadowland at the beginning of the 20th century, relatively dense coniferous forests now dominate the Stavsåkra area. The environmental history data that emerged from the analyses indicate that the grave monument at Stavsåkra was well exposed in the landscape and that the Bronze Age mounds were likely visible far and wide.

Suggested readings

Bartholin, T. S. 1978. Alvastra pile dwelling: Tree studies. The dating and the landscape. *Fornvännen* 73, 213–219.

Browall, H. 1986. *Alvastra pålbyggnad – social och ekonomisk bas.* Theses and Papers in North-European Archaeology 15.

Bell, M. and Walker, M. J. C. 2005. *Late Quaternary Environmental Change – Physical and Human Perspectives.* Pearson Education Ltd.

Greisman, A. 2009. *The role of fire and human impact in Holocene forest and landscape dynamics of the bore-nemoral zone of southern Sweden – a multiproxy study of two sites in the province of Småland.* University of Kalmar, Faculty of Natural Sciences, Dissertation Series nr 62.

Greisman, A. and Gaillard, M.-J. 2009. The role of climate variability and fire in early and mid Holocene forest dynamics of southern Sweden. *Journal of Quaternary Science* 24, 593–611.

Göransson, H. 1987. *Neolithic Man and the forest environment around Alvastra Pile Dwelling.* Theses and Papers in North-European Archaeology 20.

Göransson, H. 2002. Alvastra pile dwelling – a 5000-year old byre? In Nordic Archaeobotany – NAG 2000 in Umeå, Viklund, K. (ed.). *Nordic Archaeobotany and Environment* 15, 67–84.

Jacomet, S., Leuzinger, U. and Schibler, J. 2004. *Die jungsteinzeitliche Seeufersiedlung Arbon Bleiche 3. Umwelt und Wirtschaft.* Archäologie im Thurgau, band 12.

Larsson, L. 1983. *Ageröd V. An Atlantic bog site in Central Scania.* Acta Archaeologica Lundensia Series in 8°, nr 12.

Lowe, J. J. and Walker, M. J. C. 1997. *Reconstructing Quaternary Environments.* Longman.

Olsson, F. and Lemdahl, G. 2009. A continuous Holocene beetle record from the site Stavsåkra, southern Sweden: implications for the last 10,600 years of forest and land use history. *Journal of Quaternary Science* 24, 612–626.

Olsson, F., Gaillard, M.-J., Lemdahl, G., Greisman, A., Lanos, P., Marguerie, D., Marcoux, N., Skoglund, P. and Wäglind, J. 2010. A continuous record of fire covering the last 10,500 calendar years from southern Sweden – The role of climate and human activities. *Palaeogeography, Palaeoclimatology, Palaeoecology* 291, 128–141.

Roberts, N. 1998. *The Holocene – An Environmental History.* Blackwell Publishers Ltd.

Skoglund, P. 2005. *Vardagens landskap: lokala perspektiv på bronsålderns materiella kultur.* Almquist and Wiksell International, Stockholm.

Sugita, S. 2007. Theory of quantitative reconstruction of vegetation. I. Pollen from large sites REVEALS regional vegetation composition. *The Holocene* 17, 229–241.

Sugita, S. 2007. Theory of quantitative reconstruction of vegetation. II. All you need is LOVE. *The Holocene* 17, 243–257.

2 The Mesolithic Period and the Stone Age Hunters

Mats Larsson

The earliest research about the older Stone Age, or in archaeological terms the Mesolithic period (*c*. 10000–4000 BC), was centred on 'object research', with dating and cultural concepts as primary components.

During the early twentieth century, research studies from Denmark characterized research on the Mesolithic period. The so-called Ertebølle Commission conducted extensive archaeological studies at the Ertebølle site as well as at the older site of Mullerup on Själland. Scientific influences had a strong effect on these investigations.

Studies of Mesolithic settlements did not develop in Scandinavia until after 1940 however, and then only with obvious influences from British archaeology where studies of settlements were connected with scientific investigations in order to create a picture of how people lived and what the landscape they moved about in looked like. This can be directly connected to the older Danish studies. During the following decades, a 'biological' and economical orientation began to characterize the research. At this time, Mesolithic societies were often portrayed as mobile, nomadic hunting societies with a material culture, *i.e.*, tools and other objects, which were similar across large areas. Great emphasis was placed on ecological conditions and the effect the environment had on the settlements. It was not until the 1970s before attention was given to new impulses within research on the Mesolithic. This new research came to be characterized largely by what was later called 'New Archaeology', which clearly focused on economy and settlement structure. Conclusions thus were often based on studies within social anthropology. In this research tradition, it was important to be able to establish social identities and territories. Consequently, studies of material culture were to a great extent directed towards such questions.

The period between *c*. 4600 and 4000 BC constitutes the latest part of the Mesolithic. In order to understand what happened after 4000 BC, it is important that we have a clear understanding regarding what took place in the previous period. During the Mesolithic, living conditions in the area we today recognize as Sweden underwent radical changes. We can begin by examining historical changes of the shorelines in different parts of the country. Shorelines underwent dramatic changes during this period. The melting of glaciers and polar ice resulted in a dramatic elevation of land in the north, while large areas of land in the south became submerged under water. Öresund and the Danish straits were formed, which led to an inflow of saltwater into what are today known as the Baltic Sea and the Littorina Sea. The name Littorina comes from the saltwater snail *Litorina litorea*. The salinity was approximately two to three times greater than in the Baltic Sea of today, which resulted in a much more species-rich marine fauna. The coastline of the Littorina Sea varied greatly over time and many beach ridges were formed that are still visible in the landscape. Most studies in southern Scandinavia show that five or at most seven transgressions or sea level changes occurred. The land elevation that took place around 4000 BC reached a maximum of 115 metres in northern Sweden, *c.* 55 metres in Central Sweden, and in southern Sweden reached *c.* 5 metres over today's sea level (Fig. 2.1).

During the long period of time covered by the Mesolithic, radical changes took place regarding both natural conditions and settlements. Human interactions changed and new social structures emerged. After the arrival of the first people to the area about 15,000 years ago, living conditions changed regarding several significant points: the climate became warmer, forests successively covered more land area, the number of animal species increased thus allowing the establishment of new potential prey species, and the population grew, resulting in changes in the interactions between people. Since this is quite a long story, I will therefore focus on what happened during the last 400–500 years of the period. Considerations regarding the length of the book are not the only reasons for this. As we shall see, the relationships between people and the interactions between different regions in Sweden underwent noticeable changes during this period.

The last hunters

We will begin our survey in southernmost Sweden and Denmark where we see how the late Mesolithic Ertebølle Culture changes during this period. The Ertebølle Culture occurred throughout southern Scandinavia with concentrations in the Swedish areas of Scania, Blekinge in the southeast and Halland to the west, as well as in Denmark and in northern Germany. The Ertebølle Culture existed between *c.* 5500 BC and *c.* 4000 BC The culture went through a dynamic developmental phase during this long period of time, and it is this story that follows. We can see completely new designs in the material culture, like pottery, but also how cultural contacts with the continent intensified and developed during the period (Fig. 2.2).

The name Ertebølle comes from a classic settlement in northwest Jylland in Denmark. The large shellfish banks, called kitchen middens, could sometimes stretch for more than 100 metres along the coast and were primarily characteristic of the West-Danish Ertebølle Culture. One of the most studied of these sites, Norsminde, south of Aarhus, was in use a very long time, 5050–4050 BC This indicates a more or less continuous settlement over a period of 1000 years. These kitchen middens are actually large rubbish dumps with large amounts of garbage left over from meals. One interesting element in the diets of these people was the large quantities of oysters consumed. Studies of human skeletons quite clearly show that people from this period seemed to enjoy eating shellfish, fish and marine mammals.

We have clear evidence that not only the coastal regions were used during this period, but

Figure 2.1. Map of Scandinavia around 4000 BC showing the coastline of the Littorina Sea (source: Jensen 2001).

also the inland regions. All together, the picture clearly indicates that people used a broad spectrum of resources and ecological zones, from Jylland's fjords to Scania's interior. One recognized assumption that has been held true for a long time is that populations moved around in a seasonal pattern of settlement, from the sea shore to inland areas, and vice versa. Summer/Autumn were spent inland while winters were primarily spent along the coasts. Researchers have recently begun discussing whether people actually followed a movement pattern such as this. The material discovered at some of these inland sites like Bökeberg in Scania (for example bones from animals that had been hunted or fished) may indicate that people lived at the inland sites more or less permanently. However, the occurrence of both fish and marine mammals at other sites, Ringkloster in central Jylland for example, indicates that definite contacts existed with coastal sites like Norsminde. Indirectly, these hypotheses can be supported with measurements of carbon-13 levels in both human and dog skeletons. The analysis of a canine cranium from Bökeberg reveals low levels, which could indicate inland settlements; however, Per Karsten also draws attention to the problems with these analyses and argues that, today, we cannot clearly find support for the hypothesis of permanent inland settlement.

An important and often debated group of Ertebølle sites are the so-called 'mixed settlements' along what was then the coast of Scania in southern Sweden. One such site is Löddesborg, on the coast of Öresund. The settlement was situated on a beach ridge at Barsebäck. The shoreline at that time was about five metres higher than today's, and was characterized by bays and lagoons with extensive shallow areas. The site was excavated mostly during the 1960s. The excavation revealed that the site was complex, with traces

Figure 2.2. Example of a Ertebølle pot (source: Andersen 1981).

of several settlements. It is clear that the location was utilized over a long succession of years, from the early Ertebølle Culture and onwards. Particularly interesting is that a large amount of pottery was found. In total, 130 kg of pottery was found, with a clear majority from the Ertebølle Culture and only a small amount was Funnel Beaker pottery, *i.e.*, from the Primary Early Neolithic. The latter was mostly found in the upper regions of the site. The fact that both pottery types occurred together in most layers led archaeologist Kristina Jennbert to see the Funnel Beaker pottery as a part of the Ertebølle Culture, and that the introduction of an agricultural-based economy should be seen as a part of a gift-exchange system. This interpretation of the Löddesborg site led to a debate we will return to in the next chapter. There are other similar localities along Scania's coast, for example Soldattorpet, Elinelund (both in Malmö), Sandskogen (Ystad) and Vik (Simrishamn)(Fig. 2.3).

An important new element in the later part of the Mesolithic is that settlements are sometimes located together with grave-fields, like at Skateholm in southernmost Scania and Vedbæk outside of Copenhagen.

Skateholm, which was excavated by Lund researcher Lars Larsson at the beginning of the 1980s, includes three localities with a large chronological distribution. In general, the sites Skateholm I–III extend over the entire Ertebølle Culture. Radiocarbon dating using C^{14} dated the first site to between 5600 and 5400 BC Skateholm I dates to between 5200 and 4800 BC The youngest of these dates is also the endpoint for settlement at Skateholm I. The youngest site is Skateholm III. The site had been destroyed by a gravel pit, but by using a preserved skeleton has been dated to *c.* 4700 BC A large number of graves have been examined at Skateholm. Skateholm I included 64 graves with a total of 63 people and 7 dogs, while Skateholm II included 22 graves and 2 separately buried dogs. Interestingly, one

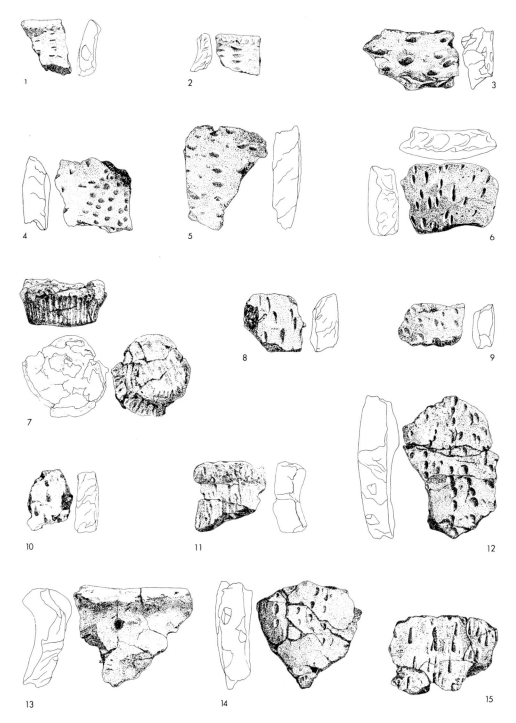

Figure 2.3. Ertebølle pottery from the Löddesborg settlement in Scania (source: Jennbert 1984).

of the graves richest in findings was a dog burial site. Based on preserved human skeletons, we can create a picture of how people lived as well as what they looked like. The individuals buried here reveal rather large variations in bodily constitution. Some individuals were more powerfully built, while others were more fragile. Men had an average height of 168 cm, but there were individuals who were 181 cm. Women had an average height of 155 cm, with variation between 150 and 160 cm.

Regarding average lifespan, men lived to be about 45 years old and women, 40 years old. One large problem when estimating average lifespan is infant mortality, which we assume was high.

One important aspect at Skateholm, as well as at Vedbæk, is the combination of settlements and grave-fields, which creates the impression that this was the normal arrangement for this period. We are able to study changes in burial rituals, social status and health in the material found.

The question of how people lived during this period is a major issue for researchers. There is no clear evidence that people actually lived at or near the kitchen middens. Apart from hearths, there is no clear evidence that houses or huts have been documented near the kitchen middens. During recent years however, our picture of the Ertebølle Culture's settlements has changed. One of the most exciting new discoveries is thus the excavation at Tågerup in western Scania, where a number of houses and huts have been excavated in connection with the extensive archaeological excavations. House I is a circular structure and House II is a rectangular longhouse with an area of *c.* 85 m² and with a line of centrally placed posts holding up the roof. House III measures 15 × 4.5 metres, with an opening towards the south. Dating of the houses is not so straightforward; it is based on flint tools such as transverse arrowheads as well as pottery found in House III. Pottery was not produced in southern Scandinavia before 4600 BC at the earliest. If this interpretation is correct, then the hut is younger than this.

There is also additional evidence for assigning the huts to the Ertebølle Culture. One example is the round hut from Bredasten, outside Ystad in Scania. It is older than the one mentioned above, however.

What kinds of contact networks did these people have? We can see that they had contacts with groups of people on the European continent who were already farmers. These groups are often collectively labelled Linear Pottery Culture. The unfamiliar objects that turn up in Denmark and Scania may be different kinds of ground stone axes and antler axes, whose origins can be traced to central parts of Europe. As far as we can judge, the motivation to begin making pottery came from the farmers on the continent as well as perhaps from the east.

What does the situation look like in other parts of Sweden? Interestingly, the groups of hunters that lived north of Scania have not received any kind of collective cultural name. There are historical reasons for this.

We begin our survey in the areas northeast of Scania – in Blekinge, Småland and on the island of Öland. The archaeological picture of the period is clearly much poorer here than in Scania and Denmark. One often hears of a research shadow over these areas. However, during the past few years this shadow has begun to dissolve. New studies have changed our picture regarding the late Mesolithic in these regions.

In Blekinge, the area most discussed has been the area around Siretorp in Listerlandet. The settlements here are located on coastal embankments and have a complex sequence of deposits. Archaeologists Axel Bagge and Knut Kjellmark conducted the most extensive studies of the area in the beginning of the 1930s. A settlement in the area called 'Furet' has been chiefly discussed. Ertebølle pottery has been found here between two strata containing Funnel Beaker pottery. This is the only evidence for such a sequence of deposits, and later studies, including excavations located near the one in question, have not been able to produce any kind of similar results. It has been suggested that these results might be due to rearrangement caused by violent storms or erosion.

During the later part of the Mesolithic, most of the objects typical for the Ertebølle Culture are absent from the area around the Kalmar Strait. One exception are the specially shaped arrowheads called transverse arrowheads, which are commonly found at settlements on Öland and in the southern part of the Kalmar Strait region, but are much more uncommon in the northern parts of the region. The settlement pattern in the Kalmar Strait region is characterized by large sites rich in findings, which are near estuaries and lagoons along the coast. Archaeological investigations at Hagbytorp south of Kalmar indicate that the large site can be divided into several smaller settlements that gradually grew together. This is very apparent when we look closer at the distribution of the finds. At these large base sites, the stone material is dominated by Kristianstad flint, which is a special type of flint from the area near Kristianstad in northeast Scania.

The largely unpublished material from the Alby site has long dominated the discussion about settlements from this period on Öland. A large amount of the material was uncovered in connection with excavations during the 1970s where in addition to a great deal of material from the Mesolithic, material from a later site belonging to the Primary Early Neolithic was also found. One interesting discovery was a grave containing the skeleton of a *c.* 30–year-old man. The skeleton was dated to 4300–3900 BC, which indicates the later part of the Mesolithic and would also be in agreement with the other material found at the site. The dating of a single human mandible from Köpingsvik to *c.* 4400–4200 BC clearly points to the same period. One additional grave should be mentioned. During an excavation in 2007 at Tings Ene (Köpingsvik), parts of a thick settlement deposit (or culture layer using the archaeological term) were examined, under which a grave was discovered. Unfortunately, the grave was so severely damaged that it could not be dated using the ^{14}C method. A piece of coal from the grave has however been dated to 4230–3970 BC, which is in clear agreement with the above-mentioned graves. Such a placement in time is also supported by the findings of transverse arrowheads in the culture layer.

In recent years, other localities from the late Mesolithic have also been discovered on Öland. In 2003, a culture layer of about 40 cm was excavated in a small area at Tingsdal in Köping. Using ^{14}C dating as well as the occurrence of transverse arrowheads, the site can be dated to the same period as those mentioned earlier.

We should also mention the site of Lilla Mark at Oskarshamn, located in the northern part of the Kalmar Strait region. The site was restricted to the coast and divided into three terraces. However, no chronological differences can be found between them. There are a significant number of ^{14}C dating analyses that can help us regarding dating of the site. Dating analyses from Terrace 1 stretch from 6000–4000 BC, which indicates the late Mesolithic. The area has obviously been visited and utilized a number of times during this long time period. Interesting to note is that flint occurs, but not in the same amounts as in the southern parts of the Kalmar Strait region. The people who lived at Lilla Mark have for the most part relied on local kinds of rocks such as quartz and quartzite.

In West Sweden, studies of the period began with extensive landscape inventories, which facilitated the continuance of the work. Studies of the inventory and attempts at compilation were begun as early as in the 1870s by Oscar Montelius and ended in 1923 with Georg Sarauw and Johan Alin. After extensive excavations at sites such as Sandarna, three decades of work systematizing the material followed. In many ways, one can see Åke Fredsjö's dissertation from 1953 as an epoch-making work that resulted in the division of this period in West Sweden into three periods. The oldest was labelled the Hensbacka Culture, after that came the Sandarna Culture, and finally the Lihult Culture.

The settlements from the later part of the last mentioned period are coastal bound; however, a new element is that the inland settlements are becoming more common. As a rule, inland settlements are located near larger bodies of water. Waterways have been important in allowing people to move between different locations and settlements as well as for simple ecological reasons. Via waterways, people with boats have been able to access more ecological zones, something that is beneficial in many ways, for example in making and maintaining contacts and for hunting/fishing.

It appears that the Lihult settlements disappear around 4500 BC and a new group emerges – the first transverse arrowhead settlements in Bohuslän and in northern Halland. The oldest of these is ^{14}C dated to *c.* 4600–4500 BC There are however very few sites from the youngest phase, *c.* 4600–3800 BC

It is interesting to note that development regarding the introduction of the transverse arrowhead cannot be compared directly with development in Scania/Denmark, but comes significantly later. We can also note another difference – the typical Ertebølle pottery is absent.

However, regarding the Ertebølle Culture, it is interesting that we find typical Ertebølle objects in the form of, among other things, a Limhamn axe and transverse arrowheads at the Breared site at Varberg. Together with sherds from a characteristic Ertebølle pot (which was probably imported) from a nearby site also containing material with Lihult characteristics, these objects might indicate southern Scandinavian influences.

Our journey now continues north towards what is usually called eastern Central Sweden. In this context, the area is a geographical region that stretches from Uppland in the north, via the island of Gotland, to Östergötland in the south and Närke in the west.

We will begin on Gotland. The picture of the late Mesolithic is multifaceted here. The large 'axe settlements' found at among other places Tofta on the western part of the island are particularly interesting. Ground stone axes are described in the literature as being similar to Limhamn axes, a type of axe associated with the Late Ertebølle Culture in Scania and East Denmark. There is an abundance of round stone axes however. It is believed that the axes were intentionally left at the sites and that there is a difference between the settlements that might indicate different handicraft traditions. Settlements have also been discovered in the interior of Gotland, for example at Mölner. Strictly speaking, one cannot refer to inland regions of Gotland, since people were never far from the coast during this period.

In eastern Central Sweden one can easily argue that Sten Florin, who was primarily active during the 1940s and 1950s, dominated the older research. His greatest contributions were studies concerning changes in sea level and the studies at among other places Dammstugan and Hagtorp, which were the first sites studied where in addition to pottery, axes and flint, also worked quartz was found. After Florin's time, Stig Welinder had great influence on the research concerning the Mesolithic in the region. During the 1970s, Welinder led a project that resulted in claims that he could distinguish between two partially contemporaneous culture groups, which he called the quartz group and the flint group. The former can be said to be typical for sites in what can be called the archipelago region, *i.e.*, today's Södermanland, while the flint group settlements were primarily located in what can be called the mainland region, *i.e.*, the inland areas of Närke, Östergötland and Dalarna.

In this section, as in previous sections, emphasis will be primarily placed on the later part of the Mesolithic. The archipelago continues to grow during this period as new land areas are exposed creating a larger continuous land mass surrounded by larger and smaller islands.

Knowledge about the late Mesolithic in Östergötland is still relatively poor, not the least concerning the period in question, 4500–4000 BC The recently studied settlement at Motala came to an apparent end right before this time, about 5000 BC However, there are several sites around Lake Tåkern, Holmen for example, where objects have been found that can be dated to the Late Mesolithic. A series of radiometric dating analyses place the settlement in the interval 5600–4800 B.C, that is to say, somewhat older. When discussing the Late Mesolithic in this region, the well-known discoveries from Åby Fyrbondegård not far from Ödeshög are of particular interest. Among other things, flake axes characteristic of the Ertebølle Culture have been found here. However, it may be that these are from the older part of the Primary Early Neolithic since a number of smaller fragments from knapped flint axes have also been found here. If these actually did come from the end of the Mesolithic, it might be evidence of contacts between the people of the region and people farther to the south.

In summary, we can say that knowledge about the younger part of the Mesolithic in Östergötland includes large gaps. This is due to many factors, like the relationship between land/water as well as perhaps an earlier lack of interest for the period. Gradually, as inventories are made and new investigations conducted, these gaps will surely be filled.

In the area north of Östergötland, *i.e.*, Södermanland and Uppland, several excavations have provided us with a fairly detailed picture of the period in question. It should be noted however that this has been much influenced by increasing development, which in this region is greatest near Stockholm. This is problematic from a source criticism point of view, as our picture of the Mesolithic society in eastern Central Sweden is based primarily on Södertörn, which was only a small part of the archipelago at that time.

In order to gain a better understanding of what happened, and of the extensive changes that we can see after *c.* 4500 BC, we should take a quick look at one of the larger sites from the time just before this. The very large site discovered at the Jordbro industrial estate at Södertörn is at least 7000 m² and has a deposit strata at least one metre thick, rich with finds. The site is about 45 metres above sea level and during the period in question was located in a smaller bay in the outer archipelago. The site has been ¹⁴C dated to *c.* 5500–4500 BC The large area, together with the abundance of finds, is an indication that the site was a gathering place for a larger group of people in the area. One characteristic feature is the occurrence of large pits dug at the site. Bone material from here as well as other sites clearly indicates that people of that time and in that region for the most part lived on what the sea had to offer. The aquatic contributions to the bone material from the sites comprise up to 95 percent of the total number of bones found.

The compilation of finds from these sites that can be dated to the later part of the period, after 4500 BC, differ somewhat from the older sites. The finds are still dominated by knapped quartz, but it is clear that the technology has changed. Neither do flint microblades occur any longer. Previously, abundant and significant categories of finds become fewer in number or are completely missing, axes for example. On the other hand, we now find transverse arrowheads, which are a kind of arrowhead very common in the Ertebølle Culture discussed earlier, but which also existed during the Primary Early Neolithic.

Examples of larger sites dated to the period after 4500 BC are also absent. The settlement's areas give the impression of becoming smaller, about 1500 m². The large pits, which were found for example at the Jordbro site, disappear and instead we find hearths or hearth-like constructions. Interesting to note is that ¹⁴C dating analyses from two of the sites (Söderbytorp and Åby allotment-garden area) indicate that these were also utilized during the next period, the Early Neolithic.

At the sites that have been excavated, clear traces of dwellings have seldom or ever been discovered. There are however exceptions and one such site is Pärlängsberget at Järna in Södermanland. This settlement was also located on the coast during the later part of the Mesolithic. At the site, which is dated at the oldest to *c* 4200 BC, four definite huts and one structure that might have been a hut were discovered. The huts were all approximately the same size with an inside area of 7–8 m². All were excavated with surrounding wall trenches with post-holes. It is also interesting that transverse arrowheads were discovered at this site as well (Figs 2.4 and 2.5).

During the last few decades, the view of Norrland's older Stone Age has markedly changed. From seeing the region as a more or less late-colonized region, we know better today. As in the previous sections, focus here will be on the period around 4600–4000 BC In order to gain a better perspective regarding development here, it is worth mentioning the sites with finds of so-called blade cores, which in South Scandinavia are usually placed in the middle part of the Mesolithic, and have been dated to *c.* 6000–4500 BC It has often been argued that Norrland's first colonization can be connected to a migration of people from the Norwegian Trøndelag region. This is a very likely description of a complex course of events and therefore the blade core tradition can be associated with development in southern Scandinavia.

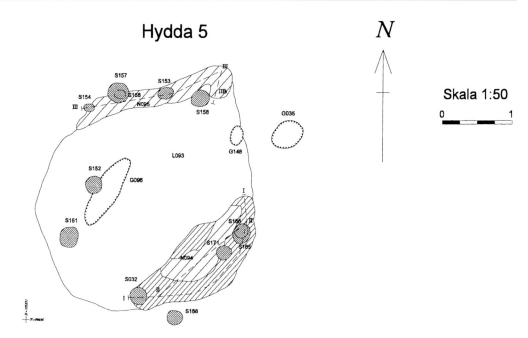

Figure 2.4. Hut 5 from Pärlängsberget in Södermanland (source: Hallgren, Bergström and Larsson 1995).

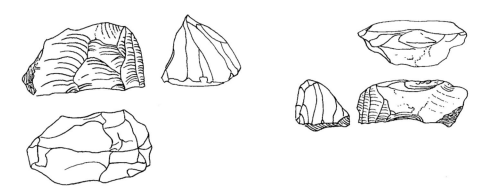

Figure 2.5. Examples of handle cores (source: Larsson 1994).

In Norrland, this tool form has been found at sites like Garaselet in Västerbotten, which has been dated to *c.* 6000 BC However, Kjel Knutsson has emphasized that the blade core tradition in Norrland perhaps should be primarily connected to the later part of the Mesolithic. This is controversial however.

During the period 5000–4000 BC, a transition took place from the use of dense fine-grained material such as *hälleflinta* (rock flint) and porphyry, to quartz. During the period 4750–4000 BC, we also begin finding bones from Eurasian elk and beaver at settlements.

How did the people in Norrland live during the late Mesolithic?

In his survey from 1992 over Norrland's prehistoric times, Evert Baudou wrote that knowledge about the settlements in the interior of Norrland is poor, and the assumptions we make about how the society was organized is greatly based on anthropological ideas about human social organization. Regarding hunters/gatherers, one often talks about band societies, which are loose societal organizations. During recent decades, knowledge about settlements and social organizations has grown. This is chiefly due to inventories, but also several larger archaeological excavations.

The so-called semi-subterranean houses make up one special type of settlement. The oldest have been excavated at Alträsket. They are oval-shaped and measure 10 × 7 metres and 12 × 7 metres. Today they are located in a forested area at 98 metres above sea level, but at the time of the settlement they were located on the coast. They have been dated to *c.* 5000 BC Sites such as Lundfors and Vuollerim at Skellefte and Lule Rivers are somewhat later and have been dated to around 4200 BC

The Late Mesolithic – a few trends

In this section, focus has largely been on the period around 4600–4000 BC in different parts of Sweden. During this period, far-reaching changes occurred in human societies. Old structures disappeared and new ones were built. Tools and materials, *i.e.*, the material culture, changed in form and content. Pottery appeared and contacts with the European Continent intensified in southern Sweden. We have seen how old settlement patterns changed and the large grave-fields; Skateholm for example, came to an end. We see similar patterns also in other parts of the country. In West Sweden, the Lihult Culture disappeared and the transverse arrowhead cultures came onto the scene. Contacts with other parts of South Scandinavia increased as is indicated by the discovery of Ertebølle pottery in Halland. In the Kalmar Strait region, we see an establishment of large settlements at estuaries as well as an abundance of transverse arrowheads. In central Sweden, a distinct shift from large to small settlements takes place and the common greenstone axes also seem to more or less disappear in the material while transverse arrowheads appear.

A shift in the material culture also occurred in Norrland during this period. A transition from *hälleflinta* and porphyry to quartz takes place. New game species such as European elk and beaver became more common. An interesting idea put forth by, among others Kjel Knutsson is that the blade core tradition disappeared during this period and was gradually replaced by new shapes and materials, shale for example, but also in the form of new kinds of semi-subterranean housing. Some argue that this had to do with people wanting to create a new and unique identity clearly differentiated from that existing in South Scandinavia.

In summary, developments during the late part of the Mesolithic indicate extensive changes on several different levels in society. In my opinion, these should be connected to what was happening in southern Scandinavia, namely the introduction of agriculture, or what in archaeological terms is called the Neolithic period.

Suggested readings

Andersen, S. H. 2001. Danske kökkenmöddinger anno 2000. In Jensen, O. L., Sörensen, S. and Hansen, K. M. (eds) *Danmarks Jægerstenalder – status og perspektiver*. Hörsholm: Hörsholms Egns Museum, 21–42.

Baudou, E. 1995. *Norrlands forntid – ett historiskt perspektiv*. Umeå: CEWE förlaget.

Fischer, A. 2001. Food for feasting? An evaluation of explanations of the neolihisation of Denmark and southern Sweden. In Fischer, A. and Kristiansen, K. (eds) *The Neolithisation of Denmark. 150 year debate*. Sheffield: Sheffield University Press, 343–393.

Jensen, J. 2001. *Danmarks Oldtid*. Stenalder 13000–2000 f.Kr. Copenhagen: Gyldendahl.

Larsson, L. 1988. *Ett fångstsamhälle för 7000 år sedan*. Kristianstad.

Larsson, M. and Olsson, E. (eds) 1997. *Regionalt och interregionalt. Stenåldersundersökningar i Syd- och Mellansverige*. Riksantikvarieämbetet. Arkeologiska Undersökningar. Skrifter nr 23. Stockholm.

Welinder, S. 2009. *Sveriges Historia 13000 f.Kr.–600 e.Kr.* Stockholm.

3 From Hunter to Farmer

Mats Larsson

One of the most debated questions within Scandinavian archaeology is the transition from hunters to farmers. This process brought many radical changes such as agriculture, livestock farming and eventually a completely different societal structure in which humanity's view of ourselves as well as the world around us changed. This period in history has been the object of the occasional heated debate among archaeologists. In archaeological terms, the period is referred to as the Neolithic (Younger Stone Age) and can be divided into three main periods: Early, Middle and Late Neolithic, and covers the period between *c.* 3950–1700 BC New cultural terms are introduced and dealt with, for example the Funnel Beaker Culture, Pitted Ware Culture, Battle Axe Culture and Late Neolithic Culture. The Funnel Beaker Culture is the group associated with early agriculture in southern and central Sweden.

In the context of this book, it is not possible to take into account the abundance of source material available today from the Middle East, Southeast Europe and Central Europe. Instead, I focus on changes in Scandinavia, primarily Sweden. In order to make the story understandable however, I will begin with a brief look at the changes that took place on the European continent during the period 4600–4000 BC

Northern Europe

The culture associated with early agriculture in Central Europe is labelled the Linear Pottery Culture. This culture probably originated in western Hungary around 5500 BC and spread quickly across central and northern Europe. It reached Holland and Holstein and Pomerania in northern Germany as early as around 5000 BC The material culture of these people was initially very similar throughout this large geographic region. This included pottery and stone/flint tools as well as dwellings and graves.

Characteristic for this culture are also the large monumental longhouses. At several sites belonging to the Linear Pottery group, dozens of houses have been discovered. At first, this led archaeologists to believe that they were dealing with large villages with populations of hundreds of individuals. Today, there is another view of these sites. Careful analyses of pottery for example, as well as ¹⁴C analyses clearly indicate that the houses were not built at the same time, but that we are perhaps dealing with two farms that relocated within a limited area over the course of several hundreds of years (Fig. 3.1).

Figure 3.1. Example of typical Linear pottery (photograph: M. Larsson).

The grave fields are adjacent to the settlements and are characterized by graves containing skeletons buried in flat ground, often forming larger grave fields.

The early view of this swift colonization was that it resulted from migration from Southeast Europe. In this context, it is interesting to highlight the DNA analyses conducted on these early farmers. The results show that only 20 percent of the modern European genetic make-up can be dated back to the Neolithic migration. The result of this is that today, one emphasizes an alternate development and we see a background for the hunter societies that lived in Europe.

In around 4950 BC, we see how the Linear Pottery Culture has fragmented into a number of local groups such as the Gatersleben, Cerny, Lengyel, Rössen, Michelsberg and Baalberg. The primary difference between these local groups is in the design and shape of their pottery. The reasons for this are debated, but old values and social connections had obviously changed (Fig. 3.2).

In order to place southern Scandinavia in a larger context of development, it might be interesting to touch on the development along the southern shore of the Baltic Sea. Through extensive studies in central Poland, at Brzesc Kujawski in particular, we now have a detailed picture of what contacts between the local hunter populations and the farmers looked like and what this meant for development in northern Europe. The area around Brzesc Kujawski is significant since it was part of a region where an almost symbiotic relationship arose between the local hunter population and the agricultural population. The occurrence of T-shaped antler axes and different kinds of stone axes at their settlements indicate that contacts occurred between people in this region and the Ertebølle population farther to the north.

Figure 3.2. Reconstruction of a longhouse from the Linear Pottery Culture.

It is chiefly during the period 4500–4200 BC that we see these contacts. We can also see how a local variation of what is today called the Funnel Beaker Culture emerges during this time in an interaction between the farmers from the Lengyel Culture (a later part of the Linear Pottery complex) in for example Brzesc Kujawski, and a local hunter population. This means that we can see a fully developed Funnel Beaker Culture in this region between *c.* 4200 and 3900 BC We can also observe this development and successive changes in nearby regions. At sites near the island of Rügen, isolated sherds of late Linear pottery have been found.

We also see definite signs that something is happening at this time in other areas of North Germany. From the Parow site in Mecklenburg for example, ^{14}C-dated early Funnel Beaker pottery has been found. The dating of these vessels places them at around 3900 BC

In summary, we can say that the transition to an agricultural economy in northernmost Germany takes place somewhat earlier than in southern Scandinavia, perhaps around 4100 BC This is not surprising when you consider the proximity to neighbouring agricultural groups. Recent debates often emphasize the Michelsberg Culture. Its name comes from the village of Michelsberg outside of Karlsruhe in Germany and the culture has a wide distribution, from Belgian to southern Germany. Rectangular house foundations, preferably situated on an elevated location, characterize the culture. Long-necked beakers with curved edges around the opening are characteristic for the pottery. Much indicates that the Michelsberg Culture expanded towards the north. It is obviously now that people from this agricultural culture come in contact with the hunters along the coast, thus beginning a wider process.

More about this will be presented in the next section. Our story begins with the Primary Early Neolithic and ends with the transition to the Bronze Age. Each individual section is organized geographically, beginning in southern Sweden and ending in Norrland. Each section has a similar structure with several thematic subheadings that address chronology, material culture, settlement, economy as well as burial customs and rituals.

Paths towards a new world

In this section, we will look at the history of the first farmers. The collective name for these early farmers is the Funnel Beaker Culture, and they lived in an area encompassing southern Poland, Denmark to northern Uppland in Sweden and southern Norway to the west. The period is known as the Primary Early Neolithic, but for the sake of brevity, I will use the term Early Neolithic in the text. The text is arranged chronologically, thematically and geographically, which means that the journey will begin in southern Sweden. The chapter begins with a brief history of how archaeological research has viewed this period. The following themes are addressed: ecology, chronology (in which the material culture is included), settlement, economy as well as burial customs and rituals.

One of the most discussed questions within Scandinavian archaeology is the Neolithisation process, *i.e.*, the transition between the Mesolithic Period and the Neolithic Period. This debate has a long history; however, in this context I choose to begin with the classic discussions between the Danish archaeologists Carl Johan Becker and Jørgen Troels-Smith at the end of the 1940s and beginning of the 1950s.

Scientific investigations characterized a great deal of the early discussion. These investigations were primarily studies of pollen diagrams that showed a 'landnam phase' or colonization phase, which was interpreted as pronounced evidence of an invading farming population who, with axe and fire, cleared the forest in order to use the land for agricultural purposes. The debate, which was basically about views of people's ability to change, continued for several years. In his dissertation from 1947, Becker wrote that he considered the early farming culture (Funnel Beaker Culture) as a culture of invaders, with roots in Southeast or East Europe. This view differed from that of Troels-Smith, who based his on very meticulous excavations and observations in Aamosen (Muldbjerg) on Själland and who saw the Funnel Beaker Culture as developing from the Ertebølle Culture. During the following decades, it was primarily Becker's viewpoint that dominated the outlook on the Early Neolithic. His division of the early Funnel Beaker Culture into three groups – A, B and C – became classic. It was revised however during the 1980s.

Little by little, as the archaeological material grew, more views were voiced in the debate, and particularly during the 1970s, new hypotheses were proposed that were strongly influenced by what has been called the 'New Archaeology', where economic and ecological factors were seen as decisive. The largest part of the research surrounding the transition to an agricultural economy takes its starting point in the late Ertebølle Culture's settlement patterns that were based on large, permanent settlements. Grave fields were also associated with some of these, *e.g.*, at Skateholm in southern Scania.

The debate regarding how the transition to the Neolithic should be interpreted has been, and still is heated. Going back several decades, we see that there are primarily two different positions that can be discerned. One position is the idea that a Neolithic economy arose because of a lack of resources and an increasing pressure on the population. The other position places emphasis on studies of social relations and gift exchanging as important factors in the development of an agriculture economy.

In several studies, the three phrases *accessibility*, *compensation* and *consolidation* are used. The main problem with these however is the question of how quickly the new economy became established. From the point when agriculture was introduced in what is now central Germany, it was almost 1,300 years before the native hunters/gatherers adopted farming. What caused this can naturally be discussed, and it is here that the three distinguishable phases have been a point of reference. Marek Zvelebil and Peter Rowley-Conwy, who together created the model in the middle of the 1980s, claim that it was due to the late Ertebølle Culture's stabile settlement patterns, the fact that they were tied to the coastal region and that hunters primarily utilized resources obtained from the sea. It is obvious that during the period 4600–4000 BC a sharp increase in how people utilized resources from the sea occurs, and the large kitchen middens rapidly grew.

One provoking factor, according to Zvelebil and Rowley-Conwy, may have been a decrease in the availability of shellfish, primarily oysters. This is something that we actually find in several kitchen middens, for example at Norsminde, where around 4000 BC cockles and other smaller crustaceans replaced oysters. What might have caused this decline? We now know that a climate change took place at that time. An obvious rise in temperature can be seen around 4000 BC simultaneous with significant changes in the relationship between land and water, especially in eastern Denmark. We must remember that the coastline at that time was about five metres above present-day sea level in the south, about 40 metres above sea level in central Sweden and about 60 metres above sea level in the north. An increase in sea level led to substantial changes in the geography of beaches and shorelines, which or course must have caused the landscape to appear very different. An increase in the mean annual temperature would have also made it easier for people to grow crops. We can see that people reacted quickly to external changes and adapted to a new age and a new landscape. Was it changes in the climate that caused the hunters to abandon their lifestyle in order to become farmers? In my opinion, it is an important aspect of this era, however it is not the only reason behind the transition.

In an important book from the early 1990s, the English archaeologist Julian Thomas discusses the beginning of the Neolithic in England. Thomas sees the process as a complete transformation of social relations because a social system already existent on the continent was adopted. He emphasizes the symbolism in this and argues that since cereal grains and livestock have mostly been found in the large ritual monuments in England, they have only had significance in ritual acts and as a part of the exchange between different groups of people. This is of course a controversial viewpoint and therefore has also been questioned. However, Thomas' ideas were very significant for the discussion, especially within Swedish archaeology.

Trading relations may also have been an important part of this transition. The German archaeologist Lutz Klassen maintains that during the period 4300–4000 BC, which he calls Import Phase 5, we can see a clear rise in the number of what are called prestigious goods, for example, T-shaped antler axes and certain types of stone axes. The latter were all imported from the region south of the Baltic Sea. They were foreign objects that when they turned up in the hunting society we can assume they had strong symbolic significance and were charged with foreign images and meaning. Thus, they played an important role in the transformation of the hunting society, something previously discussed by Anders Fischer and Kristina Jennbert.

In my opinion, it is not possible to consider only changes in the climate and economic changes, but we must also see that the trade goods like those mentioned above have had an important role in the transformation of the hunting society that existed around 4000 BC

In other words, we have moved from an almost nature-deterministic interpretation to one today that takes into account ideological, ritual and social interpretations. Within archaeological research, one sometimes talks about the 'Neolithic package', which implies that it is a complete package of objects, rituals and ideas that becomes generally accepted.

The early farmers and their contemporaries

This section is thematically organized, so by way of introduction, we will briefly describe and discuss the changes in climate and vegetation, which have been discovered thanks to scientific investigations.

The period we are most interested in here is between *c.* 4200 and 3900 BC In other words, we are looking at a period that brought about great changes for the people of that time. A fitting starting point is the Danish Quaternary geologist Johannes Iversen's epoch-making work from 1941, where he mainly discusses the so-called elm decline. This was a very sharp decline in the levels of elm pollen in the pollen diagrams, which Iversen associated with human activities in the late Mesolithic virgins forests. Pollen diagrams are compilations of different kinds of pollen taken up in a core sample from a lake bottom for example. At first, they were used to show the immigration of different species of trees. He later distinguished three phases that he attempted to link with the elm decline:

- The clearing phase
- The Landnam phase
- The regeneration phase (regrowth).

This pattern was interpreted as support for a colonization phase (*landnam* phase) of an immigrating population, the Funnel Beaker Culture. Clearing of the forests was considered as resulting from slash-and-burn agriculture. This quickly became standard for the understanding of landscape changes during the transition to the Neolithic. Dissenting opinions emerged at the beginning of the 1950s however. It was also here that, based on his very detailed investigations at Aamosen (Muldbjerg) on Själland, the Danish researcher Jørgen Troels-Smith also saw small but methodical clearings in connection with the elm decline. He proffered the explanation that people had gathered leafy vegetation in order to use it as winter fodder for livestock. Troels-Smith saw a connection between these small clearings and that which Becker characterized as the A-phase in the Funnel Beaker Culture. The significantly more distinct second colonization (*landnamet*) that Troels-Smith claimed he could see in his studies was linked to the B-phase of the Funnel Beaker Culture that had been perceived by Becker.

In Sweden, it was perhaps mainly Lund researcher Björn Berglund who worked with similar questions. During the 1960s, he discussed the consequences of the elm decline based on pollen diagrams from the lake at Bjärsjöholm Castle in southern Scania. He claimed that he could perceive four, what he called expansion stages, which were thought to be the results of human actions on the landscape. The first of these was dated to the oldest part of the Early Neolithic. Berglund's work had great impact during the coming years' discussions about the introduction of agriculture in southern and central Sweden.

During recent decades, view about the introduction and development of agriculture have changed. Hans Göransson has presented a partially different picture based on extensive studies during the 1980s, especially from Östergötland for example. He claims that already at the end of the Mesolithic, hundreds of years before the elm decline, forests were subjected to strong human influence in the form of fires and clearing. During the Early Neolithic, this was to have developed into what Göransson calls 'gardening farming' (*trädgårdsbruk*).

In Björn Berglund's later work from the 1990s, it is evident that he considers the elm decline as being caused by several interacting factors, primarily fungi and elm bark beetles. The fungi cause the elms to become diseased and the leaves to dry up during early summer, and the elm bark beetles spread the fungal spores when the beetles gnaw on the bark of living branches in the crown of elm trees. Berglund essentially calls it an ecological catastrophe. He also argues that a few more minor traces of human influences on the landscape can be seen already at the end of the Mesolithic, but it is not until after the elm decline that the evidence becomes clear, this being a result of small-scale agriculture on small fields. Here, Berglund and Göransson agree. In summary, we can say that devclopment during the period *c.* 4800–3900 BC was very complex and, as we have seen, not easy to interpret.

Time and artefacts

The Danish archaeologist Carl Johan Becker was mentioned earlier as being the one who created the first practical classification of the older Funnel Beaker Culture into the three groups A, B and C, where A was the oldest. He based his classification on comparative studies of pottery found in Danish bogs. This classification had a great impact and was used for several decades. It was not until the end of the 1970s and the beginning of the 1980s that something new occurred. During the previous decades, a new, large collection of material from the Funnel Beaker Culture had been uncovered; this thanks to the large and widespread archaeological excavations in both Denmark and Sweden. During the early part of the 1980s, this material was subjected to studies, which essentially led to Becker's classification being questioned. In addition, we should also add the development of the ^{14}C method, which made significantly more accurate dating possible as well as the possibility for dating food crusts from the inside of containers (Fig. 3.3).

Based on the site material from the extensive investigations undertaken during the 1960s and 1970s, a new classification of the early Funnel Beaker Culture was presented in 1984, and with certain modifications, it is still used today. The study was based on the occurrence of different kinds of decorations on the containers as well as their different shapes, and led to a division into three groups named after sites in southern Scania:

- The Oxie group
- The Svenstorp group
- The Bellevuegård group.

The frequency of different kinds of decorations, combined with the then relatively few ^{14}C dates resulted in the two first groups being seen predominately as concurrent. However, later dating analyses have strengthened the idea that the Oxie group is the oldest of the Early Neolithic Funnel Beaker groups. ^{14}C-dating places this in the interval of about 3950–3700 BC The decorations were sparingly used and occur only along the actual mouths of the vessels. A type of decoration created with cord is prevalent on

Figure 3.3. Funnel beaker from Önsvala, near Malmö, typical for the Oxie group (photograph: I. Kristiansson).

Figure 3.4. A selection of pottery sherds from the Svenstorp site (photograph: I. Kristiansson).

the vessels from the Svenstorp group. Overall, the decorations in this group are significantly more complex.

The Bellevuegård group, which is the youngest and dates to the period *c.* 3700–3300 BC, shows a rich variation regarding pottery decorations. What has been called twisted cord decorations, string tightly wound around a stick or piece of bone, and different kinds of impressed decorations commonly occurred. The variation in the shapes of the pots was also much greater. Here we see a whole array of both drinking vessels and containers used for cooking and storage (Fig. 3.4).

To complicate the picture further, the existence of the Mossby group was established in the early 1990s. The name comes from a site near Ystad, Sweden. This can be seen as a group parallel with the Svenstorp group, but with more cord decoration. It also had a more eastern area of distribution.

Unsurprisingly, it easily becomes a complicated story, and in order to simplify things a bit the period is often divided into two main groups:

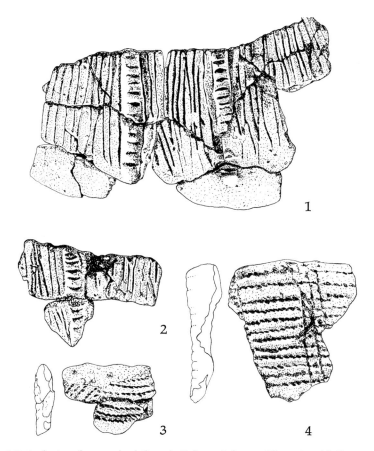

Figure 3.5. A selection of pottery sherds from the Bellevuegård group (illustration: M. Centerwall).

- TN I, which includes the Oxie, Svenstorp and Mossby groups.
- TN II, which includes the Bellevuegård group.

If we add the Danish material as well, then Oxie/Svaleklint/Volling belong to TN I, while Virum/Fuchsberg are placed in TN II. The boundary between the two is around 3600 BC; however, the boundary is not razor-sharp (Fig. 3.5).

If we look at the flint and stone tools, an interesting picture emerges. A noticeable continuity exists between the late Ertebølle Culture and the Oxie group as regards certain kinds of tools: flake axes, transverse arrowheads and isolated core axes. Polished pointed-butted axes, which are basically polished core axes, and stone battle-axes are new types of axes during this period. The kinds of tools mentioned above can only be linked to the Oxie group and to some extent the Svenstorp group. Thus, in primarily the flint tools there is a clear link back in time to the late hunter/gatherer groups.

On the other hand, if we look at the kinds of tools in the late Bellevuegård group, we find

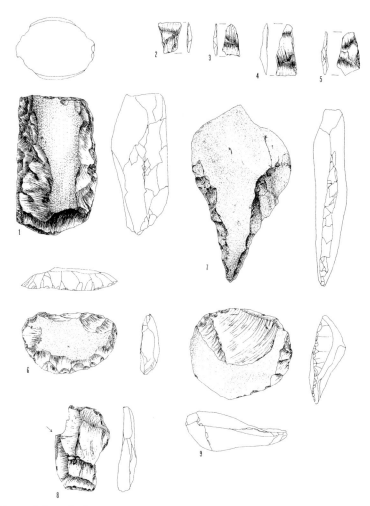

Figure 3.6. Flint tools from the Oxie group.
1. Part of a point-butted axe; 2–5. Transverse arrows; 6. Scraper; 7. Bore; 8. Burin; 9. Scraper (illustration: M. Centerwall).

a clear difference when comparing with the older groups. A new type of axe is found, the thin-butted axe, which was usually polished. Tools such as flake axes, pointed-butted axes, core axes and to some extent, transverse arrowheads have all disappeared, while scrapers completely dominate the finds. What caused this change is difficult to say. One reason may be a changed economy where cattle became more important and thus skin preparation; however, this is difficult to prove (Figs 3.6 and 3.7).

Where did they get their material, especially all the flint? Some flint could be found as loose, smaller chunks in glacial deposits; however, evidence of plain industrial mining has also been found. In the Malmö region, mining at Kvarnby and Sallerup can be verified. Mining of chalk has occurred in these areas for a long time, and in connection with this,

Figure 3.7. A selection of flake axes (photograph: I. Kristiansson).

Figure 3.8. Thin-butted axe (photograph: I. Kristiansson).

artefacts have been found that can be dated to the Neolithic as well as more recent times. Findings include raw material for axes as well as antlers used to hack away the chalk. Hundreds of mine shafts in Sallerup indicate that flint mining was important as well as widespread. Dating indicates that this mining may have begun as early as in the late Mesolithic, but that it is primarily during the Early Neolithic and later periods that it became truly important.

In northern Jylland, a region of Denmark, mine shafts have been found that were *c.* 5–6 metres deep with side shafts that were up to 8 metres long.

The main purpose of this enormous effort of labour was to produce raw materials for the manufacturing the long thin-butted axes, measuring over 25 cm long.

One interesting group of artefacts that should not be neglected are the copper axe blades found in both Sweden and Denmark. Finds of polygonal battle axes of copper have also been made. One find from Oxie, near Malmö, should particularly be mentioned here. Few of these can be dated more specifically; however, a discovery of several axe blades and other copper objects buried in a large funnel beaker at Bygholm on Jylland can be dated to the later part of the Early Neolithic.

Where did these objects come from? Chemical analyses of copper objects from the period indicate a high level of arsenic, which points towards Poland and Bohemia. It is quite possible that the objects originated from these areas of Central Europe. This also implies that people of the Early Neolithic did not live in a vacuum, but had wide spread contacts with other regions and other people (Fig. 3.8).

What is the situation like in our neighbouring country Denmark? During the early 1980s, Torsten Madsen came up with a classification of the Danish Funnel Beaker pottery that has certain similarities with that from Scania:

- Oxie
- Volling/Svaleklint
- Virum/Fuchsberg.

This is not the place to go into detail regarding these groups, but they can generally be seen as being parallel to the ones from Scania. However, one big difference is that they are regional in character. The Oxie Group can be found throughout Denmark, while the Volling Group is a local group found on Jylland. The Fuchsberg Group can also be seen as a southern Danish group, but clear influences on the pottery can also be seen in southern Sweden.

The picture is somewhat different if we continue moving north into central Sweden towards the northern boundary of the Funnel Beaker Culture. Sten Florin, who was a very active archaeologist during primarily the 1950s, divided the Funnel Beaker Culture into two groups he assumed existed at different times: Mogetorp and Östra Vrå. Florin chose to call this early Funnel Beaker Culture the Vrå Culture. Both of these sites are located in Södermanland. Round-bodied pots characterize the first mentioned site and ornamentation is very scanty, in the form of small pits, lines and cord decorations. The pottery from Östra Vrå has a richer ornamentation, with among other things both cord and twisted cord decorations. A third group can perhaps be added, Frotorp. This is an inland site located in Närke, Sweden. The pottery from the site can be most closely compared with the Oxie Group of southern Scandinavia.

Investigations during later years however have clearly demonstrated that this division cannot be used to distinguish between local groups or chronological differences. On the contrary, the pottery finds from the separate sites are similar, despite the fact that according to ^{14}C-dating the localities were used during a long sequence of years. Later studies have provided ^{14}C-dating that can place parts of the Östra Vrå site in the period 3650–3500 BC

If we look at flint and stone material, both similarities and differences are seen in comparisons with southern Scandinavia. Thin-butted flint axes occur while the pointed-butted type axes are uncommon. Stone battle-axes are found, just as are transverse arrowheads, scrapers and knives. Studies of the manufacturing process show that it was often the thin-butted axes that were used as raw material for tool making. It must be pointed out that all of the flint in the area was imported, since flint did not occur naturally in Central Sweden. In addition to the imported flint, quartz is also found, although not to the same extent as during the Mesolithic. We can also see thin-butted axes made of ground stone and ground stone axes with bored holes (Fig. 3.9).

What dates do we find for the central Swedish Funnel Beaker Culture? Absolute dating in the form of ^{14}C-dating is abundant, but the results are in no way in agreement. Based on the dating information it is very difficult to differentiate between the three groups mentioned above. Based on the dating results, it is not possible today to distinguish between the different sub-regions. Archaeologist Fredrik Hallgren claims that based on the dating results we have,

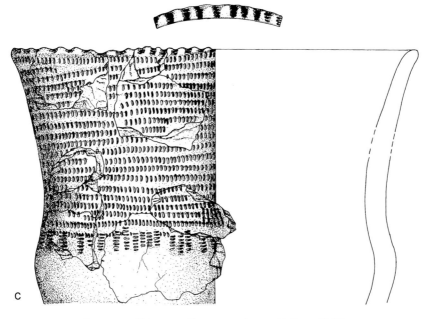

Figure 3.9. Vrå pottery, Skogsmossen (source: Hallgren 2008).

we can delineate the Early Neolithic to the period *c.* 4000 BC to 3300 BC, which is well in agreement with the dating results from southern Scandinavia.

Now our journey continues northwards in Sweden to northern Uppland and southern Norrland.

We will now take a closer look at the chronological perspective and the material culture. For example, north of Mälaren Valley it seems that agriculture did not gain a foothold until about 2300 BC Neither do we see any signs of the Funnel Beaker Culture here. The northernmost known site is near the Bälinge Bogs. What kinds of cultural expressions and societies do we find in the areas in northern Uppland and northwards? We will examine these issues in the following pages.

As pointed out before, archaeologists have often wanted to see a more or less clear connection between, for example, the southern Swedish Funnel Beaker Culture and the eastern Central Swedish early farming culture called the Vrå Culture. This connection is not always that obvious, as there are distinct differences in the shapes of the pots for example. If we look at northern Uppland and southern Norrland, it is even less clear; here, there is no direct connection found. There is much in the artefacts from the sites studied in eastern Sweden that points towards people having contacts not only towards the south, but also to the north and east. This can be seen primarily in the different kinds of material culture, *e.g.*, pottery and tool making.

This is evident in the choice of ornamentation on pots for example. At sites such as

Anneberg in northern Uppland, which can be dated to the Early Neolithic, decorations using comb impressions and pits are common. These characteristics become even more apparent at the somewhat later sites like the high bogs.

Based on what the pottery looked like, the archaeologist Niclas Björk has distinguished five different chronological horizons. Of these, only the three first (4000–2800 BC) are of interest in this chapter.

What primarily distinguishes the different horizons is the occurrence of various kinds of decorations, the composition of the pottery (solid or porous) and the shapes of the vessels. Here, I will not take the time to describe the different horizons in detail, but will only provide a general description.

During the oldest horizon, the vessels have an obvious almost bell-shape and have a rounded base. Ornamentation varies from simple insets to decorations that almost completely cover the surface of the vessels. The pottery is solid.

The second horizon is characterized by bell-shaped pottery, but the bases tend to be flat or only slightly rounded. The vessels are generally richly decorated with ornamentation that often covers the entire surface. Different kinds of cross-hatching and rows of crosses are most common. This kind of ornamentation is often seen on Funnel Beaker pottery in southern Sweden. The pottery starts becoming more porous, which is an important change.

The third horizon easily includes the largest amount of material. For example, Högmossen belongs to this horizon. The shapes of the vessels tend to be more profiled and the bell-shape is no longer as common. Looking at the decorations, we now see evidence that stamped comb decorations experience an obvious upswing, while at the same time cord, linear and twisted cord decorations are becoming much less common. The pottery shows great variation regarding additives, the mixing of different materials into the clay, but the porous pottery is predominant.

Tools are almost exclusively made of quartz, and flint does not occur at all. Stone axes, for example round stone axes, are abundant in the region.

If we follow the coast northwards, we eventually reach Norrbotten and Lappland. During recent decades, sites investigated here have changed our views on Norrland's prehistory. Evert Baudou, the father of Norrland's archaeology, claims to be able to distinguish several different kinds of settlements:

- seal hunter settlements along the coast
- base settlements inland from the coastal regions
- inland settlements at lakes and other bodies of water.

It is not only along the coasts that we find traces of settlements in Norrland. In several places in inland Norrland and Lappland, a number of shelters, so-called burnt mounds, have been examined. They are generally found on well-drained land close to water. Three to five shelter foundations are commonly found at the same location. They have obviously been used primarily during the winter, which has led archaeologist Åsa Lundberg to call them 'winter villages'. European elk was clearly the most important animal that was hunted. Subterranean floors characterized these shelters. These were surrounded by several burnt stones, *i.e.*, rocks used in hearths and cooking pits, which made up the burnt mounds. The size of the shelters varied between 7 m² and 50 m², with an average of 20–24 m². Cooking pits were located in the central part of the shelter or near the entrance. These shelters were obviously utilized over a long period, 4600–2500 BC; however, several of them are dated to the period around 4000 BC.

What was life like for the early farmers?

How did the first farmers live? Since the 1980s, studies of a great deal of material from settlements dating from the Early Neolithic in southern and central Sweden has provided us with much new knowledge about how people lived during that time. I will describe these sites in the following section. How did people of this time live and what kinds of landscape did they prefer? We will begin in Scania and work our way north.

Our knowledge about how the first farmers lived however has not always been very good. In connection with older archaeological excavations in both Sweden and Denmark, what some would interpret as being buildings or huts have been discovered. Many of these are difficult to understand and interpret, which also led researchers to dismiss them in most cases. Classic examples of this are the re-interpretations of the Danish locations Barkær and Stengade. Both of these were seen as longhouses when they were discovered, but have later been convincingly re-interpreted as being, in fact, grave monuments.

The most part of the early Funnel Beaker sites in Scania included only a few hundred pits that had been dug and not much of anything else. How should we look at and understand this abundance of pits? In older research, the pits were seen as being completely functional in nature; they were simply pits that were dug in order to collect sand or clay and which were then filled with garbage. In recent years, they have been re-interpreted and are now sometimes seen as a kind of ritual structure. Intact objects, both stone/flint tools and even entire pots, are often found in the pits. Several of these 'pit sites' are located on hills in the often rather flat Scanian landscape. One exception however is the site at Almhov in Malmö, which we will address later. However, the majority of these sites were situated on heights that were visible from great distances, as well as in dense woods. Perhaps these places had a special significance that the hunting societies had discovered. In this case, we should see these locations as a way for people to feel at home in the landscape, as well as a way of returning objects of stone/flint and clay to the earth, from which they had once been taken.

The question was, "How did people live during this period?" If we look at Scania, it is clear that changes occur in settlements at the transition to the Neolithic. The people abandoned the large coastal settlements, even if they still used them for hunting and fishing, and made a new start farther inland. People chose to settle on sandy heights located close to water. The inland regions were not unfamiliar, but as we have already mentioned, were utilized by the hunting societies earlier. It was perhaps not such a great change for people then, since they were moving to a familiar landscape. People had been moving around here for a long time; paths had been created that linked the different settlements. The people gave names to easily recognizable landmarks and in this way became important for how well they felt at home in the landscape. We can see the large 'pit sites' as being a part of this.

Studies of settlement patterns have also revealed that people chose with great care the areas where they settled. They sought out not only nearness to water, but also substantial variation in the surrounding environment. In this manner, a number of ecological zones could be utilized, for cultivation, livestock, hunting and fishing. This indicates that people then made conscious decisions guided by the knowledge they had accumulated over the centuries. It may have been individuals or groups of individuals who controlled these choices.

Consequently, we can say that the Primary Early Neolithic was characterized by both change and continuity. New parts of the landscape came to be used and new kinds of settlements were formed and established. The familiar sites at lakes and seas were also utilized. Huts and pit-houses that were similar to those from the Mesolithic are still used; while at the same time, oval two-aisled houses and D-shaped huts turn up at sites considered to belong to the Older Neolithic.

In the following section, we will look closer at how these early farmers lived. A simple way to begin is to look at the models archaeologists have used in order to classify and categorize different kinds of settlements.

One model that is frequently used divides settlements into three main categories:

1. Permanent settlements
2. Hunting settlements
3. Central sites.

Settlements from the first category were located on flatlands, often near watercourses, but not directly adjacent to seas. The settlements have often been considered small, 600–700 m², a view that is debated today. This debate has come about due to of the large sites where several possibly contemporaneous houses are being investigated, for example, along the west coast in Scania (Dagstorp). In the second category, settlements were located on the seacoast or near an inland lake, often the same places previously used by the people of the Ertebølle Culture. The third category should be seen as gathering sites, and they were very large, 10–50,000 m². We should see these as ritual gathering places for a larger section of the population. Sometimes one sees the designation Sarup style, which we will examine more closely later.

In the 1970s, Stig Welinder distinguished two primary kinds of settlements in central Sweden:

• Inland settlements for cultivation and livestock raising
• Coastal settlements for hunting and fishing (with mostly catches from the sea).

During later years, Fredrik Hallgren has chosen to call these land-facing and sea-facing sites.

It is important to remember however that what can be called inland settlements is a bit complicated. The majority of what can be called inland settlements were sometimes, like at Mogetorp, no closer than several hundred metres from the sea. Fredrik Hallgren sees the terraces along the slopes of the sandy ridges as communal settlement locations. Even the coastal sites are generally located on sandy ground and often on peninsulas and islands formed by boulder-ridges (eskers).

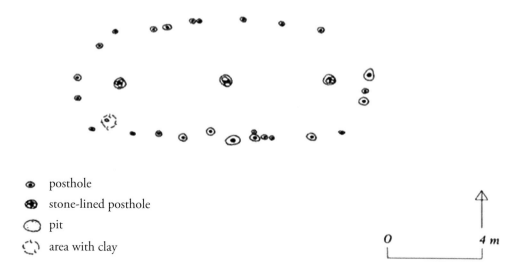

posthole
stone-lined posthole
pit
area with clay

0   4 m

Figure 3.10. The house from Mossby in southern Scania (source: Larsson 1992).

Looking at the landscape of the inner archipelago of the time in western Södermanland, we see that it is one of the region's central areas during the Early Neolithic. We base this on the occurrence of isolated finds and known settlement sites in the area, such as Mogetorp and Östra Vrå. The settlements in the area are all located a distance from the shoreline of the time. They also give the impression of having the distinct quality of agricultural sites judging from where they are located, impressions from grain corn in the pottery, pollen analyses and a few finds of bones from domestic animals from archaeological excavations. It is not clear however how people utilized the landscape during this period. However, it is clear that not only the well-drained sandy soils along the boulder-ridges (eskers) were used, but also other areas characterized by clay soils. Perhaps even here there were smaller hunting and fishing stations, similar to the coastal sites that occurred more often in the eastern parts of the archipelago.

One of the most important discoveries in recent decades is the longhouse. In the following section, I will discuss these as well as looking at the settlement patterns.

The first longhouse from Mossby in southern Scania was excavated in 1986 and measured *c.* 12 × 6 metres (Fig. 3.10).

Three large posts supported the roof. The walls were poorly preserved, but what could be seen was an almost oval series with shallow postholes. A layer of sooty sand covered an area of about 70 m² inside the walls and made up the remnants of the floor. Few objects were found in the house and those found were isolated pottery sherds, some with cord decorations, and a small amount of flint. ¹⁴C-dating performed on remnants of food from the vessels as well as on burnt cereal grains has indicated the dates 4100–3900 BC These dates are among the oldest from the Funnel Beaker Culture in Scandinavia. The oldest (4100 BC) has been questioned however. Although, it is clear that the house can be dated to the oldest part of the Early Neolithic. This kind of house has become a 'type house' and is commonly known by the name *Mossby house*. Seventeen of the 36 houses from the Neolithic we know of today (2011) are of the Mossby house type.

Since the Mossby house was discovered, several similar houses have been studied in both Sweden and Denmark. Our exposé begins in Scania, where several houses of this kind have recently been excavated. We can begin with the excavations at Dagstorp in western Scania, where a large area was excavated in connection with the construction of the West Coast railway in 1995–1998. The total area excavated was 35,000 m². A number of houses from both the Early Neolithic and from a somewhat later period were studied, perhaps 10 houses total. This is most likely the largest number of houses from this period that have been excavated in Scandinavia. Based on these excavations, three different kinds of houses have been distinguished (Fig. 3.11):

- Two-aisled houses with rounded ends – Mossby house
- Two-aisled houses with trapezoid shape – Dagstorp houses Type I
- Two-aisled houses with rectangular shape, with or without wall trenches – Dagstorp houses Type II and Limensgård houses.

In the context of this chapter, we are only interested in dwellings of the Mossby type. We will deal with the other kinds of houses in more detail in following chapters.

In addition to these types, one can also add a number of huts generally found in connection with longhouses. What we should make of the huts is not completely clear.

The Mossby house is *c.* 20 × 5–8 metres, with an area of between 100 and 160 m². Results from absolute dating (¹⁴C) of this type of house from Dagstorp indicates an age of between *c.* 3800–3500 BC

A majority of the houses from Dagstorp, as well as from other sites, were covered with, or connected with the culture layers that are actually layers of garbage linked together with pits. Based on these investigations, we can see that the houses were relatively empty of artefacts; few objects were found inside of the walls. We can interpret this as meaning that most human activity took place outside of the actual houses.

In the area around Malmö where for several years, extensive archaeological excavations have taken place, we also find evidence of houses similar to the Mossby type. In Svågertorp, located in the southern part of Malmö, a very large area was excavated in 1999–2000. Houses from several periods have been found; however, in this context it is a house dated to the older part of the Neolithic which is most interesting. The house was *c.* 11 metres long and 6 metres wide, and unfortunately, we cannot say anything about the shape of the short ends of the house since postholes have not been discovered. A ¹⁴C-analysis points towards a date of 3790–3650 BC

Apart from this house, there are not many from this period that we can discuss. This is notable in many ways, especially considering the large amount of material uncovered over the years in the form of settlements, with pits and culture layers, and the abundance of isolated finds. Archaeologists Nils Björhem and Björn Magnusson Staaf write in the book '*Långhuslandskapet*' (The Longhouse Landscape) that perhaps the Funnel Beaker Culture's longhouse settlements might be associated with larger watercourses such as the stream

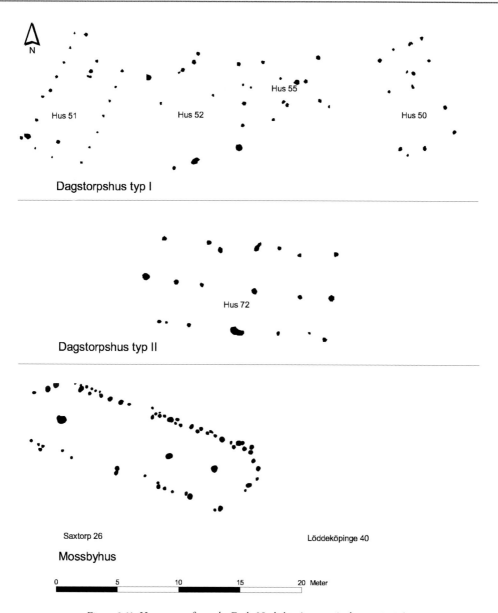

Figure 3.11. House types from the Early Neolithic (source: Andersson 2003).

Välabäck at Dagstorp, mentioned above. The houses at this site were located near the stream Saxån-Välabäcken. According to Björhem and Staaf, people utilized perhaps different parts of the landscape at that time. This is an interesting thought, which is possibly an answer to why traces of for example the early Mossby houses are largely absent from the area around Malmö. This makes Svågertorp extra interesting as there was supposed to be a larger wetland area adjacent to the ridge on which the remains of the settlement were located.

What did other parts of Sweden look like at this time? We can start on the island of Öland. Until a few years ago, we had a poor understanding of the Older Neolithic; however, the situation today is much better. Sites such as Runsbäck and Resmo have provided us with knowledge about how people lived on Öland during the period 3600–3300 BC, *i.e.*, the end of the Older Neolithic. Most interesting is the Mossby type house discovered at Runsbäck. The house was *c.* 12–15 metres long and the width is estimated as being about 5 metres. Twisted cord dominated the ceramic decorations, which fits well with both the dating and the Bellevuegård group from Scania. Today, this house is one of the few Funnel Beaker houses known from Southeast Sweden.

Knowledge about early Funnel Beaker houses in West Sweden primarily comes from the region of Halland. The most persuasive are those from Hästhagen and Slottsmöllan, near Halmstad. The first is a 17 × 5.5 metre-wide longhouse with a row of centrally placed poles. The house is ^{14}C-dated to 3626–2905 BC The dimensions of the second house were 13 × 5.5–5 metres. A ^{14}C analysis has dated it to 3754–3531 BC

The house from Hästhagen is of a type that resembles the Mossby house; however, there are differences. The walls are not elliptical, as they often are, and the poles were arranged more erratically. The dating of the house from Slottsmöllan is more uncertain however. The connection between culture layers and the house is not clear and the house is also of a type that cannot be clearly compared with other known houses. However, it is still relatively certain that the house belongs to the early Funnel Beaker Culture.

In eastern Central Sweden, there are currently several houses known to be of the Mossby type. The first of these was excavated in 1993 in Brunneby in the western part of Östergötland. Since then, similar houses have been excavated at, among other places, Bleckenstad and Kimstad, as well as other locations in the region.

The houses are very similar to those mentioned above. The size of the houses varies between 9 × 4 metres (Brunneby), 10 × 5 metres (Bleckenstad) and 15.5 × 6.5 metres (Kimstad). All had a row of centrally placed poles that held up the roof. These three houses represent one kind of inland settlement, *i.e.*, they are not connected with the sea, as we shall see is the case farther north. As mentioned, the three houses are similar, as are their ages. From Brunneby we have no ^{14}C-dates, but the pottery provides possible dates at the middle or later part of the Early Neolithic. We have two dating results from the house in Bleckenstad, 3650–3300 BC and 3770–3490 BC The pottery from here is the same kind as that from Brunneby, including twisted cord pottery. From the third house, we have dating results that indicate an age around 3790–3630 BC Also interesting is that there is not much material found at the three houses, except for the large amount of pottery from a pit dug in the house at Kimstad.

In summary, we can therefore say that the Early Neolithic settlement pattern in Östergötland is easily comparable to that in southernmost Sweden; smaller isolated farms with few finds. Those finds that we have uncovered come from pits or culture layers outside the actual houses.

Our journey continues northward towards eastern Central Sweden (Södermanland, Västmanland, Närke and Uppland). For a long time the only known houses were Mogetorp (Katrineholm) and Östra Vrå (Stora Malm) in Södermanland.

Figure 3.12. Reconstruction of the farm at Brunneby in Östergötland (illustration: T. Morisse).

The settlements were located in what was then the inner archipelago, in other words, near the coast without being on it. House II from Mogetorp is the most well known of these early excavated ruins, which were excavated already in 1936. The structure guessed to be a house was rectangular in shape and measured 18 × 8 metres.

Östra Vrå comprised three primarily four-sided stone constructions with marked kerbstones. Only one of these was completely studied, and it was made up of a rounded four-sided stone frame measuring 5 × 4 metres.

It is quite clear however that both the actual excavations and the descriptions of these 'houses' are full of inconsistencies and not very reliable. Therefore, we should not see them as being characteristic for houses during this period. However, it is interesting that in recent years Fredrik Hallgren has interpreted the structure at Mogetorp as being part of a grave structure, a so-called long barrow (Fig. 3.12).

There are however houses from the area that can be dated to the Early Neolithic, 3950–3650 BC We should especially mention three sites: Skumparberget, Skogsmossen and Fågelbacken. The first is located in Närke, while the other two are in Västmanland and are quite close to each other.

The first house is 12.5 × 6 metres and is quite similar to the Mossby house. Work areas for activities such as cooking, axe manufacturing and a place for burning scraps left over after slaughtering animals surrounded the centrally located house. At Skogsmossen, which can be dated to 3800–3300 BC, we have indications that perhaps four houses were located there. Only one of these was found at the place the excavators believed was the central living site. It was difficult to determine the size of the house since it had sustained much damage. Near this centrally located house were different work areas for cooking and for manufacturing axes.

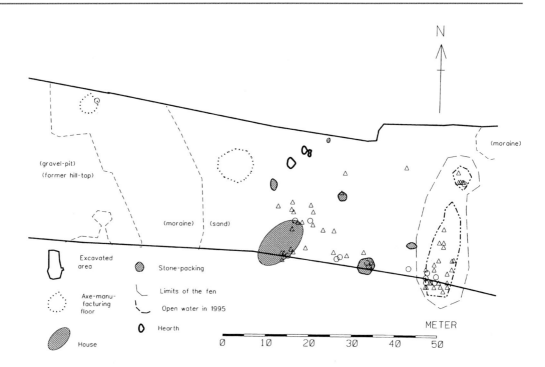

Figure 3.13. The area around the settlement at Skogsmossen showing the work areas (source: Hallgren 2008).

It is interesting to note that three heaps of stone with traces of erected poles marked off what has been interpreted as the yard area. East of the house, excavations have uncovered what we understand to be a sacrificial fen with a large number of discarded pots and stone tools. There had also been a platform supported by poles at the edge of the fen. Archaeologist Stig Welinder has described how life here progressed on three levels. In and around the house were various work areas with household garbage and traces from tool manufacturing (level 1). Finds from these activities were also discovered among the stone-packing layer (level 2). The third level is the fen, where people together with the deities down in the bog ate their meals. Finally, I should add that the house burned down, which was most likely intentional (Fig. 3.13).

Fågelbacken is different. The site is located on an island formed by the north-south orientation of Badelunda boulder ridge. Here, four D-shaped huts were excavated. The site is dated to 3800–3600 BC It is obvious that if we place the huts together we have a Mossby house! The site has a clear spatial structure and has been considered to be a gathering place close to the coast used by several inland farming settlements and which were visited with some regularity with breaks in between. What is perhaps most interesting with Fågelbacken are the traces of ritual activities found. A large quantity of burned human bones have been found at the site as well as what can be seen as a death house, *i.e.*, a storage place for dead ancestors (Fig. 3.14).

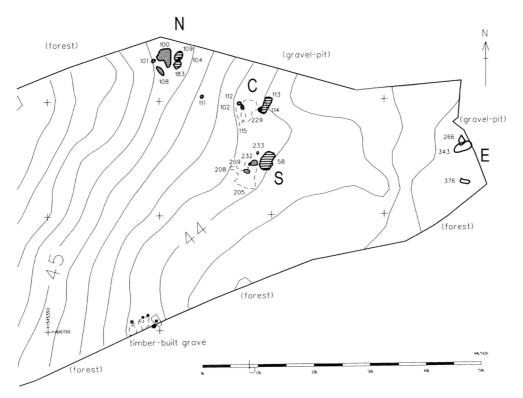

Figure 3.14. The burial site at Fågelbacken N, B and C showing the concentration of burned human bones found at the site (source: Hallgren 2008).

The three sites mentioned above are all located near one another; the two first sites are located inland, while Fågelbacken is oriented towards the sea. As opposed to the most likely small settlements from Scania and Östergotland, those from Mälaren Valley give the impression of having been quite large; Skogsmossen is estimated to have covered an area of about 30,000–45,000 m². It is difficult to determine whether these sites were the result of the relocation of settlements or if they represent several contemporaneous settlements. This is actually the same problem we have with, for example, the large excavations at Dagstorp in Scania. Is what we see a contemporaneous group of settlements or is it a result of the farm moving to a new location?

We will now take a closer look at how people lived in the area north of Mälaren Valley – Uppland and southern Norrland.

Several different kinds of settlements have been recently studied after the extensive excavations in connection with construction of a new section of European route E4. Thanks to this, our picture of societal development and use of the landscape in these areas has changed and taken on a completely new dimension. In this context, it is not possible to discuss all of the material that has been published. However, to provide insight into the development of this region during the younger Stone Age, I have chosen to take a closer look at one of these sites: Högmossen.

Settlements are located near the coast during all of the period addressed in this chapter (4000–3300 BC). On what were once the islands and peninsulas in the archipelago, settlements have been found and excavated. There is also evidence that the population of that period to a certain extent also utilized inland watercourses and lakes. Several different types of settlements have been found. These can be compared with the types of settlements discussed earlier in southern and central Sweden. The three main types we can discern are:

- Complementary sites (small)
- Actual coastal settlement sites (medium)
- Gathering sites (large).

Högmossen, which will be described shortly, is a good example of an actual coastal settlement site.

What did the landscape look like at this time? During a greater part of the Stone Age, most of Uppland and the surrounding areas were covered by water. In 4000 BC, the shoreline was about 40 metres higher than it is today, after which it receded eastwards due to the geological uplift of the land. During the Early Neolithic, Uppland was an extensive archipelago with a large number of islands and rocky islets. Pine dominated the vegetation, but hazel, alder and birch were also present.

Now we will take a closer look at the settlement.

Högmossen is an example of an actual coastal settlement site and had an area of 2,000 m². The settlement can be said to contain all the components one would expect: seasonal indicators that indicated year-round settlement, evidence of housing, various work areas and a gravesite. It is also worth mentioning that Högmossen is the first large archaeological excavation in the rich Neolithic settled country that was located near the mouth of the river Dalälven. More than 100 Neolithic settlements have been discovered in this region.

The settlement at Högmossen was located about 45–47 metres above sea level, along what was once a bay. The settlement area was *c.* 90 × 225 metres, that is to say the actual culture layer. At the site, five huts situated along the banks of the river were excavated. The huts were *c.* 10–25 m², with dimensions of 4–6 metres.

Interestingly, the settlements are obviously divided into a northern section and a southern section. In the area between these, which was apparently empty of finds, a grave-field was found with at least four confirmed graves.

The people at the settlement at Högmossen lived an organized life. Around the huts were different areas for cooking and tool manufacturing. Large garbage piles were located in front of the huts, facing towards the beach. Thus, it was an ordered life with separate areas for different activities for the perhaps 15–20 people that lived here (Fig. 3.15).

So, how old is Högmossen and what was it like for the people living here? Based on radiocarbon dating and the shape and design of the pottery, we estimate that the settlement was used between 3500 and 3300 BC, with a special emphasis on the time around 3400 BC In other words, the site can be placed in the previously mentioned chronological horizon 2. For tool making, people chiefly used quartz, which was worked in different ways and using different techniques. Stone axes have also been discovered. The people at Högmossen used pottery with a varied design – from small to large containers with a diameter of 2–16 cm for small vessels, 17–33 cm for medium sized and 34–44 cm for large ones. Using analyses of the fat content (lipids) of the pottery, we can see that primarily the small and medium sized pots were used for cooking (Fig. 3.16).

Do we know what the people of Högmossen ate? The abundance of bone remains clearly indicates marine animals, fish and seals among others. They probably also ate a large amount of vegetable foods, although they did not cultivate any cereal crops. All together, the evidence points towards a year-round settlement.

Our journey now continues north towards the upper reaches of Norrland where we find some characteristic settlements that date to this period.

Vuollerim in Lappland is the first of these sites. The settlement, which included 3–6 hut-foundations, is located at the confluence of the Greater and Lesser Lule Rivers. Dating analysis places the site at *c.* 4000 BC The hut walls were quite low and difficult to see. Inside the walls was a sunken floor measuring 11 × 5 metres. Inside the house, postholes, cooking pits, storage pits and a hearth were found. What is especially notable is the 3 metre-long covered entrance along the eastern side of the house. Under this, a subterranean flue was discovered, which led away from the fireplace, in other words, an early form of central heating.

Quartz dominated the material tools were made from, similar to what was found at Högmossen, but stone and slate were also used. The people who lived at Voullerim hunted mostly European elk, but also beaver, game birds and salmon. Taken together, this indicates a winter settlement. Evert Baudou claims that this is typical of base settlements in the inner coastal region.

The second settlement we will look at here is Lillberget at Överkalix in Norrbotten. The settlement belongs to the Comb Ware group, having an eastern distribution. It was situated on a slightly sloping hill, *c.* 58–64 metres above sea level, and had no direct connection with a larger body of water. However, near Lillberget there were a couple of smaller lakes and the settlement faces a larger wetlands area. There are several things interesting about this site – nine dwelling structures and finds of comb pottery, flint, copper and a grave-field.

The nine, or possibly ten, dwellings are grouped around a *c.* 0.6 ha large depression that has a marsh-like quality. Interestingly, the houses are situated right next to each other. The houses vary in size between 21 × 13.5 metres on the outside and 14 × 5 metres on the inside. The smallest house is 8 × 7 metres and 5.5 × 3–5 metres respectively. On the inside, the houses are almost rectangular in shape, with sharp corners. The shape of the houses has led to the interpretation that they were probably built with logs, a kind of blockhouse. In addition, the floors are somewhat sunken. Several fireplaces were found in the houses.

The eastern-influenced comb decorated pottery is the oldest in northern Sweden and, like the entire Lillberget site, can be dated to about 3900 BC As mentioned above, flint has been found here. The flint found at Lillberget is of a different kind than for example that found in southern Sweden. The colour of the flint from southern Sweden is generally greyish blue to black, while that from Lillberget is almost light brown to greyish purple. What is interesting is that this type of flint originates from Russia. Also within the site is a smaller grave-field with four identified (probable) graves. I write 'probable' as no human bones have

Figure 3.15. Reconstruction of what the settlement at Högmossen may have looked like c. 5,500 years ago (source: Björk and Hjärtner-Holdar (eds) 2008).

Figure 3.16. Different kinds of clay pots (reconstructed) from the settlement at Högmossen (source: Björk and Hjärtner-Holdar (eds) 2008).

been found. What do we base this assumption on then? The fact that the four shallow pits with stones contain traces of red ochre powder makes it possible to interpret them as graves. This is something considered typical for the late Mesolithic graves at Skateholm in Scania and Vedbæck in Denmark.

Ove Halén, who excavated Lillberget, claims that the settlement should be seen as being permanently inhabited over a long time. He also sees the choice of settlement location as strategic from several different points of view – communication, but also a rich abundance of game animals. What did the people hunt and eat at Lillberget? The clear majority (81 percent) of the burned bones come from different species of seals, followed by European elk and beaver in significantly smaller amounts. The same was true of fish, where pike was the dominant species.

Settlement trends

We have now come to an end of this part of our journey. I have described settlements, with or without huts or houses, from Scania in the south to Lappland and Norrbotten in the north. I have decided which sites to visit; however, I do believe that they present a representative picture of how people lived during the period 3950–3650 BC, in other words, the Primary Early Neolithic period. Is it possible to see any clear trends in settlements? Of course, it is not so simple to present a clear and unequivocal picture of how people lived during this long period based only on the material presented here. There are however clear trends.

Around 4000 BC, a shift clearly occurs in the focus of settlements in southern Sweden – from the coasts to more inland sites. The change has been associated with the first farmers and has received the collective name of Funnel Beaker Culture. This can be seen in may different ways, like from the distribution of certain kinds of flint and ground stone axes as well as in the pollen diagrams that show that new areas had been cleared. At the same time, the first longhouses of the Mossby type begin to be built. The question is of course whether these were the first longhouses. We should not forget the houses from Tågerup that belong to the late Ertebølle Culture. The techniques used in house building were not completely unfamiliar. The Mossby houses were being built throughout southern, central and western Sweden during this time. There are however areas where few or no houses of this type have been found. One such area is the Malmö region, which seems quite remarkable. Several explanations for this exception have been discussed, for example, that these early farmers utilized areas of landscape with a predilection for ridges close to waterways. This is quite apparent if we compare the results from the archaeological excavations in the Malmö region with those conducted in connection with the West Coast railway in western Scania. In the latter region, a number of Mossby-type houses and similar houses have been examined. Close proximity to waterways is very apparent in this area, within which most of the early longhouses have been excavated.

One important and much discussed question concerns how big the settlements were. A usual estimate is that they were rather small, 5–600 m², and were made up of isolated farms inhabited by an extended family of perhaps 8–10 people. The large excavations in recent years have changed this picture to some extent. Both in southern Sweden and in central Sweden, very large settlements have been excavated. The problem is that it is not that simple to be able to say that there were several farms existing at the site simultaneously. It is possible that the farms moved periodically around within a larger area. This is something that can be difficult to determine and date.

The people at these settlements were essentially farmers, a subject that will be addressed in the next section. We see a completely different picture however, if we look north of the Funnel Beaker Culture's northern boundary in northern Uppland. The extensive excavations in connection with the new construction of European route E4 have provided us with a large amount of new knowledge about how people lived in the region that today makes up northern Uppland and southern Norrland. Here, we can also see the emergence of permanent settlements with houses and huts, like at Högmossen for example. This settlement, which dates to the end of the period, is characterized by pottery as well as a very well-ordered way of organizing daily life. The people who lived here were not farmers, but were hunters and fishermen.

Farther to the north, we encounter large settlements such as Voullerim and Lillberget, with their well-built houses and sometimes even with associated grave-fields. The latter site, with its 9–10 likely log houses, is very large, and with the rich occurrence of eastern pottery called comb ceramics, the Russian flint and copper, this site was very special. The dating result of about 3900 BC is early for Norrbotten. The people who lived at these sites were hunters and fishermen who primarily hunted European elk in addition to seal.

What did they eat?

In this section, I will address the difficult question of what people ate, hunted and cultivated during the period 4000–3300 BC. Our knowledge about living conditions and diet has increased markedly over the past 20 years. Knowledge in this area comes from many different sources. We have impressions of cereal grains in the ceramics, evidence from pollen diagrams as well as residues from plants, bones and other materials found during excavation of the settlements. During recent years, we can also add results from the natural sciences in the form of DNA-analyses, lipid analyses and chemical analyses of human bones. These results have greatly revolutionized our knowledge of human living conditions.

Today, we can see clear trends as well as local and regional differences. In the following section, we will examine this closer. In this chapter, we will look at all of Sweden and not divide our survey into geographical regions.

Stone Age food

In order to gain perspective on the developments during the Early Neolithic, we should turn the clock backwards to the Late Mesolithic. At the beginning, I mentioned that there is evidence that people of that time (4600–4000 BC) knew about agriculture. Some of the more clear evidence for this is the impressions of cereal grains in a few typical Ertebølle potsherds from Scania, a discovery published by Kristina Jennbert. These finds indicate that knowledge of cereal cultivation existed – but were people already farmers then? No, the archaeological finds clearly dispute this. Does evidence exist that the hunters kept domesticated livestock? From parts of Denmark, there are several dated finds of bones and teeth from cattle. They date to between 4900 and 4600 BC However, DNA-analyses of these have clearly shown that the material comes from aurochs and not from domesticated livestock.

As early as *c.* 4600 BC, we also see evidence of domesticated livestock from sites in northern Germany (Grube-Rosenhof). Naturally, we should adopt a critical attitude to some of these dating results since it can be difficult to see the difference between domestic cattle and aurochs.

We should also remain critical of the number of pollen diagrams from both Denmark and Sweden; however, from Central Sweden there are indications that cereal cultivation there may have been considerably older than the early Neolithic. In many ways, it can be difficult to distinguish between for example wild species of grass and different kinds of cereal.

We can begin by looking at what is today a classic find from Dragsholm on Själland (Denmark), which in an illustrative manner lifts several important questions. During the early 1970s, three graves were excavated: two of them contained women. One woman was around 18–years-old and the other was middle-aged. They had been buried in the same grave with rich grave goods, for example in the form of tooth beads. Dating analysis of the two women has been debated, but new radiocarbon dating results place them between *c.* 4950 and 4730 BC This means that the graves are considerably older than what was previously believed. The third grave, which was located two metres from the women's grave, contained the skeleton of a 30-year-old man. Placed in his grave was a rich and varied collection of grave goods such as funnel beakers, a battle-axe, an armguard and transverse arrows, which reveal traces of bows and arrows. This grave is dated to between 3780 and 3640 BC Thus, there is a difference of almost 1,000 years between the individuals.

In addition to the rich grave goods found, the dead have been able to tell us much about the food they ate during their lives. Using chemical analyses combined with radiocarbon dating, we can see great differences in what these individuals ate during their lives. At the transition to the Early Neolithic, both in Scandinavia and in Great Britain researchers have been able to see a clear change in what people ate; they went from a diet of chiefly seafood to one containing more protein from land-living animals and plants, like cereals. By measuring the amount of carbon-13, which shows this difference, we can see a clear change in what they ate. The analyses indicate that the women's diets included about 70 percent seafood, while the man's diet included only about 15–20 percent. This shows a very clear change in what people ate when comparing the Mesolithic with the Neolithic.

What were the reasons for this change? When humans began cultivating crops and keeping livestock, their lives rapidly changed. From having been hunters and fishermen, they became farmers. What do we know today about the cultivation of crops and the raising of livestock during the period between 4000 and 3300 BC? In addition to the impressions of cereal grains in potsherds, we also have finds of large amounts of charred grains from many sites in Sweden. The finds contain very small amounts of weeds, which may indicate that the material was picked over. Simple kinds of wheat such as einkorn wheat, emmer, spelt and barley were grown. Oats and rye came much later. The fact that few weeds are among the finds could indicate that our image of a kind of gardening with well-kept, enclosed fields may be correct. Interesting however is that in the pollen diagrams from a number of Danish graves from this period, we can see that people cleared, burned and then grew crops in thin birch forests. That it was just birch forests might indicate that it was not the first time the forest was cleared at these locations. However, this does not exclude that gardening methods were also used.

There are still relatively few radiocarbon-dated burnt cereal grains from Sweden, but the dating results we do have indicate that they had already begun cultivating grain crops early in this period. From Almhov in Malmö as well as from Mossby in the southernmost part of the region, we have dating analyses from cereal grains indicating the period 3900–3630 BC.

An interesting picture of the changes in settlement patterns in Scania has been established. From the inner parts of Scania, the hilly region, we find that a change takes place at around 3500 BC The settlements are concentrated along the coasts, and it is apparent that plant cultivation also gains increasing importance, which can be seen in that the ard, or scratch-plough, begins to be used. An ard is a simple kind of plough that breaks up the soil without turning it over. This innovation was a significant development in the history of agriculture.

In central Sweden, finds of burnt cereal grains are also relatively common and the dating of these are well in agreement with those from Almhov and Mossby. This indicates that the people in Central Sweden began cultivating cereal crops just as early as did the people in Southern Sweden.

Today we have a good knowledge regarding the raising of livestock, which not only included cattle but also pigs and sheep/goats, as well as about how important the different animals were. The oldest dated finds of cattle from Scania and Denmark are from *c.* 3960 BC, and the same goes for sheep/goats. We do not have very exact dates from the remains from pigs and they were utilized as hunted game already during the Mesolithic. Here, we have problems discriminating domestic swine from their wild relatives. In central Sweden, there is a clear difference between settlements that can be called base or land-facing settlements, and hunting or sea-facing settlements. At the first mentioned settlements, cattle, sheep/goats and domestic pigs are predominant; while at the latter, primarily sea animals are in majority, *i.e.*, fish and seals. Dating results from the bones of cattle show that they are approximately the same age as those from southern Sweden and Denmark, perhaps somewhat younger.

The distribution of the different species is based on a combination of archaeological material and what we assume the surrounding landscape looked like – open or with dense forests. In other words, there is no doubt that the early farmers in Denmark and southernmost Sweden kept cattle, pigs, and sheep/goats, and grew different kinds of crops. The distribution among the different species of animals is, as mentioned, difficult to ascertain. However, there are many indications that pigs were common during the oldest part of the Neolithic, and were later supplemented by cattle. This agrees with how the landscape changed and the clearing of the dense forests, as well as the view of cattle as a sign of prosperity.

Analyses of isotopes from skeletons found in graves in Västergötland and on Öland clearly indicate that there were differences between both different geographic regions and between people within the same district. In Västergötland, people mostly ate meat as well as freshwater fish, while those on Öland had a much more varied diet with food originating both from land and sea.

In an important article from 1981, the British archaeologist Andrew Sherratt described what he called the *secondary products revolution*, or the time when humans began using dairy products. This is something that has recently been intensively debated and significant new results have emerged. This research uses modern DNA techniques and genetic research to examine whether the younger Stone Age population utilized milk and whether they had the ability to make use of it physiologically. In other words, what the distribution of lactose tolerance/intolerance was or, whether the population tolerated drinking milk at that time. The results of the analyses clearly show that the Funnel Beaker population on Öland obviously tolerated milk. The results are quite similar to that found in the current Swedish population. We should understand however that these studies concern graves that were created about 3600 BC and can therefore not be seen as representative of the entire period 4000–3300 BC.

North of Uppland, which is the northern boundary of the Funnel Beaker Culture, we have no evidence of agriculture before *c.* 2500 BC, which we will return to later. In this vast area, hunting and fishing was still predominant. Seal hunting in particular was an important part of peoples' strategy for obtaining a food supply. There are however large regional and seasonal variations. In northern Sweden, we can see that during the summers, people lived at the coast and hunted seals and fished, while during the winters, they lived partly at inland locations and hunted primarily European elk.

In summary, we can say that already during the oldest part of the Primary Early Neolithic (3950–3650 BC), people in southern Sweden and in Denmark began growing different kinds of cereal crops as well as keeping cattle, pigs and sheep/goats. At approximately the same time, the people in central Sweden also began growing crops and keeping livestock. It is difficult to provide a clear answer to what the distribution was between growing crops and keeping livestock. If we look at evidence from the pollen diagrams, it is a question of small clearings in the forests, which indicates that the importance of growing crops was relatively insignificant during the period 4000–3600 BC Results from the analyses from skeletons from graves in Västergötland and on Öland suggest that keeping livestock was more important; however, there are large regional differences. In Sweden north of Uppland, there are no traces of agriculture before *c.* 2500 BC and people were still hunters/fishermen and gatherers where different areas were used during different parts of the year.

4   The Dead and the Afterlife

Mats Larsson

In this chapter, I will discuss how people dealt with the dead during the first part of the Early Neolithic period and correspondingly, the rituals and sacrifices associated with this. During the early part of the Funnel Beaker Culture, there were three main kinds of graves:

- long barrows
- flat graves
- dolmens.

Long barrows

The different kinds of graves follow a certain chronology and it is therefore appropriate we begin with the long barrows. What is a long barrow? Geographically, we find them from central Poland to France and England in the west. We have also found them in North Germany, Denmark and Scania, in other words, quite a large geographical area. The length of a long barrow varies greatly – from 20 metres to over 300 metres, while they rarely exceed 10 metres in width. Their shapes can vary from oval to rectangular or triangular. Thus, they are generally long, narrow mounds of earth that covered one or more graves, in addition to having a pole structure, a façade, on the eastern side.

There were three clear ways to demarcate the actual mounds – using trenches, stones or timber palisades. In many cases, these long barrows form actual 'burial grounds', with up to 17 long barrows, like at Balloy not far from Paris. This site is also interesting in that several of the long barrows were constructed directly on top of older settlements with houses from the Linear Pottery Culture. The graves were constructed c. 4500–4450 BC and should therefore be about 200 years younger than the houses. This connection between houses, settlements and graves is often emphasized. The exterior similarities between these long barrows and the houses belonging to the Linear Pottery Culture are often striking – regarding both shape and size. Because of this, archaeologists sometimes refer to them as 'houses for the dead'. In most cases however, we see a difference of several hundred-years between these houses and the long barrows. This is especially evident in Denmark and Scania. Therefore, we must find other explanations for why people built these burial monuments.

In Scandinavia, it was not until the latter part of the 1970s that the long barrows were identified, first in Denmark. In an earlier chapter, we described how sites such as Barkær and

Stengade went from having been identified as longhouses to becoming long barrows. During the following years, archaeological excavations clearly indicated that the long barrows were complex constructions. This resulted in that we often talk about 'a monument's biography', *i.e.*, its life history. We can see that the long barrows have a long and complex origin. They can start out as being a simple wooden palisade that encloses a grave. Like at Bygholm on Jylland, it may have been a former house that was incorporated into the long barrow. The house from Bygholm, which is similar to the Mossby house we discussed earlier but is unusually small, had been torn down and a young person of about 13–15 years old had been buried on the floor of the original house, most likely in a wooden coffin that had completely decayed. Consequently, the house should be considered a house of the dead. Time passes, we do not know how long, and another grave is constructed. In this case, four adults buried in pairs, one pair with their heads towards the east and one pair with their heads towards the west. Two smaller houses are built, and after that, everything is cleared away and the actual barrow is constructed. In the eastern part of the long barrow, an oblong pit was discovered with traces of large, strong posts. Here, ceremonies were most likely conducted in connection with burials. For example, clay pots have been placed in the barrow.

Several long barrows have been excavated in Scania during recent decades, most of these in connection with the important studies in the Malmö region and in western Scania. Researchers have only been able to identify them thanks to pits and postholes in the eastern edges of the long barrows. Only a few excavations have taken place in and around the long barrows in the countryside. These were smaller excavations at Örnakulla and Jättegraven near Malmö and Trelleborg.

Concerning more recent excavations of long barrows, Almhov in Malmö is particularly interesting. Within a quite large area, *c.* 10 ha, artefacts from mainly the Early Neolithic were uncovered. Especially interesting for this chapter were the remains of four or possibly five probable long barrows. I write remains as we have only uncovered the eastern facades with their sacrificial pits and traces of 'facades' in the form of sturdy posts. Regarding the presumed long barrows, one of them is credible, since preserved artefacts from the filling of the barrow were found. As far as the others are concerned, there are objections. Are they long barrows or 'only' palisade constructions with associated graves? It might be that there are two stages to the burial customs. The first involving the grave and palisade, and for some, a barrow is added (Fig. 4.1).

Presumed graves were investigated in several of the constructions. Human bones were primarily found in a rectangular dark-coloured area that measured 2.9 × 1.4 metres. The skeletal remains were poorly preserved, but they are from two individuals perhaps, one who was about 30–40 years old and the other about 30 years old when they died.

In another long barrow, a thin-butted axe was found in a presumed grave, but no traces of skeletons were uncovered.

Several, what can be interpreted as sacrificial pits were excavated near the long barrows. The one richest in artefacts (A19049) contained over 30 kg of pottery, at least 60 pots, which is quite a large quantity of pottery. Archaeologist Elisabeth Rudebeck considers this large amount of pots, and other artefacts such as flint tools and bones, as evidence of large commemorations in connection with burials.

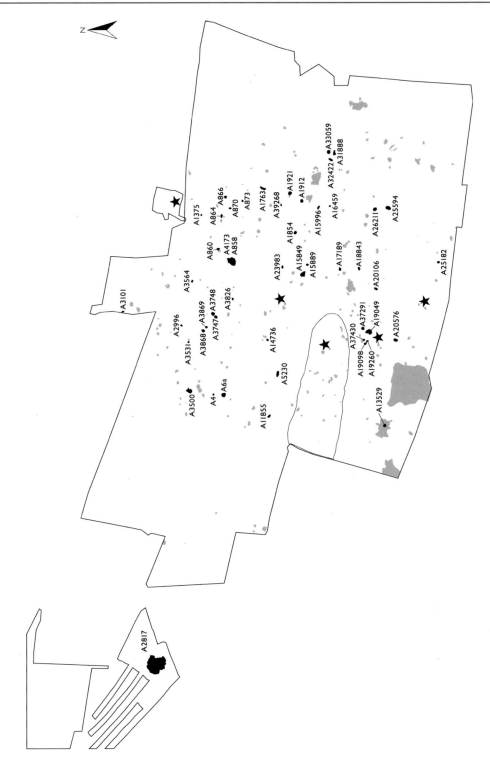

Figure 4.1. The excavated site at Almhov in Malmö, with the long barrows marked (source: Rudebeck 2010).

Based on several ^{14}C-analyses, we can date the presumed long barrows at Almhov to between *c.* 3970 and 3700/3500 BC Both interesting and thought provoking is that these dates are among the oldest we have from long barrows in northern Europe. In other words, we may be dealing with two stages that directly follow each other. We cannot see any direct evidence from settlements during this time, but the site gives the impression of having been an area where people gathered for burials and to conduct various ceremonies in conjunction with them.

Flat graves

A flat grave is, to put it simply, a skeleton buried in a grave beneath the topsoil. The grave may contain wooden or stone coffins. They are primarily skeleton graves, even if burning of corpses, cremation, took place as early as in the Early Neolithic. Compared with Denmark, relatively few flat-ground graves have been excavated in Sweden.

One problem with this kind of grave is that in only a very few cases is the skeletal material preserved. A few cases from Malmö (Almhov) were mentioned above, where skeletal remains have been found. As I said, this is uncommon. Often, more or less undefined pits are interpreted as being graves – sometimes with, and sometimes without typical artefacts such as pots and different kinds of axes. Such uncertain but probable graves have been studied in several places in Scania and other regions.

One nice example of a flat grave is a burial site that measured 3.5 × 1.7 metres and 0.8 metres deep from Oxie near Malmö, which was excavated at the end of the 1970s. A thin-butted flint axe almost 30 cm long was found in the pit. Together with the axe, excavators found a special kind of pot, a so-called collared flask. These small vessels with small openings have often been considered drinking-vessels and are generally associated with graves.

As mentioned above, the burning of corpses or cremation was practiced during this period. A good example is found at Fågelbacken in Västmanland. The site and its huts can be seen as a temporary abode in connection with burials and ceremonies. Fredrik Hallgren vividly describes the site:

> For an early Neolithic traveller who came wandering over the ice or paddling across the fjord, the row of gravesites with erect posts must have been a striking sight, especially when they were shrouded in smoke from the crackling flames of the funeral pyres.

In other words, it was a very special place. In conjunction with the excavations in 1993, excavators discovered 21 structures with charred human bone. These have been classified in three groups:

- post structures
- bone pits
- fire pits.

Post structures were substantial stone-filled postholes, sometimes placed in groups of threes. Bone pits were pits with clean bones, *i.e.*, without soot and charcoal. The third group is made of pits with bones with a great deal of soot and charcoal. Not only human bones were found in these, but often also elaborately decorated funnel beaker pottery. An estimation

Figure 4.2. Collared flask from the Oxie grave (source: Larsson 1979).

of the number of individuals represented among the bones is at least 20–22 people, both men and women (Fig. 4.2).

Traces remain from a kind of timber structure that can be interpreted as a grave or a 'house of the dead'. If this interpretation is correct, it may indicate that the dead were first stored in this building before being cremated.

Fågelbacken is not the only place where burial pyres or cremation have been studied, as there are several more sites in Central Sweden. One such site is the settlement at Östra Vrå in Södermanland, which we visited earlier. As is often the case in the history of archaeology, the discovery was made in connection with development plans. In this case, it was in connection with new running of cables. The graves were made up of two 2.5 × 4.5 metre pits, which were interestingly enough covered by stone packing composed largely of broken as well as whole grinding pebbles. At the bottom of the pits, charred and un-charred bones were uncovered. In this case, it was not adults, but children between 0–7 years old that were found. Among the stone packing, excavators uncovered parts of small funnel beakers as well as stone artefacts. Some charred grain seeds were also found. One of these has been ^{14}C-dated to 3510–3120 BC.

Dolmens

We have now come to the third type of grave from the Early Neolithic – dolmens. What is a dolmen? Megalithic grave is a collective term for the different kinds of large stone chamber graves. The word megalithic is from the Greek word for large stone. Dolmens are known from large parts of Western Europe, from the Iberian Peninsula to southern Norway.

The typical grave chamber of a dolmen is covered by a capstone (a large horizontal boulder), which rests on several upright wall stones. Often, the stone chamber is part of a rectangular or round barrow – long dolmen and round dolmen respectively – which is demarcated by erected boulders. Originally, such barrows probably covered most of the dolmens; however, the earth mounds have disappeared or eroded in most cases today.

There are a hundred or so preserved dolmens in Sweden, found in Scania, Halland, Bohuslän as well as on Öland, Gotland and in Östergötland. However, it is not completely clear whether in the latter three mentioned regions we are actually dealing with dolmens or some other kind of megalithic graves. The number of undiscovered finds is also probably quite large. Through studies of older surveyor's maps as well as through archaeological studies, we know that originally there were significantly more dolmens than what we see in today's landscape.

Figure 4.3. Round dolmen at Hofterup in Scania (photograph: M. Larsson).

Figure 4.4. Long dolmen at Skegrie in Scania (photograph: M. Larsson).

The relative few that have been preserved in Sweden today can be compared with Denmark, where as many as 7,000 have been preserved and estimates suggest that there may have been up to 27,000. Quite an amazing number, not the least when you consider that the estimated working time needed to build a dolmen is about 10,000 working hours.

We should also not forget that a significant number were removed or destroyed during previous centuries. Through studying older surveyor's maps, we can sometimes see where the missing megalithic graves were marked out. If they were not placed on the map, their names can sometimes reveal where they were located, for example Dyseåkern (dolmen field). Megalithic graves can also be uncovered in connection with archaeological excavations. For example, in the long dolmen at Hindby Mosse near Malmö, which was excavated by Göran Burenhult at the beginning of the 1970s, a very rich find of material was made including pottery, flint and skeletal remains, even though no visible signs of the dolmen remained. We will look at other such sites later (Fig. 4.3).

Few archaeological excavations have been done around the megalithic graves in southern Scandinavia, but what has been done indicates that different activities took place at the gravesites, not only in the direct vicinity of the graves, but also within a larger area surrounding them. Finds of pottery, charred flint axes, *etc.*, indicate that we are dealing with different sacred acts such as sacrifices and depositions (Fig. 4.4).

In the literature, we see that archaeologists often write about two main types of dolmens:

- round dolmens
- rectangular dolmens.

Previously, archaeologists believed that there was a chronological difference between these two types, but it is difficult to find support for this view today. It is obvious, however, that the oldest dolmens had a rectangular burial chamber, approximately the same length as a man. These were seldom larger than 2 × 1 metres. Unfortunately, what we know about these original interments is poor. This is because after the first burial, additional burials were conducted. Because of this, of course very few dolmens have been excavated where the first burials have been intact.

In order to study one such grave, we will need to travel to Denmark, southern Fyn, and a dolmen called Klokkehøj. The dolmen is missing one supporting stone as well as the capstone. Between the supporting stones, archaeologists discovered a carefully laid dry-stone walling composed of reddish-coloured sandstone particles. Dry-stone is a building technique where stone structures are constructed without using mortar. The floor of the chamber consisted of several elements: flakes, coarse gravel, a clay layer and charred flint, with the latter uppermost. The skeleton in the primary grave, which was almost completely preserved, lay in the northern part of the chamber. Interestingly, a large part of the skull and the four most proximal vertebrae were missing. This may indicate that the skull was removed immediately after the man's death. The skeleton is from a man who was 20–35 years old and *c.* 175–180 cm tall. The only artefact that can be connected to this grave is a dagger-like object. Also found in the grave chamber were poorly preserved remains from two additional burials – a child and an adult. I should point out that aside from these three graves, there were remains from at least 11 additional burials, which occurred later and which are dated to the late part of the next period, the Middle Neolithic, 3300–2700 BC

The primary grave is dated to *c.* 3250 BC Worth noting is that ^{13}C levels indicate that the man had eaten food primarily taken from food sources on land (Fig. 4.5).

One nice example of a dolmen in Scania is from Trollasten, east of Ystad, which was excavated by Märta Strömberg in 1965. However, an earlier excavation had taken place already in 1855. In conjunction with the excavation in 1965, not only the actual burial chamber but also a larger area around the dolmen was excavated. In the area in front of the dolmen a large amount of stone packing was discovered, which was also found behind and around the sides of the dolmen. In front of the stone packing, three substantial postholes were excavated. The chamber of the dolmen is constructed of six stones, which had supported a capstone. The chamber has a regular shape and measures 2.4 × 2 metres. Exactly like at Klokkehøj, the floor of the chamber was built up of several different layers of stone, sand and clay.

A great many finds were discovered in the chamber, mostly in the sandy layer that had been placed on top of the stone packing. Discoveries of probable skeletons, pottery and stone/flint tools were discovered here.

As is often the case, significant amounts of the finds were discovered outside the opening in the stone packing mentioned above. Not only pottery and flint/stone artefacts, but also

Figure 4.5. The Trollasten dolmen (source: Strömberg 1968).

axes, often damaged by fire, and charred human bones were found. The phenomenon of charred flint axes is something I will return to later.

The oldest pottery from Trollasten can be placed in the Late Early Neolithic, *c.* 3400 BC (the Bellevuegård group), while clearly the largest part of the finds belong to the Middle Neolithic, which will be addressed in the next chapter. The Trollasten dolmen thus gives an impression of having been constructed and used during the latter part of the Early Neolithic, which is in agreement with results from Danish and Swedish studies.

Döserygg (Dolmen Ridge)

Sometimes, archaeological excavations can completely change the established picture of a time period. Such was the case with the fantastic finds resulting from the construction project of European route E6, south of Malmö and Vellinge in southern Scania. During 2006–2008, archaeologists conducted significant excavations, resulting in astounding discoveries. Archaeologists Magnus Andersson and Björn Nilsson from Lund write that already during the pilot studies preceding the excavation, they could see traces of what were most likely dolmens on the surveyor's maps from the 1770s. The map referred to the area as *Döserygg*. We will know look at the events that followed.

What archaeologists found here was not 1 dolmen, but 20 dolmens. All of them were damaged in some way – supporting stones and capstones were missing. However, dark impressions in the sand showed where the supporting stones had originally stood. Artefacts found in the dolmens were mostly axes, fragments of axes, scrapers and flakes, as well as an abundance of pottery of different kinds and quality; however, there were no traces of human remains (Fig. 4.6).

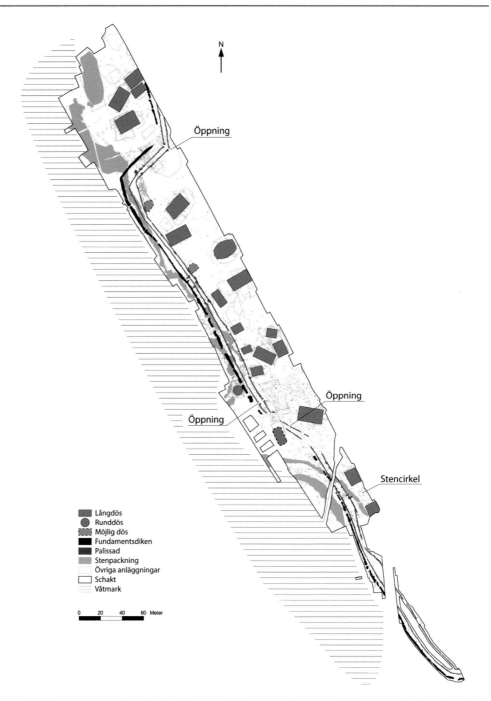

Figure 4.6. Döserygg in southern Scania. Overview of the excavated area with dolmens, palisades and wetlands marked on the map (source: Andersson and Nilsson 2009).
■ *Long dolmen;* ● *Round dolmen;* ▦ *Possible dolmen;* ■ *Foundation trench;* ■ *Palisade;* ■ *Stone packing;* □ *Other structures;* □ *Shaft;* □ *Wetland; Öppning = entrance; Stencirkel = Stone circle.*

Figure 4.7. Döserygg. Re-creation of what the site may have looked like 5,500 years ago (source: Andersson and Nilsson 2009).

Almost all of the dolmens have been deduced as being rectangular, and only two can be construed as round dolmens. In addition to the 20 dolmens, the most startling find was of two parallel stone-filled trenches. Three ^{14}C dating analyses (3980–3760 BC, 3500–3100 BC and 3350–3020 BC), together with the other finds place the trenches in the period between the Early Neolithic I and Middle Neolithic II. The earliest dates imply that the trenches, with their tightly placed posts, should probably be seen as one of the first building phases at Döserygg and that this was among the first structures built there together with the first dolmens.

The trenches were aligned north to south across the entire large area studied and were between six and eight metres apart. Several poles and standing stones had been erected in the trenches. Findings were uncovered in the palisade trenches including traces of axe manufacturing as well as an abundance of charred flint. Remains of two openings in the palisade could also be seen.

Archaeologists found several flint axes as well as scrapers and pottery out in what was once the wetlands. A significant number of the axes showed signs of damage from fire (Fig. 4.7).

Taken as a whole, the area is adjacent to an earlier marshland to the west, and along this, outside the palisade, traces of about 300 erected stones were discovered. The archaeologists excavating the site interpreted the rows of stones as a kind of 'wall' or demarcation from the water. It comprised an elongated and dense area of stone packing arranged in recurring square formations. The artefacts found in the stone packing were from the younger Stone

Age and included mostly objects made of flint, and are easily comparable to finds from the dolmens and the probable procession road.

In summary, we can say that the excavations at *Döserygg* have provided us with a completely different picture of Early Neolithic society. We see a complex and well-organized society in which care for the dead and ancestor worship were central and important elements. To this, we can also add the widespread placement of axes and other objects as well as pottery in the adjacent marshland, which can be considered ceremonial elements.

In order to see anything similar to *Döserygg*, one must look to the British Isles and locations with procession roads, for example, Avebury and Stonehenge. However, we should remember that these are younger than Döserygg.

Meeting places for the living and the dead – Sarup structures

Before we leave this period, we should look at a few additional things. Among these are the types of structures that in the past were seen as fortifications, but that today we consider to have been ceremonial meeting places for a local society. In today's archaeological literature, they have the collective name Sarup structures, named after a location on the Danish island of Fyn. They have been dated to the latter part of the Early Neolithic, but younger dating results have also been reported. Unfortunately, no similar structures from this period have yet to be discovered in Sweden, but as we shall see, there are younger structures. For this context, we will therefore remain in Denmark as we examine the *c.* 20 such structures that are today known to exist there. If any one of these is to be mentioned, it should be the only one that is fully excavated, that is Sarup itself.

The site was located on a sandy peninsula surrounded by two smaller bodies of water. Worth noting is also that the site was located in the centre of a densely populated district with several settlements, dolmens and places of sacrifice nearby. Also worth noting is that the site is not located centrally in the district, but lies on the outskirts (Fig. 4.8).

Construction at the Sarup site began around 3400 BC and it is a very impressive structure. A palisade was constructed with enclosures and large pits on the inside. The area that was thus enclosed measured *c.* 8.5 ha. Niels H. Andersen who led the excavations at Sarup between 1971 and 1984 notes that the palisade was built with split oak logs that were approximately 2 to 3 metres long. It is an impressive site! It is estimated that 1,300 oak logs were cut and shaped. There was only one narrow entrance to the inner part of the structure. This was located in the middle of the palisade and was 1.6 metres wide. The entrance was shielded on both sides by fences, and a 2–3.5 metre-wide path led into the inner area. The Danish archaeologist Jørgen Jensen has expressively called the interior of Sarup 'the village of the dead'.

What actually took place here? Thanks to the very meticulous excavations, we know a great deal. Inside the palisade were two parallel rows of large pits, 15 × 4 metres, which were 1 metre or occasionally 2 metres deep. Associated with these pits were different kinds of fencing making up a complex system. At the bottom of these pits, different kinds of stone constructions, charcoal layers and hearths were found, as well as concentrations of artefacts.

In some places, archaeologists also found human bones from both children and adults. It could also be seen that after an object was placed in the pits, the pits were then filled in, and after a few years the process was repeated. How long was the site used? It is estimated that it was only used for 30–40 years, which is a very short time considering the enormous efforts of labour required to build the structure.

Are there any traces left from different events that may have taken place inside the 8.5 ha enclosed area? There are certainly traces of some pits that might be seen as being sacrificial pits, containing for example vessels that were sometimes filled with cereal grains. However, traces of houses or other buildings were not discovered. We really can call this 'the village of the dead'.

By way of introduction, I mentioned that Sarup structures were seen as fortified villages in the past, but that today they are seen as ceremonial gathering places for a region. They were used for a short time during the same period dolmens were being constructed and used. What we can see as ceremonies are associated with both, and there are explanations that argue that they are places to which the dead were brought in order to be placed in the large pits – the uncovered skeletal remains can corroborate this. After they became skeletonized, the dead were taken to the dolmens for final burial. Here we can return to the skeleton at Klokkehøj, with the missing skull. Perhaps it was placed at Sarup, which is not far from the dolmen (Fig. 4.9).

Intensive archaeological work in the Sarup region has provided an abundance of new data concerning settlements, sacrificial findings as well as dolmens. The number of known dolmens has for example increased from 4 to 175.

Burnt axes and ceremonial deposits

In this section, we will look at the different kinds of ceremonial depositions that are so characteristic of this period.

We can begin with the burnt flint axes. We mentioned earlier that burnt flint has been found in several different places, for example at settlements, but also as a part of the construction of the dolmens (Klokkehøj). In the 1980s, a new category of sites was discovered. Pronounced ridges or nearness to watercourses characterized the location of these sites. One such site is Svartskylle in southern Scania. A significant number of severely burned fragments of mostly thin-butted axes have been discovered at this site. They were primarily concentrated to two smaller areas. Lars Larsson interpreted Svartskylle as a place for the deliberate destruction of mostly axes for ceremonial purposes. He points out that burnt flint is often found in many contexts that are commonly interpreted as being ceremonial. The site was deliberately selected due to its very pronounced elevation, which meant that people could see the fires from a great distance.

It is not only in Scania that we see this phenomenon of burnt flint axes. During recent years, excavations at Stensborg in Grödinge (Södermanland) have shown that extensive depositing and burning of axes also occurred in Central Sweden during the Early Neolithic. This site can be dated to *c.* 3400 BC More than 500 fragments of flint axes have been found here. Most have come from thin-butted axes, but fragments of pointed-butted axes have also been found. Several of these

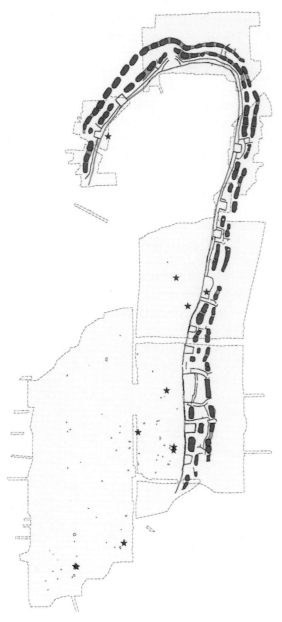

Figure 4.8. Sarup I. The stars indicate the so-called sacrificial pits (source: Andersen 1997).

are over 30 cm long. Also interesting are the pits that have been excavated. They were very difficult to see against the background of the light clay, but after going looking closer, it turned out that the pits had been refilled with the same clay found naturally in the area. Under this 'clay lid', pieces of finely ornamented pots and fragments of fire-damaged axes were found. We should also mention the large amount of burnt cereal grains found. This is actually the largest find of such material in Sweden and perhaps even the largest ever found in Scandinavia. Of the grain-types identified, the common type of wheat called emmer was most abundant.

How should we interpret and understand all of this? Lars Larsson, the archaeologist who conducted the excavation, maintains that we should see the burning of flint axes as a form of cremation. As mentioned earlier, cremation commonly occurred in Central Sweden during the Early Neolithic, and this may be a complement to the burial rites.

The sacrificial acts conducted in marshlands comprise a large and significant subject concerning sacrificial acts. In an earlier chapter, we mentioned the Danish archaeologist Carl Johan Becker and his work with pottery found in Danish bogs. The greater part of these pots, as well as other artefacts such as axes, has been found in connection with peat harvesting and therefore does not have a clear context of discovery. What we have been able to see is that the objects have usually been deposited along the edges of an overgrown lake or smaller watercourse, sometimes even on a constructed wooden platform.

Per Karsten, who has conducted quite a comprehensive study of Neolithic sacrificial

Figure 4.9. Sarup I. Re-creation of what the site may have looked like and how it may have been used (source: Andersen 1997).

finds, claims that there is an obvious connection between the placing of sacrifices during the Late Mesolithic and in the Early Neolithic. However, we know very little about the former, although we obviously see site continuity.

Not only axes and ceramic pots are sacrificed however, also people. We should look at one such find from Denmark. In 1948 at Sigerdal on the island of Själland, two skeletons from what were likely two women were discovered. Both had been young, about 16–18 years old, and one of them had obviously been strangled, as there were remnants of a rope around her throat. Radiocarbon analysis gives the date of *c.* 3500 BC.

From Swedish territory, we have a significant number of finds of human bones, particularly from Scania. Unfortunately, the majority of these are not datable; however, finds from Näbbe bog and Sandåkra (Skurup) have dates that indicate that the same sacrificial customs occurred in South Sweden. In both the Danish and Scanian examples, there is no doubt that we are dealing with human sacrifices.

What do we see here? Undeniably, we see a picture of an apparently extremely ritualized society, where ancestors and the care of them are quite significant. We can see this in the burial customs, the Sarup structures and in the depositions discussed above. Rituals are usually considered important parts of society, particularly during periods of uncertainty and stress. During the transition to the Early Neolithic with its new economy and a largely new way of perceiving the world and humanity's role in it, people must have experienced uncertainty and a sense of disjointedness. Jørgen Jensen writes that the depositions in watercourses can be seen as 'sacred meals', where the living met their dead ancestors.

It is obvious that people created a new world for themselves, but also that they consciously formed links with the older one. The rites conducted at different places were important for how societies were constructed, but also how they could be reworked. In this way, they helped people not only to connect with the past, but also with the future. By placement of objects, and for example the burning of flint axes, people connected back to stories and myths that had guided them towards an uncertain future. Religion researcher Catherine Bell claims that rites have such profound support among people that they rarely change.

The Early Neolithic – a few trends

We have come to the end of the first part of our long journey through the younger Stone Age (the Neolithic Period). Above, we have for example discussed different aspects of material culture, settlements, chronology, burial customs, economy and religious sacrifices.

As we have seen, the period between 3950 and 3300 BC, called the Early Neolithic, was an eventful epoch. Great changes in peoples' lives can be observed throughout Sweden, from Scania in the south to Lapland in the north. We can conclude that the introduction of an agricultural economy is a much-debated issue. In my opinion, this change was a rapid one. We can see that there really were no chronological differences between southern and central Sweden, rather that the processes start at approximately the same time, 3950–3800 BC There are also similarities, both in material culture and in what the settlements looked like. For example, we have been able to see that similar houses (Mossby houses) were built throughout the distribution of the Funnel Beaker Culture. The settlements also give the impression of being rather small, with one farm. Different kinds of settlements for farming and hunting/fishing existed in both areas.

Differences in various parts of society existed however. For example, it is uncertain whether the large burial monuments in Central Sweden were constructed as long barrows and dolmens, even if there is evidence of this in Östergötland and on Gotland. They most likely belong to the next period – the Middle Neolithic. Burial customs were also different. It is apparent that burial customs involving cremation were prevalent in Central Sweden, while in South Sweden the internment of skeletons was clearly most common.

Suggested readings

Andersen, N. H. 1989. Sarup: *befæstede kultpladser fra bondestenalderen*. Aarhus: Aarhus Universitets-forlag.
Andersson, M. 2003. *Skapa plats i landskapet*. Tidig- och mellanneolitiska samhällen utmed två västskånska dalgångar. Lund.
Andersson, M. and Nilsson, B. 2008. Döserygg: den skånska myllan gömde sex långdösar. *Populär arkeologi* 2008(26), 1, 16–17.
Björhem, N. and Magnusson Staaf, B. 2006. *Långhuslandskapet: en studie av bebyggelse och samhälle från stenålder till järnålder*. Malmö: Malmö kulturmiljö.
Cronberg, C. 2001. Husesyn. I Karsten, P. and Knarrström, B. (eds) *Tågerup specialstudier*, Skånska spår – arkeologi längs Västkustbanan. Stockholm: Riksantikvarieämbetet, 82–154.
Fischer, A. 2001. Food for feasting? An evaluation of explanations of the neolithisation of Denmark and southern Sweden. In Fischer, A. and Kristiansen, K. (eds) *The Neolihisation of Denmark. 150 year debate*. Sheffield, 343–393.

Hallgren, F. 2008. *Identitet i praktik. Lokala, regionala och överregionala sociala sammanhang inom nordlig trattbägarkultur.* Uppsala.

Jensen, J. 2001. *Danmarks Oldtid.* Stenalder 13000–2000 f.Kr. Köpenhamn: Gyldendahl.

Karsten, P. 1994. *Att kasta yxan i sjön. En studie över rituell tradition och förändring utifrån skånska neolitiska offerfynd.* Lund.

Larsson, M. 1984. *Tidigneolitikum i Sydvästskåne.* Kronologi och bosättningsmönster. Malmö.

Larsson, M. and Olsson, E. (eds) 1997. *Regionalt och interregionalt. Stenåldersundersökningar i Syd- och Mellansverige.* Riksantikvarieämbetet. Arkeologiska Undersökningar. Skrifter nr 23. Stockholm.

Malmer, M. P. 2002. *The Neolithic of South Sweden.* TRB, GRK, and STR. Stockholm.

Nilsson, B. and Rudebeck, E. (eds) 2010. *Arkeologiska och förhistoriska världar.* Fält, erfarenheter och stenåldersboplatser i sydvästra Skåne. Malmö.

Price, T. D. (ed.) 2000. *Europe's first farmers. Cambridge: Cambridge University Press.*

5   Science and the Neolithic

Kerstin Lidén

DNA, or genetic information, can be preserved under favourable conditions in diverse prehistoric remains, primarily in skeletal material such as bones and teeth. In addition, in remnants from plants and combinations of things like food scraps and faecal material, DNA from the original organisms can be preserved. This DNA is much degraded and therefore special methods and laboratories are needed in order to extract and interpret the information preserved; thus, it is anything but simple to conduct these kinds of investigations.

The material containing the best preserved DNA, and which is therefore predominantly used for the analysis of prehistoric remains, are teeth. This is due to the fact that the protective enamel around teeth is the body's hardest material. However, the teeth must not have been exposed to fire, since DNA and proteins are destroyed by fire and heating. This means that a large part of the prehistoric human remains cannot be used for DNA analyses since cremation was the predominant burial form during certain periods.

So, what kind of information can be produced using DNA analyses? What first comes to mind are of course the different kinds of kinship, both distant and close. The DNA studies that have attracted the most attention are those looking at the relationship between Neanderthals and anatomically modern humans. Findings regarding their kinship vary depending on whether the analysis has been based on mitochondrial DNA, which is only inherited through the maternal line, or whether it is based on nuclear DNA, which is inherited both maternally and paternally. The entire genome has now been analysed and it is obvious that the picture is a little more complicated than what was previously thought.

Close kinship has been studied in single graves where, in an analysis of a German Neolithic burial with four interred individuals, it was established that the two young individuals were the children of the adult woman and the adult man.

DNA can also be used to study different characteristics, hair or eye colour for example. This has also been done on a few Neanderthal individuals where results revealed that these individuals were redheaded. DNA can also be used to determine biological sex, which could be difficult to do based on skeletal parts when only isolated bones are found or where the individuals found are too young to have developed morphological sexual characteristics. When isolated bones or bone fragments from animals are found, DNA can be used to determine the species. For example, it is very difficult to tell the difference between sheep and goats based on skeletal parts, and DNA is a great help in these cases. The occurrence of illness and diseases can of course also be studied using DNA, regarding both hereditary diseases and bacterially transmitted diseases such as tuberculosis and leprosy.

As far as the situation in Scandinavia is concerned, researchers have used DNA to address the long debated relationship between Neolithic cultures characterized by different styles of pottery – the Pitted Ware Culture and the Funnel Beaker Culture. What do the different styles of pottery represent – are they separate ethnic groups or are they the same people, perhaps pursuing different activities at different places? We now have DNA analyses of skeletons buried in different contexts, *i.e.*, individuals buried with elements belonging to one or the other cultures, indicating that the people belonged to different genetic population groups. Therefore, the different styles of ceramics also represent the different population groups.

Domestication

That we took control of our own food production was a large step in our pre-history. When, where and how this took place is something that has interested many archaeologists as well as researchers within other disciplines. In recent years, the use of DNA has been a very powerful aid in understanding and answering these questions. Here, researchers have studied when cattle were domesticated, *i.e.*, when people took control over cattle reproduction and started breeding for certain sought after characteristics such as milk production, size and even colour. Using bones from northern European aurochs and cattle dated from 9500 to 1000 BC, researchers have been able to see that while the domesticated cattle in Europe originated from cattle from the Middle East and Asia and were brought here by farmers, people have also over a long period of time, consciously or unconsciously, used wild bulls for breeding purposes. Furthermore, researchers have discovered that pigs have been domesticated at several different times in different geographic locations, and that people have mixed domestic pigs with wild boar.

In horses, coat colour has been studied and researchers have for example found genetic evidence for the occurrence of spotted or multi-coloured horses, something seen in French cave paintings and which scientists were uncertain if this was due to artistic licence or a natural depiction. Through DNA analyses of horse bones dated to the same time as the paintings, researchers have determined that the gene that in modern horses leads to spotted coat colour, and which also leads to night-blindness, occurred relatively frequently in the recovered horse bones.

Adaptation

There are a few genetic changes in the human genetic material that can be argued are connected to changes in our diet. One such important change is the ability to break down lactose as adults, what we usually call being lactase persistent. The ability to utilize milk products is strongly associated to the introduction of agriculture, *i.e.*, when people begin keeping livestock. The milking of cows certainly requires that cattle have first been domesticated. The problem is only that the natural condition of more than 90 percent of the world's population is to be lactose intolerant, that is, they are NOT able to break down lactose as adults. The ability to break down lactose as adults arose through a mutation in a special gene that controls the production of the enzyme lactase, something that only a few people had and which obviously, during a certain period in prehistoric times, was so advantageous that there was strong selective pressure favouring this characteristic. Today, this characteristic is common among northern European populations. In a study of this particular gene in one of the Neolithic cultures in Scandinavia, the Pitted Ware Culture, researchers found that the ability for adults to break down lactose was uncommon compared with today's Swedish population. This might mean that in this particular hunter/gatherer culture it was not advantageous for adults to be able to drink milk, perhaps because they did not usually use milk products, since there is very little evidence that they kept any livestock.

Kinship

The big question of how the different Neolithic cultures are related to one another has also been addressed with the help of DNA studies. In this case, a study was conducted with DNA taken from teeth from two groups of people, one belonging to the Funnel Beaker Culture from the Swedish mainland and the other belonging to the Pitted Ware Culture on the island of Gotland. Here it was found that the two groups were genetically separate. They also found that the individuals who were buried in a megalithic tomb, and who thus came from a funnel beaker context, were more genetically similar to the current Swedish population. This could be interpreted as meaning that the individuals who came from Gotland and who belonged to the Pitted Ware Culture in this study were replaced by, or assimilated into the population of the Funnel Beaker Culture.

The future

The techniques and methods used today for studying the genetic make-up of prehistoric humans are continually being developed and becoming more refined. Knowledge concerning how we interpret the enormous amount of data and information produced is also increasing exponentially. This means that, today, what limits the information we can produce from prehistoric material lies rather in how well the material is preserved. However, perhaps even more important is how we use this information ethically, *i.e.*, what questions we ask of the material.

Isotopes

'You are what you eat' is the saying within the field of research that uses stable isotopes for studying the food and food cultures of prehistoric humans. This is because the food one eats is used to build the skeleton and other tissues in our bodies. This means that the isotope composition of the different elements of which food is composed, and which an individual then eats, is reflected in the same individual's skeleton and other tissues in a typical manner.

Isotopes are atoms of the same element with different numbers of neutrons and different mass. There are some isotopes that are radioactive and decay, like carbon-14, and which can thus be used for dating, while others are stable isotopes. The stable isotopes are the ones used in studies of diet and mobility. The elements that have isotopes commonly used for studying prehistoric remains are carbon, nitrogen, oxygen, sulphur and strontium.

Diet

When isotopes are used to study prehistoric diets, it is mainly carbon and nitrogen isotopes that are used. The isotopes provide different information regarding what people ate and carbon is used to identify whether the food came from land or sea. Nitrogen is used to study from which level in the food chain the food originated, and it can even be used to determine whether the food came from a freshwater environment. In isotope studies, it is most common that skeletal material is used in the analyses. Here, a special protein from bone and teeth called collagen is used. This means that the information obtained comes from the proteins in the food according to the principal 'you are what you eat'.

In research concerning the Stone Age, stable isotopes have been used to study when agriculture was introduced, *i.e.*, when people increasingly started using domesticated products like cereals and livestock. In one study of several individuals from various Neolithic cultures on the island of Öland, researchers could see that an agricultural diet became generally accepted *c.* 1,000 years later than what was found in material from England using the same kind of analysis. It is also apparent that marine resources take on less importance than before.

Since different tissues in the body are renewed at different rates during the life of an individual, some actually not at all, one can use isotopes to study changes in diet during one individual's life. This means that age-specific diets can be studied, something that can vary between different cultures or between different geographical regions. Thus, in the same Stone Age people from Öland, researchers found that some individuals during a revolutionary period, the Middle Neolithic (3300–2350 BC), had undergone significant dietary changes during their lives.

Mobility

Because certain tissues are not replaced or renewed, teeth for example, one can use the isotopes of certain elements whose variation is dependent on variation in geology in order to study whether an individual at different times has spent time at different geographical locations. Researchers have taken samples from both teeth and bone of individuals in order to analyse strontium and sulphur when they want to study mobility in the prehistoric past.

Using both strontium and oxygen isotopes (oxygen is used here as an indicator of the local temperature), researchers have for example found that two archers who were buried near Stonehenge in England sometime around 2400 BC actually grew up somewhere on the mainland and not at all on the British Isles. They had however spent their adult lives in what is now England.

Strontium and sulphur have also been used to study mobility in Sweden, where researchers have found that several individuals buried in one of the megalithic tombs on Öland did not spend their first years on Öland. They also found that the number of non-local individuals, that is individuals from the mainland, increased in the later burials in these megalithic tombs.

The future

Just like with DNA, it is the degree of preservation that sets the limits for the kind of information that can be extracted using isotope analyses. Neither in this case can bones that have been exposed to fire be used for analysis. However, one can always imagine that isotopes from other elements can be used to add knowledge about other components in the diet or specific local conditions. Here, I am primarily thinking about calcium, where milk and milk products are the single most important source of calcium in diets. In this case, a routine sampling of several samples from each individual representing different biological ages and analysis of several isotopes will contribute to an increased understanding regarding the diet, changes in diet and mobility of individuals as well as groups of individuals. This knowledge must naturally be place in relation to the cultural context in order to gain a full understanding of what it means and how it should be understood.

Suggested readings

Eriksson, G., Linderholm, A., Fornander, E., Kanstrup, M., Schoultz, P., Olofsson, H., and Lidén, K. 2008. Same island, different diet: Cultural evolution of food practice on Öland, Sweden, from the Mesolithic to the Roman Period. *Journal of Anthropological Archaeology* 27, 520–543.

Evans, J. A., Chenery, C. A. and Fitzpatrick, A. P. 2006. Bronze age childhood migration of individuals near Stonehenge, revealed by strontium and oxygen isotope tooth enamel analysis. *Archaeometry* 48, 309–321.

Götherström, A., Anderung, C., Hellborg, L., Elburg, R., Smith, C., Bradley, D. G. and Ellegren, H. 2005. Cattle domestication in the Near east was followed by hybridization with aurochs bulls in Europe. *Proceedings of the Royal Society series* B 272, 2345–2350.

Jones, M. and Brown, T. 2000. Agricultural origins: the evidence of modern and ancient DNA. *Holocene* 10, 769–776.

Lalueza-Fox, C., Rompler, H., Caramelli, D., Staubert, C., Catalano, G., Hughes, D., Rohland, N., Pilli, E., Longo, L., Condemi, S., de la Rasilla, M., Fortea, J., Rosas, A., Stoneking, M., Schoneberg, T., Bertranpetit, J. and Hofreiter, M. 2007. A melanocortin 1 receptor allele suggests varying pigmentation among Neanderthal. *Science* 318, 1453–1455.

Larson, G. 2011. Genetics and Domestication Important Questions for New Answers. *Current Anthropology* 52, 485–495.

Linderholm, A., Fornander, E., Eriksson, G., Mörth, C. M. and Lidén, K. 2010. Increasing mobility at the Neolithic/Bronze Age transition – sulphur isotope evidence from Öland, Sweden. In Fornander, E. *Consuming and communicating identities Dietary diversity and interaction in Middle Neolithic Sweden*. Doktorsavhandling. Stockholm.

Malmström, H., Linderholm, A., Liden, K., Storå, J., Molnar, P., Holmlund, G., Jakobsson, M. and Götherström, A. 2010. High frequency of lactose intolerance in a prehistoric hunter-gatherer population in northern Europe. *BMC Evolutionary Biology* 10, DOI: 10.1186/1471–2148–10–89.

Malmström, H., Gilbert, M. T. P., Thomas, M. G., Brändström, M., Stora, J., Molnar, P., Andersen, P. K., Bendixen, C., Holmlund, G., Götherström, A. and Willerslev, E. 2009. Ancient DNA Reveals Lack of Continuity between Neolithic Hunter-Gatherers and Contemporary Scandinavians. *Current Biology* 19, 1758–1762.

Pruvost, M., Bellone, R., Benecke, N., Sandoval-Castellanos, E., Cieslak, M., Kuznetsova, T., Morales-Muniz, A., O'Connor, T., Reissmann, M., Hofreiter, M. and Ludwig, A. 2011. Genotypes of predomestic horses match phenotypes painted in Paleolithic works of cave art. *Proceedings of the National Academy of Sciences USA* 108, 18626–18630.

6   A Time of Change

Mats Larsson

In this chapter, we will address a very complex period, the Middle Neolithic. During the period 3300–2350 BC, significant changes occur in both culture and in the way of life. We see the emergence of three separate groups of people in southern and central Sweden, while agriculture is established in southern Norrland. During a short period of time, three groups live side by side but with completely different cultural characteristics. In the archaeological literature, they are referred to as the Funnel Beaker Culture, the Pitted Ware Culture and the Battle Axe Culture. We have already discussed the first mentioned culture, but the latter two emerged from quite different conditions. We will examine these changes in a wider European perspective. On the continent, we see the development of groups such as the Single Grave Culture, the Corded Ware Culture and the Bell-Beaker Culture.

The archaeological material from this period is very plentiful today, which requires us to limit our selection. The division of the period into the two sub-periods MN A and MN B has been used for many years and it is this classification that I will use here. First, we will take a look at the MN A in Sweden, followed by the MN B. At the end of the chapter, we will summarize the greater trends in this history.

The MN A (3300–2700 BC) includes the Funnel Beaker Culture and the Pitted Ware Culture, and the MN B (2700–2350 BC) covers the Battle Axe Culture. This classification is of course not without problems, which will be apparent, but it does make it easier for the reader to follow the story.

Farmers and seal hunters

For many years, researchers in Scandinavia have been involved in a lively debate regarding the relationships between the Middle Neolithic cultures. The relationship between the Funnel Beaker Culture (TRB), the Pitted Ware Culture (GRK) and the Battle Axe Culture (STY) has been considered extremely complicated. The differences have been thought to be chronological differences or remnants after different 'cultures', in reality ethnic groups. The 'cultures' mentioned above have also been associated with different economic strategies.

The continuation of our story begins with the farmers of the Funnel Beaker Culture and their material culture, settlements, economy, graves and rituals.

Time and objects

The Middle Neolithic Funnel Beaker Culture is to a certain extent a clear continuation of the Early Neolithic culture; however, a number of distinct differences are apparent. I hope these will be clarified as we continue.

MN Ia	Troldebjerg
MN Ib	Klintebakke
MN II	Blandebjerg
MN III	Bundsø
MN IV	Lindø
MN V	Store Valby

Table 6.1. Middle Neolithic Funnel Beaker Culture.

As usual, the temporal, or chronological, classification of the period is based on material from Denmark. In this case, it is based on the classification of pottery from Danish settlements together with pottery from the large grave monuments of the period, the passage graves. Similar to the situation in the previous period, Carl Johan Becker is the actual creator of the chronological classification still in use (Table 6.1).

As we shall see, the classification is only valid for the southernmost part of Scandinavia, including Denmark and South Sweden.

The pottery from this period has a quality probably never again reached during our prehistory – this regarding both form and technological quality.

A rich flora of shapes and ornamentations existed and this can be seen across a large area, even if there are regional differences. In addition to Denmark, we see these shapes and ornamentation in Scania, in Västergötland, Östergötland as well as on Sweden's west coast and on the islands of Öland and Gotland as well as in northern Germany. Ornamentation was done using a number of different techniques such as cord, twisted cord and imprints of different kinds, for example combs. It is also apparent that some of the vessels were only made in order to be deposited in the graves. This is the case for vessels with names like pedestalled bowls as well as brim-beakers. Vessels of these shapes are not found very often at settlements (Fig. 6.1).

It is also clear that an internal development of design language culminates during the middle part of the period. If we look at the pottery from the MN IV and V, we see that it is much more simple in its workmanship and the shapes are not so elaborate. This is particularly apparent during the youngest part of the period, MN V, when the vessels are straight-sided, almost barrel-shaped, and are mostly only decorated with pits under the mouth and on the neck (Fig. 6.2).

What does the rest of the material culture look like? We can begin with the axes. During MN I, the thin-butted type is still found, but they will eventually be replaced by another kind of working axe, the thick-butted axe. As can be seen from the name, these had considerably more substantial necks that eventually became more square-shaped.

The multiple-edged battle axes dominant during the previous period disappear now and are replaced by different kinds of double-edged axes. This is also the kind primarily found in graves and as isolated finds, possibly as grave-goods.

Other objects are generally the same as those found earlier. Tools that now take on an important meaning are the different kinds of scrapers used for example for dressing fur skins. Arrowheads, such as the previously so abundant transverse arrowheads, are hardly found at all now. It is however uncertain whether this indicates that hunting became less common.

Figure 6.1. Bowl from the passage grave at Skarpsalling from Jylland MN Ib (source: Larsen (Nationalmuseum, Copenhagen) 2012.

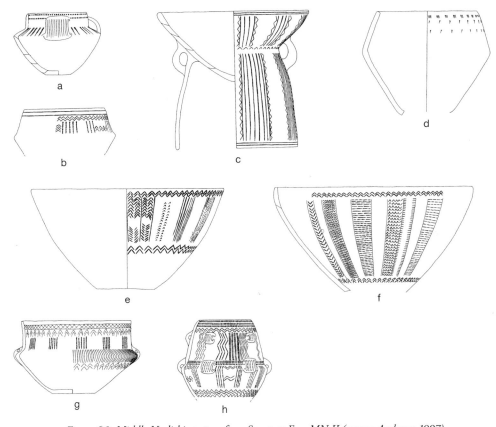

Figure 6.2. Middle Neolithic pottery from Sarup at Fyn. MN II (source: Andersen 1997).

Settlements and houses

It is more difficult to follow the development of dwellings during this period, which seems noteworthy since we do have a large number of excavated settlements. One clear tendency is that the settlements become larger. From the Danish region, we find settlements from the period that are 30,000–50,000 m², and the same developments can be seen in Scania. Here, we can see how the inland parts of the landscape are largely abandoned with the settlements becoming concentrated to the areas near the coast. One such example of a large settlement is Hindby Mosse (Hindby bog) in Malmö, which unfortunately has never been fully published, making it difficult to go into a detailed discussion about it. It is estimated that the settlement had an area of about 25,000 m². The settlement was located on a sandy peninsula in an old lake. The settlement was almost circular in shape with an empty inner area. No clear fosses or similar structures were found; instead, we see large pits and stone constructions. This has led to the location being interpreted as being some kind of Sarup construction similar to those discussed earlier. The site can mostly be dated to MN III.

Danish archaeologists can see what, for example, a concentration of buildings might look like around the abandoned constructions. Interesting however, is that these also change into ordinary settlements, which is clear when one looks closer at Sarup II. After this construction, the site develops into an ordinary, if a bit large, settlement. What lies behind this change in the settlement is debated of course, but the transformation gives the impression of a clear reshaping of the social structure, which as we shall see is also noticeable in the burial customs. Lots of time and effort were spent constructing the large passage graves.

House structures were present of course, even if not as plentiful as during the previous period. The predominant type of building is still the Mossby-type, with variations.

The Dagstorp-house Type I buildings are generally rather small, measuring between 7–10 × 4–5.5 metres. As you can see, they are much smaller and have an area of between about 28 and 55 m². They are dated to the MN I. At the site, the houses are clustered close together and seem to form an almost village-like group.

The Dagstorp-house Type II dwellings do not have any wall trenches and are almost rectangular in shape. They can be relatively large – House 74 at Dagstorp was 14.7 × 7 metres with an inner area of about 100 m². The dating of these houses is not certain, but we should be able to place them within the interval MN I–III.

The third kind of house is called Limensgård. This house-type gets its name from a settlement on the Danish island of Bornholm. These houses have straight, parallel long sides and straight short sides. The length of the houses varied between 15 and 20 metres and their width between 5.5 and 7 metres, which means that the houses had an area of between 70 and 100 m². They can be dated to the latter part of the MN A and the beginning of the MN B.

The dead and the afterlife

It is now time to see how the people of the Funnel Beaker Culture regarded the afterlife during the period 3300–2700 BC Above, I briefly mentioned that passage graves were the large megalithic tombs during this period.

In Sweden, approximately 300 passage graves are preserved today, with a significant concentration around the Falbygden area in Västergötland, where we find at least 250. This can be compared with Denmark where about 700 passage graves are preserved. Amazingly, these large monuments were obviously erected over a period of perhaps 100 years.

What exactly is a passage grave? It is composed of three elements: a chamber, a gallery and a mound. The chamber can be between 4 and 17 metres long and is generally oriented in a north-south direction. They vary between 1.5 and 2 metres wide. The gallery is generally between 4 and 8 metres long.

That people began building in this manner can certainly be connected to the European development that also affected the people here. A great number of passage graves were constructed in North Germany, northwest Holland, as well as in other regions. However, we should not see this as a shift in religious beliefs. Burial rituals similar to those witnessed in the previous period are also common now; veneration of the dead is for example just as apparent as before. Thus, there must be other reasons for why people began building passage graves. We will look closer at this in the following section.

Large earth mounds, which could be constructed in different ways, covered the passage graves; for example, burnt flint could be included in the mound as a specific layer. If we compare the size of the mounds, we see that in Denmark, the largest were between 30 and 40 metres in diameter while the largest in Sweden, and in Scandinavia, Ragnvald's grave in Karleby (Västergötland) had a mound that was *c.* 33 metres in diameter and *c.* 2 metres high. The largest in Scania is Gillhög, near Barsebäck in the western part of the region. The mound is *c.* 25 metres in diameter and is 2.5 metres high. The chamber is rectangular and measures 5.5 × 2.3 metres and is covered by three capstones that weigh several tons. The gallery, which opens towards the southeast, is 5.5 metres long (Fig. 6.3).

It is fitting that we begin with the large collection in the Falbygden region.

The Falbygden region is, for Swedish conditions, a very special region. The large table mountains of Mösseberg, Ålleberg, Varvsberget and Billingen surround the rich high plateau made up of very calcareous boulder clay and with favourable agricultural conditions. The region forms almost a triangle and is about 50 × 30 km in area. Several passage graves have been objects of study and description. As early as in 1747 during his travels in Västergötland, Carl Linnaeus described several passage graves in Falköping. Carl Gustaf Hilfeling completed the first excavation of a passage grave in Sweden in 1788, and it was from the Falbygden region. At the beginning of the 1800s, five passage graves were removed from Axvalla heath in order to construct a drill-ground. One of these, Oden's grave, is described in detail in both words and illustrations. During the following years, several excavations were undertaken that were extremely variable in quality. At the beginning of the 1960s, Carl Cullberg began his work on the Falbygden passage graves, and his complete investigation of the passage grave at Rössberga is still the most comprehensive done in that area.

In addition to Cullberg's excavations, I would also like to bring to attention to the project led by Carl-Göran Sjögren – *Gånggrifterna i centrala Västergötland och deras bakgrund* (The passage graves in central Västergötland and their backgrounds). This study began in 1985 and a total of nine passage graves were excavated and studied.

We can begin our exposé with the passage grave at Rössberga since, as mentioned above it is the only one that has been thoroughly studied. The grave was excavated during several months in 1962. The grave chamber was rectangular and measured *c.* 9 × 2 metres. The chamber was divided into at least 19 recesses, which created a spatial division in the chamber. The gallery in the east was *c.* 8 metres long and a mound of stones that was *c.* 26 metres in diameter surrounded the entire passage grave. Located outside the opening was a so-called entrance cairn.

A majority of the findings were made in and over the entrance cairn. Similar to what we have seen in Denmark and in Scania, concentrations of pottery sherds were found in front of the opening. This indicates that deliberate depositions have taken place here. The pottery, which is easiest to date, was richly decorated with mostly different kinds of imprinted decorations using comb and tooth techniques. According to Cullberg, the pottery, and therefore the passage grave, can be dated to the MN Ib–MN II. Radiocarbon dating indicates that the site was used over a long time, up to 1,000 years, but the oldest results are from about 3200 BC

As far as the number of burials is concerned, from the excavation researchers estimated that there were 16 men, 17 women and 5 children buried there. However, Torbjörn Ahlström has conducted a new examination of the skeletal material from the grave and found at least 128 individuals, which gives a completely different picture of the intensiveness of the burials. There is no clear division, but Ahlström believes that after the grave collapsed, skulls and skeletal parts were deposited in the area around the opening of the gallery into the chamber. Analyses of height and weight provide important information regarding the health of humans of the time. The estimated average height was for men *c.* 165 cm and for women *c.* 154 cm. If we look at the age of death of the people buried at Rössberga, it is clear that child mortality was high and that a great majority of the people died between 20–29 years old; however, there are individuals that died at ages over 60, even if they were relatively few (Fig. 6.4).

Kerstin Lidén has studied the diet of these people and has found that they survived primarily on land-based food sources. Analyses of stabile isotopes from skeletons clearly indicate that people ate local foods and that the people buried there were from the region, something that is clearly indicated through the analyses of sulphur isotopes conducted by Anna Linderholm. This result stands strong in comparison with the animal bones found at settlements in the Falbygden region. Mostly bones from cattle and pigs have been found here.

One important question is how the dead were placed in the chamber. Researchers have debated whether only certain parts of the bodies were deposited in the grave. In this case, this would mean that the dead were stored in another location before they were eventually placed in the chamber of the passage grave. The results from the analyses conducted on the skeletons found at Rössberga did not show that this was the case, but that all the bones from the skeletons were represented. Recently, studies conducted of the passage grave at Frälsegården, also in the Falbygden region, clearly indicate that the bodies were placed in a crouching position along the chamber walls. The remains of 44 individuals were found in the chamber. Torbjörn Ahlström calls the passage graves 'underground kingdoms of death', which is a fitting term considering the large number of individuals buried in them.

Figure 6.3. The passage grave at Gillhög in Scania (photograph: M. Larsson).

Figure 6.4. The passage grave at Rössberga in Västergötlan (source: Cullberg 1963).

It is also important to point out that the results of chemical analyses of bones (strontium isotopes) indicate that *c.* 25 percent of those buried in Falbygden passage graves spent their childhood in regions other than Falbygden. In other words, immigration occurred to the region from the surrounding areas where these kinds of graves were not constructed.

What is the situation in the other areas where people have constructed passage graves? We generally see the same picture as that mentioned above. We can look at few interesting trends and results however.

During a large part of the 1960s, Märta Strömberg conducted several archaeological studies in southern Scania (the Hagestad project), of both settlements and graves, especially megalithic graves. Earlier, we examined the excavations at Trollasten, now we will take a closer look at the story of the four megalithic graves studied by Strömberg – Carlshögen, Ramshög, Albergshög and Hagestad Nr. 2. However, we do not have enough room here to go into detailed descriptions of all of the interesting results found, so I have been forced to select a few that might be of interest.

I will focus on Carlshögen, which was excavated during 1964 and between 1968 and 1969. The chamber is rectangular and measures 5.5 × 1.8–2 metres. The gallery, which opens towards the east-northeast, is 6.4 metres long and *c.* 0.7–0.9 metres wide. Unfortunately, the capstones are missing and were probably removed during the 1800s in order to be used as building material. Seven skeletons were found in the top layer of the chamber, all of which can be dated to the last part of the Stone Age, the Late Neolithic, thanks to characteristic finds such as daggers. When the stone flagstones that made up the upper layer of the floor were removed, the excavators discovered that the chamber was divided into 9 sections, just like at Rössberga. Human skeletal remains were found in all sections, as well as a significant amount of other artefacts. Interestingly, no pottery artefacts were found in connection with the excavation of the area in front of the opening. This is otherwise something that is usually found. The dating of Carlshögen is somewhat later than what is generally reported – MN II–III, *i.e. c.* 3000 BC Estimates of the number of burials at Carlshögen indicate something between 47 and 53 individuals, with the majority being adults (Figs 6.5 and 6.6).

We should also look at a third example from a completely different part of Sweden – a megalithic grave at Alvastra in the region of Östergötland, not far from Lake Vättern. The discovery of this gravesite is interesting while at the same time tragic. It was discovered in 1916 when a farmer wanted to remove some troublesome boulders in his field by using explosives. Otto Frödin went out in the field and conducted a preliminary inspection. In his notes, he mentions that a large number of bones were found lying on a layer of stone packing.

Opinions differed regarding what the place was. Was it a Stone Age grave or was it an execution site? In order to determine conclusively what it really was, Gunborg Janzon conducted a study of the site between 1979 and 1983. Despite the fact that the structure was in ruins, interesting and important results were uncovered. It became clear that we were dealing with a megalithic grave, almost a dolmen. Radiocarbon dating of the skeletons established the date for the structure to 3500–2800 BC In what was once the actual chamber, archaeologists were able to study a carefully placed layer of stones – a floor. It was also obvious that a mound of stones composed of a local volcanic rock had surrounded the chamber.

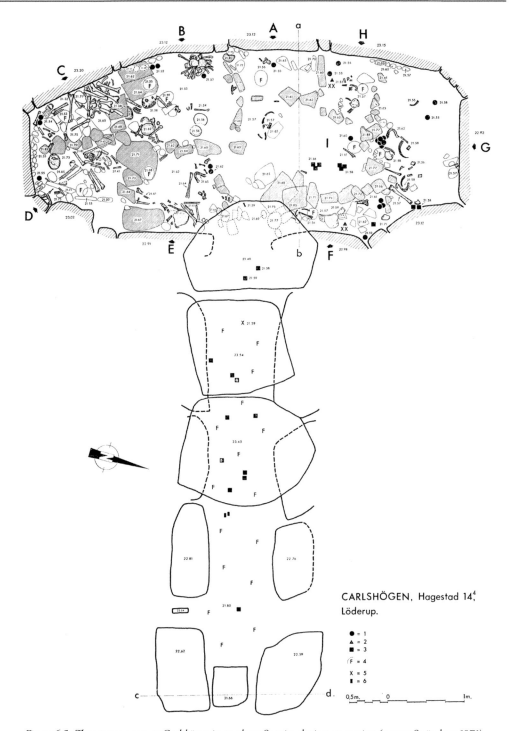

Figure 6.5. The passage grave at Carlshögen in southern Scania, during excavation (source: Strömberg 1971).

In connection with Frödin's limited study in 1916, several amber beads shaped as double-edged axes or clubs were found, which were obviously associated with the skeletal material and perhaps worn on necklaces. Some flint was found, but no intact objects. The amount of pottery found was much greater however, a little more than one kilogram. The ornamentation indicates a date during MN I or even a somewhat later part of MN III–IV. Due to the structure being so damaged, the distribution of the pottery was uneven and most of it was found in the southern part of the structure. Interestingly enough, analyses of the pottery revealed a similarity to the material from the passage grave at Rössberga, mentioned above. This is also true as far as the exterior and the addition to the clay of a kind of volcanic rock that does not occur in Östergötland. Is it possible that the vessels from the Alvastra dolmen come from Rössberga and Falbygden? We cannot say with any certainty, but indications of contact exist.

New analyses of the skeletal material have also provided interesting results. The number of individuals buried is estimated at over thirty, with both sexes represented as well as both children and adults. Analyses of stabile isotopes from the skeletons clearly indicate that the people buried in the dolmen lived primarily on a diet of meat and land-based plants. Even though it was not far to lakes like Tåkern and Vättern, fish was clearly not a part of their diets.

Extremely interesting is the fact that one of the skeletons in the grave has been radiocarbon-dated to the Mesolithic, that is, several thousand years earlier. He has been designated the 'Alvastra Man' (*Alvastramannen*). The skeleton has been dated to 6030 BC and it turns out that he was a 60-year-old man. It is very possible that some of the quartz collected here comes from the same period. A technical examination supports this. It is most likely that a settlement as well as a grave-field had been located in the vicinity.

Why did people construct these large monuments then? The dolmens were, at least in the beginning obviously intended for only one person, while we know that the passage graves were seen as collective burial grounds. One idea that has been around awhile is that the social system to which these early farmers belonged can be called *segmentary*. This is a term borrowed from social anthropology, meaning that in a segmentary society, the graves/grave sites are the central points in peoples' lives. Settlements are scattered and small, and fixed points are necessary for the sake of social cohesion. These fixed points were the graves and thus the place of the ancestors. It is of course difficult to see such a social system in the archaeological material and perhaps it is so that it fits better into the early Neolithic society with its scattered settlements. Regarding the period we are now looking at, we have more of an impression that the settlements are becoming more concentrated as well as larger. This, together with the often times greater number of burials might indicate a clan-based society in which the passage graves made up the central points.

If we take a closer look at the findings from the passage graves, which Birgitta Hårdh and Chris Tilley have done for example, it is clear that some of the passage graves have significantly larger amounts of depositions that do others. Graves such as Gillhög clearly have larger amounts of finds, especially of pottery, than in other parts of Scania. In her analyses of pottery ornamentation from a number of passage graves, Birgitta Hårdh has been able to

Figure 6.6. The megalithic grave at Alvastra, seen through the mist (photograph: M. Larsson).

see that people from northeast Scania (Fjälkinge) had actually travelled to Gillhög to deposit pottery vessels with specific shapes and decorations (Fig. 6.7).

Thus, we get the impression of a society in which certain groups may have had a more dominant role than others and where a monumental grave such as Gillhög has placed a special role.

It is now time to continue and examine other ceremonial elements of the Middle Neolithic Funnel Beaker Culture.

Sarup structures

In an earlier section, we looked at a few of these large ceremonial gathering sites, in particular Sarup at Fyn in Denmark. It is now time to see what happened here during this period.

About 100 years passed between when Sarup I and what has come to be known as Sarup II were built. Sarup II is dated to 3280 BC It is similar to the older construction, but Sarup II is significantly smaller, 3.5 hectares. The palisade was made up of small posts that were placed in a 2 metre wide belt that was 159 metres long. The enclosures connected to the palisade were also much smaller and of a much weaker construction than those from the earlier construction. Unlike Sarup I, we have been able to excavate the interior part of Sarup II. There, the excavators found pits; however, most notable were the half-circle shaped constructions discovered. Large postholes, which in one case formed a square, were found

Figure 6.7. The weight of sherds found at a few megalithic graves in Scania. 1. 0–20 kg; 2. 21–100 kg; 3. 101–150 kg; 4. Greater than 150 kg (source: Tilley 1996).

in association with these. In two of the postholes, charred human bones were among the objects found. Regarding the number of finds, there were significantly more than at Sarup I, 45 percent more. Among the finds were whole funnel beakers, richly ornamented, whole flint axes, and especially interesting, a superb double-edged battle-axe.

In the Scania region, we have a construction that is comparable to the Danish Sarup constructions, namely Stävie, west of Lund. Between 1973 and 1978, archaeologists conducted excavations here, which revealed something quite interesting. The area is located near Lödde

River and is relatively flat. In the present context, the system of pits discovered in the eastern part of the excavated area is what is most interesting. A total of 14 pits were excavated, for a total length of *c.* 250 metres. The length of the individual pits varied between 3 and 40 metres and their depth between 0.4 and 1 metre. The pits were rich in artefacts of different kinds. The flint axes comprised one large and significant category of findings. These were more or less in pieces, but with a few exceptions can still be said to belong to the thick-butted type and later variations, such as those from Lindø and Store Valby. In addition to the axes, the pottery is of great interest. Definitely, the largest portion of the pottery finds came from only a few pits. The containers are almost barrel-shaped and are decorated with pits along the edge of the mouth, while a few are decorated with fishbone patterns, imprints and diagonal lines. In addition to these barrel-shaped containers, there are also a relatively large number of so-called pottery plates that may have been some kind of lid. These were decorated with curving patterns and short strokes. All in all, the dating analyses of the finds point towards the youngest part of the Funnel Beaker Culture, MN V Store Valby phase. Radiocarbon dating from Stävie indicates a time interval of *c.* 2850 to 2350 BC

To date, Stävie is the only known Sarup construction in Sweden. So, what do other ceremonial acts look like during this time period? It is obvious that during the earlier part of the period, sacrifices continue in the marshes similar to what went on earlier; however, this tradition is broken towards the end of the period MN III–V. Per Karsten mentions that of 114 sacrificial sites from the end of the Early Neolithic to MN III, only 12 show continued use during the later periods. We clearly see that something drastic took place during this time. For example, we see that depositions of flint axes at the large megalithic graves increase during the period, and the same is true for the offering of sacrifices at the settlements. Later, we will return to the events that we see taking place at this time.

Seal hunters

I chose to give the main section of this chapter the title *Farmers and Seal Hunters*, and after discussing the farmers and their settlements and burial sites above, I have now come to the other half of the subtitle – the seal hunters. In the archaeological literature these people are called the Pitted Ware Culture (PWC); however, as we will see, the name seal hunters is not completely taken from the air.

Since the Pitted Ware Culture is difficult to understand without a more in-depth analysis, I will begin this section with an historical survey. This is a culture that is not so very easy to understand. In the eastern part of Central Sweden, where we also find the largest settlements, the Pitted Ware Culture has been defined based on the pottery and the five Fagervik periods mentioned below, while in southern Sweden and Denmark, the Pitted Ware Culture has been defined based on flint tools such as arrowheads. This means that comparisons between different regions is not so simple, as we shall see.

Studies of the Pitted Ware Culture on the Swedish mainland began early in the 1900s with Oscar Almgren's discovery of Åloppe in the region of Uppland in 1901. Excavation of this settlement was followed by Einar Nerman's excavation at Säter in Östergötland in 1911.

The initial name for this newly discovered Stone Age culture was the *East Swedish Settlement Culture*. The ornamentation on the pottery has from the very beginning been an important component in studies of the Pitted Ware Culture. Studies of the changes in sea level along the coast in the region became a very important complement to the time line that the pottery had created. In this manner, in 1927 Nerman developed his Säter chronology with its four periods, and which was a big breakthrough in studies of the Pitted Ware Culture. This division became the predominate chronology up until the beginning of the 1950s when Axel Bagge, based on his studies during the middle of the 1930s at Fagervik in Östergötland, adds an early period and a late period to the chronology. In this manner he created the even more widely used Fagervik chronology.

Bagge's chronology associated the different periods to changes in sea levels and claimed that every period was characterized by a particular kind of pottery ornamentation. He also believed that the two oldest periods (I–II) should actually belong to the Funnel Beaker Culture. Fagervik I shows many common qualities with this culture, cord decorations for example.

During the periods I–II, the pottery was made of clay that had additives, *i.e.*, clay mixed with stone, while clay in the periods II–III began becoming mixed with lime and more porous, and then continuing through period IV, where it was completely mixed with lime and bone, which resulted in an extremely porous material.

Axel Bagge's Fagervik sequence was essentially never questioned until it became possible to date them using radiocarbon dating. One interesting aspect of this is that the Pitted Ware Culture can obviously be dated to as early as the Early Neolithic, *c.* 3350 BC, continuing on through the end of the Stone Age at about 2150 BC.

There are, however, a number of problems with these early dates. Due to problems with reservoir effects of radiocarbon dating (that older material, sediment, has been taken up by both fish and seals, which have then been cooked, resulting in food encrustations coating the cooking vessels), the analyses result in dates that are too old. Therefore, we cannot say with any certainty that the Pitted Ware Culture belongs in the Early Neolithic. In my opinion, we cannot find any Pitted Ware cultures until the beginning of the MN A, *i.e.*, during the Fagervik chronology II–III, around 3200 BC We should therefore consider the Pitted Ware Culture as being a local development from the Funnel Beaker Culture.

Today, we know of over 200 settlements from the Pitted Ware Culture in eastern Central Sweden alone. Characteristic for these settlements is that they vary greatly in size, between 500 and up to 90,000 m². It is however difficult to clearly determine their actual sizes since none of them have been completely excavated. What one finds at these settlements is a layer filled with finds (a culture layer), a variable number of constructions, and often, large numbers of artefacts, mostly pottery.

In order to exemplify what the settlements may have looked like, I have chosen to focus on two different settlements in two different geographic regions: Åby, north of Norrköping in Östergötland, and Fräkenrönningen in Gästrikland. The story begins in Åby.

The settlement at Åby

> Immediately west and northwest of the schoolhouse in Åby there is an area of rolling hills covered in pine forests. Here, we have found the largest settlement in the region.

So begins the story of the Åby settlement, located north of Norrköping, which was discovered at the end of the 1920s and is mentioned by Engström and Thomasson for the first time in 1932. They had demarcated an area of *c.* 200 × 40 metres within which they had found pottery, flint and stones. The settlement is located on a sandy piece of land between 26 and 29 metres above today's sea level.

It was Axel Bagge, who at the same time was working with the excavation at Fagervik not far from Åby, who led the first larger excavations of the settlement during 1934 and 1936. Bagge excavated a total of 317 m², which is still the largest excavation at this site. The total weight of over 700 kg bears witness to the fact that quite a large amount of finds were recovered. Included in this weight are both pottery and stone materials. Not only large amounts of pottery were uncovered, but also relatively large amounts of flint in the form of arrowheads and axes.

In his reports, he briefly mentions finding two structures – a layer of stone packing and a shallowly buried area with a large number of artefacts. Both have been interpreted as being huts; however, it is difficult to discuss them today since the documentation is insufficient.

After Bagge's excavation during the 1930s, several both smaller and larger excavations were undertaken between the years 1946 and 1997. When a minor excavation was conducted in connection with the rebuilding of a school in 1995, an interesting find was made. Excavators found the remains of a hut that was about 5.5 × 2 metres in size and situated about 0.3 metres below ground, and was almost oval in shape. At the bottom of the hut as well as surrounding it were several postholes that had likely been part of the structure. Quite a number of finds were made in the hut, among them, about 14 kg of pottery. When the hut was excavated, it was soon obvious that most of the vessels had stood in one of the corners of the hut (Fig. 6.8).

I conducted the most recent excavation of the Åby site in 1997. The excavation gave rise to several interesting results, which in many ways made it possible to see the entire settlement in a new light. We have also acquired a better idea of what the people living there ate. Admittedly, the bone material is very small and burnt, but as expected, it shows that they primarily ate seal and fish, although there were also bones from terrestrial animals such as beaver and hare.

An area that can be considered a ceremonial area was also excavated. In a smaller part of the area, burnt human bones were discovered together with burnt fragments of flint axes/burins, small stone axes and pottery, whose bottoms still sat in the pits in which they were once placed. The burnt bones come from at least two or probably more adult individuals. Among the decorated pottery, we found a few sherds with a characteristic pattern that can be called 'hanging triangles'. I will return to this later. One of these sherds has been radiocarbon dated to 2880–2490 BC This date is among the youngest found at the site, and in my opinion, the area with the ceremonial deposits of human bones and burnt axes represents the last time the site was actually used before being abandoned, a form of homage to their ancestors. Similar deposits have been found at other settlements. Here we can mention a few examples

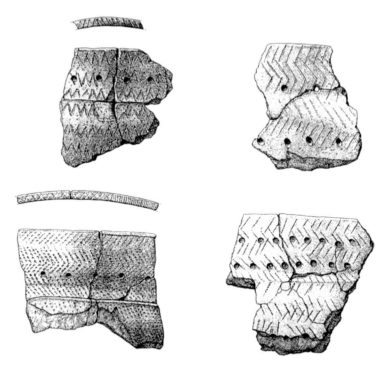

Figure 6.8. A selection of characteristic pottery sherds from Åby (source: Larsson 2006, illustration: R. Holmgren).

such as Siretorp (Blekinge) and Bollbacken (Västmanland). At the first mentioned site, two smaller pits were excavated revealing a large amount of burnt flint, among which were pieces of axes and burins as well as what was most likely burnt human bones. Radiocarbon dating results from one of the pits provided the date 3300–2700 BC At Bollbacken, a number of dwellings were excavated, and it is one in particular which has aroused the most interest – a house in which a large amount of human as well as animal bones was found. The excavators of the house have interpreted it as being a ceremonial building. The house has been dated to *c.* 2600–2300 BC, which agrees well with Åby, for example (Fig. 6.9).

In other words, it is clear that at several of the Pitted Ware Culture's settlements we find what we should consider to be ceremonial buildings or traces of ceremonial activities.

After decades of archaeological excavations, we now have a good understanding concerning the scope and organization of the Åby site. As mentioned earlier, we often see the settlements belonging to the Pitted Ware Culture as being large and lacking any clear structures. Based on the evidence from Åby, we can now see that this is not always the case. Based on the large number of excavations, it has been suggested that the settlement should actually be seen as two separate ones. One area is located in the zone that was excavated during the 1950s and during the first part of the 1990s. Here we find the remains of a hut for example. The second area includes Bagge's excavation during the 1930s and the excavations during the latter part of the 1990s. Here we find huts, graves and a ceremonial

Figure 6.9. Arrowheads made from flint, from Åby (source: Larsson 2006, illustration: R. Holmgren).

area. How can we distinguish between these two areas? Through detailed studies of pottery ornamentation, we can see that there is a detail in the decorations that, using radiocarbon dating, indicates that both of the areas were inhabited more or less during the same time. A possible explanation for this is that we are probably dealing with two groups of people who lived here and who were closely related. They chose to show their group affiliations by using differing forms of decoration along the rims of the pots.

Fräkenrönningen

The settlement at Fräkenrönningen in Gästrikland was excavated in 1993, as is so often the case, in connection with road construction. Today, the settlement is located *c.* 40 metres above sea level, but during the Stone Age, it was situated on a peninsula in the inner part of an island-rich archipelago. The total area encompassed by the excavation was 1,300 m², but one can actually say that the exact settlement was an area of about 350 m² where stones had been cleared away. It was also here that archaeologists found the large number of artefacts in the form of stone tools, bone and pottery. Beneath the settlement layer, the dig uncovered several structures of different kinds, including pits, hearths, cooking pits and postholes. Archaeologists also excavated seven or possibly eight huts. Interestingly, these huts were situated around a cleared area within which few artefacts were found. The huts were made up of round to rectangular stone boundaries with postholes inside. They were quite small with an inside area of between 2 and 7 m². As far as the artefacts are concerned, pottery clearly made up the largest group with a weight of almost 175 kg. In addition, tools of primarily flint and shale were among the discovered artefacts, which indicates wide contacts with both southern and northern Sweden.

What kind of sustenance did people utilize? If we look at the bone material, we see different species of seal and fish, as well as terrestrial animals. Dating of the Fräkenrönningen site is supported by several radiocarbon dating analyses that place the settlement within the interval 3000–2800 BC, which the excavator Niclas Björck claims indicates a relatively short but intensive period of settlement (Fig. 6.10).

Figure 6.10. Map of Fräkenrönningen (HG = hut foundation) (source: Björck 1998).

The afterlife

It is now time to take a closer look at how people buried their dead during this period. One major problem is that only a few graves with preserved skeletons have been found on the Swedish mainland. This is due to the poor preservation qualities of the acidic soil since it is composed of sand and moraine. There are graves however, for example at Korsnäs in Södermanland and Fagervik in Östergötland. At the first mentioned site, four graves have been identified, while there is one certain grave from Fagervik.

In several cases, we also find traces of red ochre, similar to the graves from the latter part of the Mesolithic at Skateholm. We can also note that there are single graves, double graves as well as occasional graves containing three individuals.

In order to gain a better picture of burial customs, we need to travel to the islands of Öland and Gotland. We can start at Köpingsvik on Öland. The settlement at Köpingsvik is quite large and is estimated to be about 70,000 m². Unfortunately, the large number of excavations since the 1920s and onward make it almost impossible to grasp the entire picture of the site today. The number of grave constructions is estimated at around twenty; however, there is quite a bit of uncertainty about this number. In this context, we cannot describe all of the graves, but there is one that is of special interest. It is a grave containing three individuals, which was excavated in 1975. It contains two adults, a woman and a man, as well as a six-year-old child. All three were buried on their backs with their arms and legs outstretched. They had been buried with a large number of burial gifts such as flint axes, bone beads, bone harpoons, two seal skulls, fishhooks and pottery. Alongside the woman, 11 bone arrowheads were found, which were clearly buried at the same time. Radiocarbon dating places the grave in the period 3000–2800 BC.

Gotland is another region with very good conditions for preservation of both burial goods and skeletal material. Similar to the situation on Öland, this is due to the soils being rich in lime, creating advantageous preservation conditions.

Naturally, we cannot discuss all of the hundreds of gravesites excavated on the island in this context, so I have selected a few that illustrate the variation that exists. A few large grave fields on Gotland have provided important results regarding different aspects of both burial customs and burial gifts. In recent years, scientific studies have provided us with an abundance of new knowledge about diets, as well as information about the movement patterns people had and what kinds of contacts they had. New DNA-studies point towards interesting contacts. I will address these studies in a concluding chapter where I will look at questions concerning how these seal hunters lived as well as some thoughts regarding how the Pitted Ware Culture developed, something which is also taken up in Kerstin Lidén's chapter.

The three largest and most well studied grave fields on Gotland are Ajvide, Västerbjers and Visby. You should know however that at least 180 graves have been found for this period on Gotland. We will now look closer at some of the results from Ajvide and Västerbjers.

We start at Ajvide. The site is located on the west coast of Gotland, opposite the islands of Stora and Lilla Karlsö. Excavations began at the beginning of the 1980s and continue today. In addition to a grave field, a very large settlement area is also being excavated, covering an area of *c.* 90,000 m². In this context however, I will primarily concentrate on the graves. The grave field is also younger that the actual settlement and can be dated to the period *c.* 2750–2300 BC Up to now, about 80 graves have been examined. Göran Burenhult, who has led the excavations, considers the grave field to be a ceremonial landscape. The graves are situated in a half-circle around an open area. In the centre of the open area, a cult site surrounded by a palisade has been excavated. Archaeologists have discovered large numbers of different kinds of artefacts here, for example animal bones (especially seal) as well as pottery and other objects.

The graves are for the most part oriented along two directions: north-south and east-west. Burenhult thinks that the latter may be the youngest. Also interesting is that at least eight of the graves are so-called cenotaphs, which do not contain any remains of deceased people. We should also note that some of the buried people were buried without their skulls. This may indicate that the dead were stored at another location in a so-called death house or on a platform before the actual burial. The skulls may have been stored somewhere else in these cases.

As Ajvide is an on-going project, we cannot refer to a final publication, but based on that which is already published, we can form a picture of the people buried there. They were men, women and children. The average age of death for women was about 36 years, and for men, about 44 years. The number of children was relatively large, which is typical of many Stone Age grave fields. However, it is interesting that quite a few people became relatively old, 50–70 years. Regarding burial gifts, we find that pottery along with different kinds of tools such as fishhooks and harpoons made from bone and antler, as well as flint and stone axes dominated the findings.

Now, what do we find at Västerbjers?

The grave field is located in Gothem's parish on the northeast part of the island and was discovered in 1886 when a grave was uncovered during the digging of a gravel pit. The actual excavations were conducted between 1932 and 1942, and Mårten Stenberger published the results in 1943. The grave field was situated on a gravel ridge adjacent to a long, narrow inlet. Results from radiocarbon dating place the grave field in the period 2900–2500 BC, which is more or less contemporary with Ajvide. There are over 50 graves in the grave field, mostly with only one individual in each grave. There are, however, a few isolated graves containing two individuals. Traces of settlement activities such as hearths, remains from culture layers and postholes were also found in the grave field. Mårten Stenberger claimed in his 1943 publication that Västerbjers should be seen as a year-round site where settlements and graves were contemporary. In the 1970s, Mats Malmer introduced an alternative interpretation for the site. He believed the site to be exclusively a grave field, which was essentially in two parts, a northern section and a southern section. Malmer based his view on the age and distribution of the burial gifts and he considered the northern part to be the oldest with its battle axes, flint axes and arrowheads, while the southern part was 'poorer' and younger with finds of for example concave-edged flint axes and objects made of antler. According to Malmer, the northern part could be dated to the Battle Axe Culture, which we well look at in the next section. He bases his conclusion on finds of two battle axes – one that was of a type made in Sweden and one that resembles a Danish type. However, new dating results do not support such a division, although there may be a certain difference in time between the two sections according to Gunilla Eriksson, who has conducted the most recent studies of the grave field.

Seal hunters or…?

We will now look closer at what these people ate and what their yearly diets looked like. Did they really eat only seal or…? We return to Västerbjers and Gunilla Eriksson's work for a closer examination. She has analysed bone from 26 individuals and determined the levels of stabile carbon isotopes and nitrogen isotopes, which have the chemical symbols ^{13}C and ^{15}N. The carbon isotope results show whether an individual ate food from seas/lakes or land. Low values indicate that the individual primarily ate food from seas or lakes. Nitrogen isotope results also indirectly show marine contra terrestrial protein intake, as land environments have shorter food chains.

The results from Västerbjers clearly indicate that the people buried there had taken their sustenance mostly from the sea. We should also point out that meat from pigs was obviously not something these people ate – this, despite the fact that a relatively large number of pig bones were found at Västerbjers. Here, we find a ceremonial element; pigs did not have any particular significance for their diet, but was used as a ritual animal instead. In several graves, archaeologists have found pig mandibles or teeth that were placed there as burial gifts, which might support such a theory. People did not eat enough meat from pigs or hogs for this to show up in the analyses. One can however wonder whether the consumption of pig meat in connection with specific festivals would leave any traces in the isotopes.

In fact, it seems as though seal meat was the primary source of protein during their entire life cycle, from cradle to grave. Analyses of stabile isotopes of carbon and nitrogen in human bone indicate unmistakably that human diets were based on marine resources.

It is also quite clear that a diet of seal is something characteristic for the greater part of the Pitted Ware Culture. Elin Fornander has found the same diet pattern in Södermanland, based on graves from the settlement at Korsnäs. These results can be compared with the analyses of lipids (fats) that have been conducted on the insides of containers from several settlement sites in Sweden. The results from these also show that humans primarily preferred food from the sea as their staple diet.

The Alvastra pile dwelling

One of the most debated and discussed structures from Sweden's Stone Age is very likely the complex pile dwelling from Alvastra in the region of Östergötland. This construction has supplied us with finds from both the Funnel Beaker Culture and the Pitted Ware Culture. As Mats Malmer has said, the pile dwelling demonstrates several of the characteristics that polarize these two Stone Age cultures. The thought-provoking site is situated near Lake Vättern, and from there, it is not far to the slopes of Mount Omberg. Northeast of the pile dwelling is Lake Tåkern. The pile dwelling was built on what is today called Dags Moor (*Dags mosse*), but which was once a bay of Lake Tåkern. To be completely correct however, it was built on a spring-fed fen that was waterlogged during the summer and stood under water during the winter. Early on, this fact led to the structure being understood as a fortification. However, this interpretation is quite unlikely since a range of hills surrounds the site causing defence of the site to be practically impossible.

Thus, today we see Alvastra pile dwelling as a part of a larger social and geographical context and generally as a ceremonial gathering place similar to the Sarup-type structures mentioned earlier. In the landscape around the pile dwelling, archaeologists have discovered several settlements that belong to both the Funnel Beaker Culture and the later Pitted Ware Culture. It is obvious that the people who lived and worked at these settlements were also the ones who used the pile dwelling as a ceremonial centre.

How then is this structure constructed? The pile dwelling actually comprises two parts, an eastern and a western, which shared a common wall. The actual floor of the structure is made of horizontal and vertical logs and covers an estimated area of about 1,000 m². This floor has rested on about 900 substantial-sized poles. About 800 m² of the area has been examined in connection with several archaeological excavations during the years 1908–1919, 1928–1930 and 1976–1980.

There is no final publication resulting from the excavations available; however, results from the excavations up to 1930, and to a certain extent even those between 1976 and 1980, have recently been published by Hans Browall, who has also previously written much about the pile dwelling. I will not go into the details regarding all of the excavations, but only limit myself to some of the more important features.

In order to reach the pile dwelling itself, a narrow footbridge stretched from the mainland to the eastern side of the structure. This crossed the entire pile dwelling, from south to north. On each side of this walkway, there were smaller 'houses' or 'rooms'. Hans Browall has identified all of 17 'rooms'. These 'rooms', which did not have any walls, have an area of about 20 m². Several hearths have been excavated in these 'rooms', in total about a hundred. As a rule, the hearths are constructed with limestone slabs on which a layer of clay has been placed. On the platform, and in the small rooms, offal and food scraps were found, as well as hazelnut shells, apples and grain. Most of these remains had come in contact with fire. A large number of bones from different animals and fish have been uncovered in connection with the archaeological excavations. The total weight of these finds is *c.* 700 kg. Of the 26 species identified, only four are domesticated animals: cattle, pigs, sheep/goats and dogs. In comparison, bones from 20 wild species of animals were found. Important to remember however is that bones from domestic animals were easily in majority.

Tools made from flint, antler and bone were also found among the remains. It is interesting to note that about 40 of the *c.* 350 double-edged battle axes made of ground stone that have been found in Sweden come from the pile dwelling. Also notable is that many of the flint axes found at the pile dwelling were damaged by fire. They obviously had been thrown in the hearths. In addition, many pottery sherds were found on the floor (Fig. 6.11).

It is thus rather obvious that people gathered at the pile dwelling in order to conduct different kinds of ceremonial acts. This means that the interpretation of the site as a gathering place for a settled countryside is likely true. Who built this structure, and when? The answer to this is debated, but a few things are evident. In this context, the dolmen at Alvastra that we looked at earlier is important. People who we associate with the Funnel Beaker Culture constructed the dolmen around 3500 BC With help from the annual rings from the posts, different stages of the building can be identified. Fire has also destroyed the pile dwelling on

Figure 6.11. The Alvastra pile dwelling (source: Browall 2011).

several occasions. What we now know is that there is a connection between the dolmen and the pile dwelling. How can we see this? Primarily through finds of similar pottery at the pile dwelling, *i.e.*, funnel beaker pottery that can be dated to MN I or about 3100 BC We can also see that the economy is unchanged. We see a combination of agricultural cultivation, stock farming and hunting/fishing.

Hans Browall has provided an interesting interpretation of what actually led to the structure being built, as well as what brought an end to the pile dwelling. As mentioned earlier, the structure is comprised of two halves that are adjoined – an eastern and a western part. Browall argues that the first represents the newer, the Pitted Ware Culture, while the latter part in a similar manner represents the older ideology, the Funnel Beaker Culture, with its orientation towards the west, towards Omberg. Several years pass and the transformation means that ceremonies take place only in the eastern part. After a few more decades, the site is abandoned; people return however, only now using the site as a burial site. The area is cleared and new poles are erected while at the same time burials take place. Examination of the bone material indicates that about 45 individuals were buried here. Most of the people buried are men; only one is positively identified as a woman and a few as children or teenagers. Clear evidence of scalping can be seen on one of the men's skulls, something that is very uncommon. Using radiocarbon dating, this individual has been dated to 2920 BC, which is also one of the youngest dates from the pile dwelling.

We thus get the impression that the pile dwelling was only used during perhaps one century, with some discontinuity. It begins as a ceremonial gathering place for the settled countryside nearby and ends as a burial site.

So, who were these seal hunters?

What were these people like and how should we view the development of the Pitted Ware Culture? These questions have engaged archaeologists for decades and in this section, I will address some of the views that have been proposed during recent years.

A few years ago, Anders Strinnholm wrote the following words, which I believe can act as an introduction to this section:

> Perhaps there is not only one story that we can tell about the Pitted Ware Culture; however, there are many important stories to tell about the Middle Neolithic Period.

Many archaeologists also emphasize that we cannot talk about a homogenous group of people who we can assign to the group called the Pitted Ware Culture. Instead, we should be talking about several local groups or societies that developed in different ways based on their own opportunities and contacts.

Other researchers, like Niklas Stenbäck, emphasize the significance of the sea and perhaps a kind of 'seal ideology', that is to say, in a similar manner as Jan Storå has suggested, emphasis is placed on the great significance seals played for humans of that time. Stenbäck also considers the rise of the Pitted Ware domain as a return to the values of an older period, *i.e.*, the time of the hunter. We can also see this in the shape of the clay figurines that are often found at

Pitted Ware settlement sites, not only in Sweden but also along the coasts of the Baltic Sea. Bozena Werbart argues, in the same sense as above, that this is both a religious manifestation as well as something that created bonds between peoples.

Alexander Gill suggested a more radical interpretation of the period, in much the same manner as Anders Carlsson earlier. Gill emphasizes the significance of sea-level effects on the coastline. He discusses how the 'gardens' of the Funnel Beaker Culture become the 'beaches' of the Pitted Ware Culture. These were not what we can call settlements, but should be understood as ceremonial gathering sites and burial sites. Lars Sundström sees the growth of the Pitted Ware Culture as resulting from social stress within the Funnel Beaker Culture – a difference between an ideal and reality.

In my book from 2006, I argued that the Pitted Ware Culture developed from the Funnel Beaker Culture. People retained parts of their material cultures and their identities as well as their thick-butted flint axes and double-edged battle axes. At the same time, they changed components of their material culture and incorporated objects such as long arrowheads made of chips using a special technique requiring a special kind of flint boulder with double platforms. We can also see that people developed their own style of pottery as well as incorporated influences from other regions farther to the south, such as a kind of ornamentation that I call the hanging triangle. This form of decoration is associated with the late Funnel Beaker Culture in South Sweden and in Denmark. It is also during the transition to a new phase, MN B, that these influences become clearly evident. I consider this addition of new influences as a way people could show their own identity, but also to show the wide range of contacts that occurred during this period. We must not forget that the Pitted Ware Culture, similar to the Funnel Beaker Culture, was part of a wider context that encompassed the entire Baltic Sea region.

In her doctoral dissertation from 2009, Åsa M. Larsson creates a clear geographic definition and argues that the Pitted Ware Culture should be regarded as from the same region within which pottery of the Fagervik II, III and/or IV kinds have been found. This would mean an area in East Sweden from Gästrikland to Scania, including Öland and Gotland. Using this definition, the Pitted Ware Culture appears around 3500/3400 BC in eastern Central Sweden and the younger phase (Fagervik IV) comes to an end *c.* 2400/2300 BC

Kim von Hackwitz can be said to argue in a similar manner to Anders Carlsson and Alexander Gill in her doctoral dissertation from 2010. She claims that the Pitted Ware pottery should be viewed as an identity object used for communication between different groups of people, as well as within groups. In this way, her interpretation is quite close to how I wrote about the pottery from the Åby settlement.

As we can see, Strinnholm's opinion that there are many stories to tell about the Middle Neolithic Period is not far from the mark!

In addition to these many stories, we should also include recent years' scientific analyses of skeletons from Pitted Ware Culture grave fields on Öland and Gotland. Isotope studies and results from DNA analyses from Köpingsvik on Öland, which has traditionally been identified as belonging to the Pitted Ware Culture, indicate that there are significant differences between these people and those who were buried in the passage graves at Resmo and who belonged to the Funnel Beaker Culture (see also Kerstin Lidén's chapter). Results show that they came from two separate groups of people with contrasting lifestyles – hunters/fishermen contra farmers. Also interesting is that on Öland, they obviously lived side by side for a period. Additionally, we can see that the same pattern exists on Gotland. Here, we are also looking at two completely separate groups of people where, to quote Gunilla Eriksson, a 'seal ideology' was predominant. This view agrees well with what was said above by both Jan Storå and Anders Strinnholm.

These results make the picture of the MN A, and the story, full of contradictions, which also makes this history even more enigmatic.

What then are the changes we can see towards the end of the MN A? In the following section, I will give my picture of what the changes may have looked like and the factors that may have caused them.

Changes and new times

We can see a rapid change in the Funnel Beaker Culture during the latter part of the MN A. In a few of the well-studied parts of Scania, we see changes in the size and placement of settlements as early as during the middle of the period (MN III). A more or less continuous pattern of settlement from the end of the older Primary Early Neolithic up to MN III is broken and new areas begin to be utilized. We can also see how settlements merged and became concentrated into larger groups. This is seen in several places in southern Scandinavia. At the same time, people also stopped building megalithic graves. It is however apparent that those already built continued to be used. This takes place sometime around 2900–2700 BC

During the period 2700–2400 BC, we can see that several local groups of people with their different material cultures exist in southern Sweden. The difference between them is primarily their technique for decorating pottery, but also the design of their flint axes.

At the settlements at Jonstorp in northwest Scania, finds have been made that are usually referred to the Pitted Ware Culture; however, there are clear influences from the Funnel Beaker Culture in the pottery decorations. The youngest of these settlements has been radiocarbon dated to *c.* 2800–2450 BC This is approximately the same period as the two groups at Stävie and Karlsfält. These settlements existed during the same time, but had very different placement in the landscape as well as different economic situations. The people living at the settlements at Jonstorp were primarily fishermen, while those living at Stävie and Karlsfält were farmers.

Between these, there are however great similarities in the material culture and they used the same kind of flint tools, axes and chipped arrowheads. We can see strong influences from the Pitted Ware region towards the north and east. My own thoughts are that in using different decorations on their containers, people clearly declared their identity and in this manner, their material cultures could distinguish between as well as unite people over great distances. One such example, which was mentioned earlier, is a special ornamentation that is commonly called 'hanging triangles' and which occurs throughout many regions and in different cultural contexts towards the end of the MN A. According to the English archaeologist Andrew Jones, the use of such a decorative motive may represent the visible part of a memory, which in this case is associated with the surface of a pot. In other words, he claims that social relations are 'inscribed' on the pot. We can also point out that the use of standardized shapes such as different kinds of axes and chipped arrowheads may have made things easier for people in a time of changes.

Most archaeologists agree that significant changes took place within societies during this time. How these can be explained or interpreted is open to discussion however. We cannot see any evidence of a large-scale migration of people, even though the above-mentioned DNA-analyses of individuals from Pitted Ware graves from Gotland indicate great mobility of people, for example, but which is perhaps not surprising.

In the middle of the 1990s, Lars Larsson writes that the discoveries imply an assimilation of Pitted Ware qualities in the late Funnel Beaker Culture. This would have been made easy in that they obviously had the same origins, which is likely true. In this context, we should mention the Norwegian archaeologist Knut Bergsvik, who maintains that the more people have in common regarding technology, economy and values, the more likely it is that they see others as being closely related and possible to understand.

In summary, the significant changes that take place within the Funnel Beaker society must have brought with them a large measure of confusion as well as certainly anxiety about what was going to happen. The changes in burial customs, sacrificial rituals and the localization of settlements probably led to a great deal of apprehension. A few years ago, Per Karsten wrote that influential people in society, ritual specialists or priests of that time, changed the ritual elements from collective sacrificial ceremonies in lakes and bodies of water to the sacrifice of axes at the megalithic graves – from the collective to the individual. The large palisade constructions should also be seen in light of these changes. They have served as relatively transitory gathering sites for the population and, as was the case at Dösjebro, were destroyed by fire after a brief time of use.

In this manner, other values and beliefs emerged. The existing societies broke down and smaller, kin-based groups such as those mentioned above appeared. We should perhaps understand these as ethnic groups. This term is difficult to use, but in this context, I am referring to social constructions that are distinguished from others through the different ways of using material culture.

Through the mixing of 'old and new', people of this time could create 'a new world', as Julian Thomas said. In a time of rapid changes, the population changed and reused principles, while at the same time they were able to communicate using a common material culture such as axes and hanging triangles.

We will discuss what these changes entailed in the next chapter.

7 New Manners and Customs

Mats Larsson

This period, which extends between 2700 and 2350 BC, is often called the MN B in order to differentiate it from the previous period, the MN A. This period is probably one of the most debated in Scandinavian prehistory and has often been subject to reinterpretation. We have gone from seeing the changes that took place as being a result of a massive invasion of an Indo-European nomads or 'Horse people', to seeing it as a society based on the earlier Funnel Beaker Culture via changes in religious beliefs to a prestige commodity-based society. In order to understand this phase and the events that characterized this period better, I will begin with a brief historiography that also places a European perspective on this historical era.

During the period 2900–2700 BC, we see how new societies or cultural groups emerged in many parts of Northern Europe. The earlier Funnel Beaker Cultures with their megalithic graves became transformed into something completely different. We call these new groups the Corded Ware Culture in Northern Germany, the Single Grave Culture in Denmark and the Battle Axe Culture in Sweden, Norway and Finland. It also seems that corded ware pottery has been found on the island of Bornholm. These events should be viewed in a larger European perspective where what archaeologists describe as corded ware is predominant in large parts of Central Europe. This style can take on regional variations, but common for all are the earth burials in the form of skeleton graves with standardized grave-goods such as pottery, flint axes and in men's graves, battle axes.

In several cases, for example in the Danish Single Grave Culture on Jylland, the graves are made up of mounds of varying sizes. On Jylland, this has given us a very good sequence of graves which has made it possible to classify the Single Grave Culture into different distinct stages: Bottom grave, Ground grave and Upper grave, each with its own characteristic assortment of grave-goods including pottery, flint axes and battle axes. It is also obvious that these objects are clearly associated with the North German Corded Ware district.

Instead of the Corded Ware Culture, we see another group emerge in Western Europe – the Bell-Beaker Culture, which however, should be dated to a somewhat later period, 2500/2400 BC.

It is obvious that people of this time chose to abandon a more collective society for one that seems to be more strongly based on individuals. Significant changes take place on many levels in society and we shall now take a look at what these were.

The Battle Axe Culture

Over the years, many Scandinavian archaeologists have worked on different interpretations of the Battle Axe Culture. We will focus on Swedish archaeology in the context of this chapter. However, in 1898 it was the Danish archaeologist Sophus Müller who was the archaeologist that presented the Jylland material from the Single Grave Culture. At the same time, he was the first to present a hypothesis concerning migration, which for a long time was the prevalent interpretation regarding the rise of the Battle Axe Culture. The first who took on the Swedish questions using a more scientific methodology was Lund researcher John-Elof Forssander, who in 1933 published his doctoral dissertation on the Battle Axe Culture, or as it was called then, the Boat Axe Culture. In his book, he primarily discusses the European connections between this culture and the cultural expressions seen on the continent. In addition, he presents the Swedish material in a methodical manner for the first time. Forssander also divides the Battle Axe Culture into two groups: an older and a younger. He bases this classification on what the battle axes looked like. He also considered this culture as resulting from migration.

Almost 20 years go by before the next extensive monograph about the Battle Axe Culture comes along. This is Andreas Oldeberg's book from 1952 entitled *Studien über die Schwedische Bootaxkultur*. In this work, Oldeberg generally follows Forssander's older classification, although with a few adjustments. Above all, he deals with the Central Sweden material in more detail. He also considers this as a migration, but contrary to Forssander who sees it as a migration from the south, Oldeberg emphasizes the similarities between Southwest Finland and the Mälaren Valley region and believes that immigration to Central Sweden was via the island of Åland. He also considers this to be the migration of two ethnic groups, one coming from the south and one from the east.

Ten more years pass and the next significant publication concerning the Battle Axe Culture comes from Mats P. Malmer and is entitled *Jungneiolitische Studien*, which is an almost 900 page book where Malmer takes on all aspects of this culture group, but perhaps mostly the graves and the artefacts. In many ways, Malmer was a forerunner in not only Swedish, but also international archaeology. His method of working with typology of battle axes for example, which were carefully measured and placed in the groups A–E (with several subgroups), influenced generations of archaeologists.

Malmer is strongly critical of Müller's and following researchers' idea that the Battle Axe Culture was a result of a migration. In a critical analysis of the arguments, he concluded that such was not the case. He bases this on the following observations:

- southern concentration of settlements
- the Battle Axe Culture has the same distribution as the Funnel Beaker Culture
- concentration to the best agricultural regions
- similarities in material culture, primarily regarding flint axes
- the change should be interpreted in economic-social terms instead of ethnic.

Based on studies of pottery, Malmer divides the Battle Axe Culture into six periods. According to Malmer, the last of these, *i.e.*, Period 6, belongs to the youngest of the Stone Age periods, the Late Neolithic.

After his pioneering work in 1962, Malmer expressed these points of view in several articles and books, the latest from 2002. In this latest book, he writes that he considers the Battle Axe Culture as very conservative, since very few changes take place during its duration of about 400 years.

One could say that Malmer's work has completely dominated research concerning this period. It was not until the 1980s that new hypotheses and interpretations were put forward. For example, based on results from the interdisciplinary Ystad project, Lars Larsson maintains that the early Battle Axe Culture settled some distance from the coast, which was dominated by the Funnel Beaker Culture's settlements and megalithic graves. He sees this new establishment as resulting from what he calls a missionary movement, where a new religion as well as a new social pattern is established, from a collective to a more individual-based society. Gradually, this model of society becomes completely prevalent.

Thus, it is obvious that significant changes take place during the transition between the MN A and MN B, that is to say, between the Funnel Beaker Culture and the Battle Axe Culture. Earlier, I brought up the idea that during the later part of the MN A, we can see a rapid change in the Funnel Beaker Culture. In a few well-investigated parts of Scania, changes can be seen as early as during the middle of the period (MN III) in the size of settlements as well as their placement. A more or less continuous settlement from the end of the older Primary Early Neolithic up to MN III was broken and new regions began being utilized. We can also see how settlements became concentrated into larger groups. This takes place sometime around 2900–2700 BC

During the period after this, between *c.* 2700 and 2400 BC, people are living with their different material cultures in southern Sweden. The difference between them is mostly in the way they decorate pottery, but also in what their flint axes look like. I have called these groups the Karlsfält, Stävie, Jonstorp/Siretorp and the Battle Axe Culture.

Regarding the Battle Axe Culture in Central Sweden, in recent years several new studies have shown that the material can be interpreted in a different way. In her work from 2009 based on material from the area around Lake Hjälmaren, Kim von Hackwitz considers the Battle Axe Culture as an expression for a social group within a larger Middle Neolithic society. She claims that they were like ambassadors in the society who were meant to maintain the social relations. It is also quite clear that they re-used the same region that the earlier Funnel Beaker Culture had used during the older part of the Early Neolithic. Various activities or events such as gathering sites, inland locations and lines of communication, which in Central Sweden were made up of boulder-ridges were spread throughout the landscape. Important centres were marked by graves and/or caches, *i.e.*, places for the deposition of different objects.

In a study from 2008, Roger Edenmo presented a completely different picture of the Battle Axe Culture. His work dealt primarily with the Battle Axe Culture's regional changes, *i.e.*, how the battle axes varied between different parts of the country. He based his results on material discovered in Närke and Södermanland. Edenmo claims that by designing their battle axes in ways characteristic for certain regions, they created and maintained regional identities within the Battle Axe Culture. These battle axes were part of an entirely new economy, which he calls prestige economy, and which was based the exchange of gifts. Edenmo means that this gradually led to a kind of hierarchical ranking between the different groups of people, and that access to prestigious goods was what led to these differences. This would eventually lead to a change in group relations and more stabile ranking among individuals and groups of people.

In her doctoral dissertation from 2009, Åsa M. Larsson studied a larger region and looked at not only Central Sweden, but also other parts of Sweden, for example Scania and Öland. What was important in her work were the studies of pottery from both the Pitted Ware Culture and the Battle Axe Culture. Both of these groups lived in eastern Sweden, side by side for about 500 years. She found that the large differences in the ceramic craftsmanship between these two groups reflect the actual historical situation. The production of a Battle Axe Culture vessel was surrounded by rules for what a vessel should look like and what kind of decorations it should have. Larsson also emphasized the eastern influences; the first Battle Axe vessels were influenced by pottery from Finland. It was from the Finnish region that people in eastern Sweden learned how the vessels should be made regarding decoration, shape as well as production.

Kristian Brink, in his doctoral dissertation from 2009, primarily examined the large and very interesting palisade structures in the Malmö region, which we will discuss in a coming section. Brink maintains that these palisades were built in a landscape with several different locations that have had a varied significance. He also emphasizes the increasingly important significance of the farm or house for people. A central fixed point comes to be established with the farm located at its centre. This becomes the central point of people's lives. This is something that, due much to the lack of source material, has not previously been discussed for the Battle Axe Culture. A closer connection between house and grave can also be seen, as they are often located in close vicinity to each other. Brink emphasizes that this is true for the latter part of this culture however.

As you can see from the above, there are many disagreements among researchers regarding how we should understand this interesting period and the historical events. We have gone from seeing the Battle Axe Culture as resulting from migration, to a local development into missionaries, ambassadors, to being a prestige-goods-driven economy restricted to a farm location and in association with a grave field.

However, we should now move on and look closer at what the situation was like in northern Sweden at this time. What changes do we see and how should they be understood in relation to what was happening farther to the south?

Events in North Sweden

Two locations with great significance in this context are Bjästamon and Kornsjövägen in the Västernorrland region, south of Örnsköldsvik. Here, we find perhaps not only the first evidence of agriculture in Norrland, but also several huts. At the settlement at Kornsjövägen, five houses were excavated within a *c.* 120 × 120 metre large area. The settlement was located in a rocky and steep area. The houses excavated all looked different – partially dug into the hillside, stone foundations and round houses. The best-preserved house (1) was dug partly into the hillside and was rectangular in shape, 15 × 14.5 metres.

The settlement at Bjästamon had a completely different kind of position on a sandy hillside facing the sea. It is also the largest archaeological excavation undertaken in Norrland of a Stone Age settlement. There were a large number of houses, 12 total, and these were also of different shapes and kinds. However, only five of these have been excavated. The houses at Bjästamon had three different shapes: round, oval and rectangular. The latter was built along the shore with the long side facing the sea.

At both of these settlements, archaeologists have been able to distinguish three phases (Figs 7.1 and 7.2):

1.   2800–2600 BC
2.   2600–2400 BC
3.   2400–2100 BC

Throughout this period, the houses changed very little. In the context of this chapter, the first two periods are of special interest. They coincide with a southern Scandinavian perspective regarding the transition between the MN A and MN B.

It is very interesting that in addition to large amounts of bone from animals such as fish and seal, cereal grains have also been found at Bjästamon. Results from ^{14}C-analysis date the site to *c.* 2500 BC This, together with the appearance of the pottery, points to contacts farther to the south and perhaps above all to the Mälaren Valley region.

Another site that is important in this context is the settlement and discovery location around Bjurselet, along the Byske River in northern Västerbotten. Large depositories of thick-butted flint axes have been found here – at least 175 axes since 1827. The great majority of these were not sharpened and many are assumed to be blanks. In connection with the archaeological excavation of the settlement at Bjurselet during the 1960s, researchers established the location of at least 13 depositories that were evenly distributed along the river terrace. Based on these findings, we can say that the area around Bjurselet played an important role in the Scandinavian Stone Age north-south trading system. In addition to these axes with southern Scandinavian origins, we also find northern Scandinavian tools made of quartz, quartzite and shale (Fig. 7.3).

Kjel Knutsson, who has worked with these finds, maintains that a small group of people from South Scandinavia settled in the region during a time that corresponds with the period discussed in this chapter, *c.* 2800 BC It is likely that these people were farmers who pursued both cultivation and stock farming as a part of their way of life. This can be seen in pollen diagrams for example from farther south. We should also mention Bjästamon farther to the south, which we looked at above. The period of cultivation here is about the same time as what we find at Bjurselet. Why did they not remove the axes from the depositories? Evert Baudou thinks that the native population fought back this early colonisation enterprise and therefore the axes were never put into use. This is a hypothesis very difficult to find a clear-cut answer for; however, we should perhaps not be too afraid within archaeological research to see war and conflicts as something that never occurred.

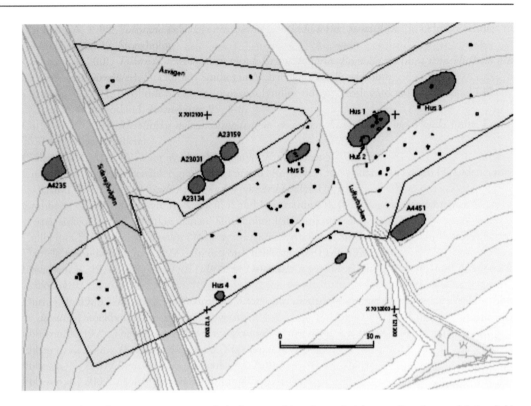

Figure 7.1. The settlement at Bjästamon with the houses and hearths marked (source: Gustafsson and Spång (eds) 2007).

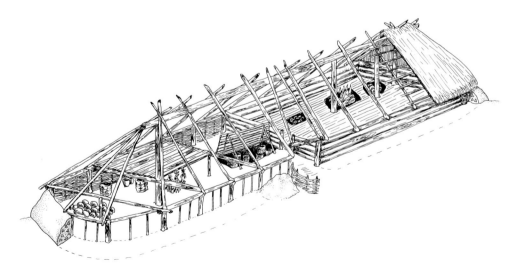

Figure 7.2. Reconstruction of House 1 at Bjästamon (source: Gustafsson and Spång (eds.) 2007; illustration: F. Sieurin-Lönnqvist).

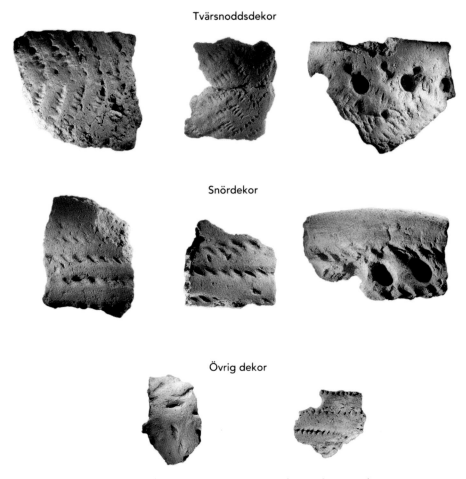

Figure 7.3. Pottery from Bjästamon (source: Gustafsson and Spång (eds) 2007).

Graves, dwellings and battle axes

It is now time to take a closer look at the remnants from the Battle Axe Culture as regards material culture, burial customs, settlements and economy.

Flint and stone

The earlier name used for the Battle Axe Culture was the Boat Axe Culture, which says much about the focus being specifically placed on the boat-shaped battle-axes. The typological classification based on the careful measurement and dating of the pottery that is used when describing these axes was formulated by Mats Malmer and includes groups A–E. The groups have names like Sösdala (C), Hurva (D) and Vellinge (E), all after discoveries in Scania.

Axes and chisels made of flint clearly dominate the different groups of finds from the Battle Axe Culture. The following types are dominant:

- thin-bladed chisels
- thin-bladed axes
- thick-butted axes.

Malmer clearly and distinctly typologically classified all of these. Here, I will not describe the various measurements he used, but instead limit myself to briefly describing typical features. All of the different kinds can be found in the graves and, based on the combinations of burial gifts, Malmer could distinguish between the different types.

A thin chisel is at the most 3 cm wide and may have a concave edge, *i.e.*, it could be used as a transverse chisel or, using a more modern term, a wood chisel.

A thin-bladed axe is at least 3 cm wide and is no more than 2 cm thick. This kind of axe may have had a concave edge. If you look at Malmer's distribution maps, this kind of axe gives the impression of being more common in the more northern parts of Sweden.

Finally, we have the thick-bladed axes, or with the term more commonly used, the thick-butted axes. This kind of axe may also have a concave edge and is at least 3 cm wide and more than 2 cm thick.

The blade arrowheads mentioned above in connection with the Pitted Ware Culture are another interesting tool we find. Malmer has also classified these into a number of different types, A–D. It is really only Type D that is found in the typical Battle Axe graves. These arrowheads are worked on all three sides (Fig. 7.4).

Together with the battle axes, pottery is what somehow defines this culture. The shapes of the vessels, decorations and even the additives in the clay differ greatly from other Middle Neolithic groups. The vessels are generally round, beaker-like, and with a short or no neck. In 1962, Mats Malmer divided the pottery into the groups A–O, including a few subgroups. To some extent, this classification also reflects a chronological division. A–B are the oldest and G–J are the youngest.

The most commonly occurring types are A, B, E, F, G, H and J. Group E is special in that it contains coarser pottery for everyday use and has consequently been found at settlements. Regarding ornamentation on the vessels, two large groups can be distinguished, groups A–B and G–J. The difference is that the former have decorations made with cords, while the latter group has decorations made with comb and cord imprints. The latter also have vessels completely covered in decorations, often in zigzag bands (Fig. 7.5).

Preparing the dead – burial customs

Graves, in the form of single or double-graves containing skeletons and lacking an earthen mound, are characteristic for the Battle Axe Culture. They are generally oriented in a northeast-southwest direction. In recent years however, graves with burnt bones have also been discovered. We should also mention that other forms of burial also existed, for example megalithic graves, stone crypts and mass graves. Also worth mentioning is that there were also graves with structures built over them in the form of tent-like constructions as well as what can be interpreted as a kind of death house.

Burial customs are often complex and, in this context, the descriptions need to be more

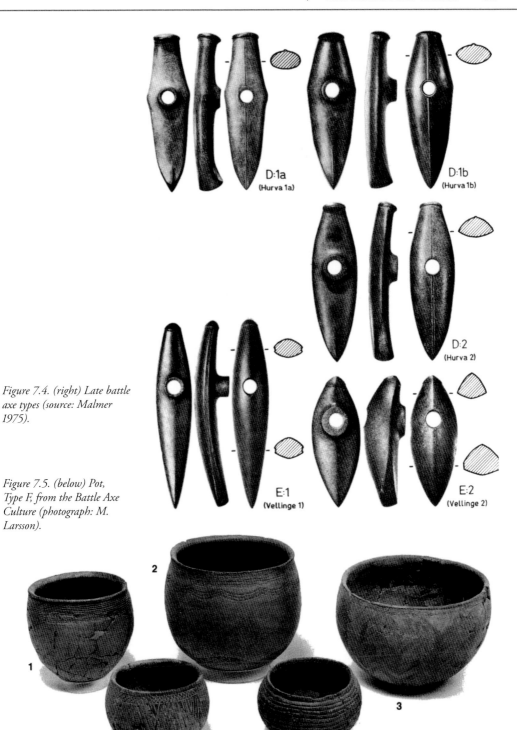

Figure 7.4. (right) Late battle axe types (source: Malmer 1975).

Figure 7.5. (below) Pot, Type F, from the Battle Axe Culture (photograph: M. Larsson).

general so that we can more easily see the differences. By way of introduction, we will look at the different kinds of graves, and in the next section, we will focus on a few individual graves that continue the story.

The dead were buried in a grave under flat ground, lying on their sides with their legs bent, a so-called hocker-position. In the graves, we find traces of different constructions such as wooden cists and frameworks made of stone. It seems like burials in wooden cists are an older form of burial than those using stone frameworks. The length of the graves varies greatly, between 2 and 3.5 metres, while they are up to 140 cm wide with a height of about 100 cm. Of course, the double-graves are larger. The longest of these is 430 cm long.

In several cases, the graves form an actual grave field comprised of a large number of graves, like at Bedinge in southeast Scania with a total of 13 graves, few of which have later dates. It is interesting that the graves form a linear grave field that was probably placed along roads and paths of communication.

Mass graves do occur and one such example is a grave from Bedinge. A stone framework surrounded a wooden cists with a lid on which large stone boulders had been placed. The floor of the box was made of thin flagstones and on these, the remains of five individuals were found: three adults and two children.

It is interesting to look at how the skeletons were placed in the graves. I mentioned earlier that Mats Malmer considers the Battle Axe Culture to be conservative; this can be seen in the placement of the dead. There were obviously strict conventions regarding how the dead should be placed – faces towards the east, the hocker-position and lying on their left or right sides. It has sometimes been suggested that placement in the grave could be dependent on the sex of the individual, and there is a tendency for the men to be placed on their left sides and the women on their rights.

We will now take a closer look at some of the graves from different parts of the country.

Our survey begins with the famous double-grave from Bergsvägen in Linköping, which is actually a triple-grave. The grave was discovered at the beginning of the 1950s in connection with road construction. The dead had been placed in a wooden cist and were oriented in a northeast-southwest direction. Regarding the placement of the bodies in the grave, the woman was placed on the east side, lying on her left side with her face towards the northeast. The man was buried in the western part and was placed on his right side with his face towards the southwest. The two adults were placed so close together that their knees were touching. In addition to the two adults, an infant was also found in the grave. Interestingly, the baby lay between the legs of a dog, north of the woman. The dead had taken many objects with them into death. The man had a battle axe, which for once was placed south of the man's skull. The woman had a flint axe, a stone axe and a flint chisel placed south of her skull. In addition, several objects made from bone and antler were found, which was unusual, but in this case was due to the favourable conditions for preservation in the calcareous soil. It was also interesting to find objects made from copper in the form of spirals and band-shaped sheet metal. The latter objects indicate extensive contact channels to the south (Fig. 7.6).

In southern Halland, there is an abundance of material from the Battle Axe Culture with

Figure 7.6. Battle Axe grave from Bergsvägen in Linköping. The child is missing in the reconstruction (source: Knutsson 1995).

several rich burial finds. In this context, we should mention a grave from Sannagård, with findings comprised of two flint axes, seven blade arrowheads of the characteristic Type D, as well as a clay pot of a late type. Unfortunately, no skeletons were found since the sandy soil is not the best for preserving organic material.

Continuing south in Sweden, we will now examine the grave field at Kastanjegården in Malmö. This grave field was excavated in 1973 and includes four graves. The graves were located on a low hill in an otherwise flat landscape. All of the graves had an underground stone construction and, in addition, were single-graves. The body in Grave 105 had been buried on its right side, with its head towards the east. Two clay pots, a flint axe and several amber beads accompanied the individual. An analysis of the skeletal remains and the teeth indicate that the individual was a woman, 25–30 years old. There were also small skeletal remains from a child in the grave.

In Grave 106, no skeleton was preserved, only teeth remained. Burial gifts included a clay pot, a flint axe, a blade arrowhead and several amber beads. In Grave 108, in addition to the stone construction, traces of a wooden box were found. The skeleton was not preserved, but one could see traces of colouring that suggests that the individual had lain on its left side with its head towards the north. Burial gifts included a battle axe and two flint axes. The last grave (109) contained only teeth from the buried individual. In this case, the burial gifts consisted of two flint axes, a few amber beads and a clay pot.

The grave field at Kastanjegården is hardly the only one in the Malmö region. In connection with recent archaeological excavations, a relatively large number of graves from the Battle Axe Culture have been excavated, among them, Svågertorp and Norra Hyllievång, both single graves, as well as other grave fields or groups of graves. The grave at Svågertorp contained the skeleton of a man who was between 30 and 39 years old at his death. He had been buried in the hocker-position, with his head towards the north and face facing east. He had a battle axe of a later type placed together with a flint axe near his head. At his feet was a clay pot, also of a later type. Radiocarbon dating of the man's bones provides a date of 2340–2140 BC This indicates that, just like the battle axe and pottery, the grave belonged to the youngest part of the Battle Axe Culture.

At the excavations at Norra Hyllievång, two groups of graves were discovered and excavated

– the southern group and the northern group. The northern group was comprised of nine stonepackings, which archaeologists have interpreted as graves. Both this interpretation as well as the dating is uncertain however.

The two Battle Axe graves in the southern group are still very interesting. The skeleton in Grave I was poorly preserved, but we have been able to determine that the body was placed with its head towards the north and facing towards the east. The individual had been between 17 and 25 years old when he died. Two flint axes lay next to the head and a clay pot of a late type was at his feet. The burial gifts date the grave to the younger part of the Battle Axe Culture.

In Grave II, only teeth were preserved, found in the north part of the grave. In this part of the grave, archaeologists also found two flint axes and a chisel, together with amber beads and a clay pot. A second pot had been placed near the hips. One unusual discovery were the eleven D-type arrowheads, which were found at the probable foot-end of the grave. It is quite unusual to find so many arrowheads in one grave. In this context, we should remember the grave at Sannagård in Halland we mentioned earlier.

As is evident from the graves presented in some detail above, variations existed primarily in the amount of burial gifts and their quality. However, the construction of the graves, the placement of the dead and the direction in which the heads were placed are all obviously guided by a strong sense of tradition and how things should be. Just as Malmer wrote, there is a strong conservatism within the Battle Axe Culture. As we shall see however, changes occur within the culture that point towards incoming influences and a different way of looking at the dead.

Houses for the dead

Experts have debated for a number of years on the presence or absence of cremation in the Battle Axe Culture. In 1975, Mats Malmer wrote that the existence of such was unlikely and that evidence of them was scarce. He still argued so as recently as in 2002, but with reservation for the 'death houses' that had been excavated.

The most spectacular of these is the one from Turinge (Gläntan) in Södermanland, excavated ten or so years ago. The structure was rectangular and was surrounded by a trench. It measured *c.* 4.8 × 3.1 metres and the trench was between 0.35 and 0.5 metres deep. Traces of stone-filled postholes were found at the corners of the building as well as in the central area. In the twenty pits with a black and sooty filling found in the structure, archaeologists found over 3 kg of burnt bone, mostly from humans, along with large amounts of pottery. The pottery was mostly broken, but three almost intact pots were discovered in one pit. In addition to the pottery, a battle axe and a few flint and stone axes were found. Results from several ^{14}C-analyses date the building to the period 2500–2200 BC, which indicates a younger part of the Battle Axe Culture.

It is also interesting to note that the pits were not evenly distributed in the building, but that the majority of them were located in the eastern part of the structure. From the large amounts of burnt bone, scientists have been able to distinguish seven individuals of different ages and probably of different sexes. However, there were probably several more individuals.

Jonathan Lindström, who was the archaeologist who excavated Turinge, believes that there might have been remains from at least sixteen individuals. After a careful examination of the placement of the bones, other interesting differences have emerged. In the pits at the north and eastern parts of the building, parts of primarily skulls were found, while the material from the pits in the southern part of the structure contained bones from other parts of the body. Lindström's explanation for the building is thought provoking. He sees this as a depiction of the Battle Axe Culture's graves, with the pits in the east showing that the dead were always facing east. The same thing is true for the skull fragments in the northern part of the building. This is a daring as well as convincing explanation of the similarities between the death house at Turinge and the graves of the Battle Axe Culture.

In this context, we should also take time to discuss sacrificial customs and the ceremonial acts associated with these customs. After concentration to the settlements during the latter part of the MN A, as well as deposits of burnt axes outside megalithic graves for example, a return to the previously used locations near bogs and wetlands occurs. The sacrifices are mostly comprised of flint axes. This obvious change in sacrificial customs has been discussed by, among others, Per Karsten, who argues that this was a way for people to manifest their affiliation and history – a kind of connection back in time, which in many ways supports Mats Malmer's views that we are dealing with a local origin of the Battle Axe Culture.

In a previous chapter, I mentioned the large discovery sites for primarily burnt flint axes in Scania and Södermanland for example, which belonged to the Funnel Beaker Culture. This also takes place during the period we are now examining. One such place is Kverrestad, in southern Scania, where a large number of burnt flint axes were discovered along with other objects. Unlike the previously discussed site of Svartskylle, this site was not located on a hill, but instead on a tableland in a river valley. Here, several axes of primarily the concave edged type have been collected, as well as even the thin-bladed type. In addition, quite a few tanged D-type arrowheads have been found, as well as a type that can be called lancet-shaped, sometimes with a small tang. A majority of the artefacts, especially the axes, were burned and destroyed. In connection with an archaeological excavation, researchers found several smaller pits in which burnt flint had been placed together with potsherds and small pieces of charred bone.

The finds from Kverrestad are interesting from many viewpoints. Dating results place it in the late Battle Axe Culture and the lancet-shaped arrowheads in particular support this dating. These arrowheads are clearly a foreign element at the site as they come from the other side of the Baltic Sea, the Oder region.

Houses for the living

Excavated settlements from the Battle Axe Culture were for a long time an unknown concept. The general view was that the people of the Battle Axe Culture were for the most part a nomadic pastoral people that did not leave any apparent traces. In 1962 as well as later, Mats Malmer writes that a settlement is a place where two potsherds from the Battle Axe Culture are found with no more than 200 metres between them. This is a definition difficult to work with, and today, our knowledge about the Battle Axe Culture's settlements are much better; however, compared with the number of Funnel Beaker Culture settlements and Pitted Ware Culture settlements, the Battle Axe Culture settlements are few in number. Here, I will concentrate primarily on the settlements where houses have been found. The main reason for this is so that we can see the differences as well as the similarities with earlier and later periods regarding how people organized their settlements. Our journey begins in the south.

Among the many extensive archaeological excavations conducted in the Malmö region during the past decade, we can assign quite a number of dwelling remains to the MN B and the Battle Axe Culture. Houses have been found at several sites, such as Almhov, Svågertorp, Elinelund, Vintrie and Dösemarken. In this context, I cannot describe all of these houses in detail; instead, I will provide a more general synopsis. All of the houses are of the Two-aisled type, *i.e.*, with a row of centrally placed poles that supported the roof. The number of roof-supporting poles varied in this case between three and five. The dimensions, when they can be determined, are between a length of 11 and 14 metres and a width of between 5.5 and 6 metres. No clear spatial details exist, but as mentioned, there is only a central area, *i.e.*, the roof-supporting area; however, the house still gives the impression of being almost rectangular.

We also see another type of house or storehouse at some of the sites. This provision-shed built on posts was almost rectangular and had four posts.

A significant number of ^{14}C-analyses have been of great help when dating the houses, since there are generally not many finds here. The oldest date comes from House 100 at the Vintrie settlement site. This house is dated to 2880–2670 BC The majority of the houses have been placed in a younger period, *c.* 2600–2400 BC The youngest lies in the period *c.* 2100–1900 BC In other words, we clearly see that these structures can be placed in the younger part of the Battle Axe Culture, just like the grave from the Malmö region that we examined earlier.

Between 1985–1986 at Kabusa, east of Ystad, archaeologists excavated a settlement from the Battle Axe Culture. The most interesting find was a dwelling structure of a somewhat different kind. It was a vaguely trapezoid-shaped underground area with associated postholes, with postholes both in the underground area and outside it. The actual underground structure measured 13.5 × 7 metres. It is difficult to gain a clear picture of what the house once looked like, but one explanation is that part of the house acted as a cellar, *i.e.*, the underground part.

Relatively few objects were found and they comprised mainly two categories: flint and pottery. It is worth noting that the majority of the flint material comes from axe manufacturing. The pottery is mostly fragmentary sherds, but the decorations indicate dates placing them in the later part of the Battle Axe Culture. Results from three ^{14}C-analyses support the dating to *c.* 2580–2330 BC

We know of similar houses from Jylland, for example, as well as from another location in Scania not far from Kabusa – Valleberga, where Märta Strömberg conducted a minor excavation during the 1970s. Like I said, the excavation was not large, but a rectangular underground structure found, rich with finds, is quite similar to the one at Kabusa. The finds indicate the later part of the Battle Axe Culture and ^{14}C-analyses support the dating to 2300–2190 BC

Among the many places in Scania having houses from this period, we should mention an almost 20-metre long and 6-metre wide house from Dagstorp in the western part of the region, not far from the palisade enclosure at Dösjebro. The house was rectangular and, according to the interpretation of the postholes, the house had been rebuilt at least twice, which meant that the number of roof-supporting posts varied between three and four. Few artefacts were found here and those finds made came from the postholes and included discarded flint and some pottery. The most interesting find was a small part of a typical concave-edged flint axe, characteristic of the Battle Axe Culture. A ^{14}C-dating analysis is well in accordance with this find as well as with the appearance of the construction, *c.* 2280–1980 BC The house is situated relatively near a large axe manufacturing site and a grave field from the same time.

Now it is time to leave Scania and travel northwards.

Archaeologists have found houses only at a few sites in Östergötland – at two smaller sites in Linköping, Kv. Glasrutan and Kv. Paragrafen. At the first site, three rather defuse houses were excavated, but archaeologists were able to determine that they were rather small rectangular buildings about 9 × 5.5 metres and similar in type to those presented above from the Malmö region. Few finds were made, but an isolated pottery sherd from the Battle Axe Culture supports the ^{14}C-dating to 2468–2205 BC It is also worth noting that the settlement was located near the grave at Bergsvägen we mentioned earlier.

At the other site in Linköping, a poorly preserved small house was excavated, which actually lay under a large and well-preserved house from the end of the Stone Age. I will describe this in a later section. The discovery of pits with Battle Axe pottery support the dating of the period to 2900–2200 BC

Trends in settlements

If we briefly summarize the settlement trends during the MN B, the Battle Axe Culture, we clearly see remnants that belong to the younger part of the Battle Axe Culture (Malmer Groups 5–6) dated to the period *c.* 2600–2200 BC Our knowledge of the older part of this period is poor. Knowledge regarding the grouping and function of settlements is also still inadequate. At a few sites, Kabusa for example, we see remnants of axe manufacturing, which can also be linked to the palisade structures. What we can see is a more fixed organisation showing continuity up through the youngest part of the Stone Age, the Late Neolithic. We find this trend in both the Malmö region and in Östergötland. A focus on farms, as Kristian Brink suggests, seems likely. Proximity to grave fields also seems to give the impression of being characteristic of the late Battle Axe Culture, in both Scania and Östergötland.

Thus, we still know very little about what these early settlements looked like. We can look at the Danish island of Bornholm where extensive excavations have left a rich material from the transition between the MN A and MN B. This is the only area in southern Scandinavia where we can follow the development of dwellings from the MN A to MN B and on into the end of the Stone Age. At sites such as Limensgård and Grødbygård, archaeologists have excavated several houses from this period. At Limensgård, two houses that can be dated to the transition between the MN A and MN B have been excavated. House AA was approximately 16 metres long and 7.5 metres wide. The house had trenches for walls on three sides. ^{14}C-dating of the houses at this site places them between *c.* 2850 and 2550 BC

Sixteen houses from this period were excavated at Grødbygård. The longest of these was 22 metres long and 7 metres wide. Just as at Limensgård, wall trenches were preserved on three sides. ^{14}C-dating places the houses between *c.* 2800 and 2500 BC Two smaller round timber circles were also excavated at the site.

It is quite apparent that the settlements at both of these locations existed during the same period. In addition, according to Finn Ole Nielsen, there should have been no less than two houses at the same time, at least at Grödbygård.

Palisades and timber circles

Before we continue with our story, we have a very interesting and important group of finds left to examine. I am referring to several palisade constructions in Scania that were excavated in conjunction with the large land development for new roads, railways and especially in connection with building the Öresund bridge and its access roads. These palisade enclosures have been documented for the past 20 years primarily in Scania, but also in the northeast part of the region. Outside of Scania, we find palisade constructions on Själland and on Bornholm. There are a number of questions surrounding these constructions and we will examine them in this section. In particular, their chronological placement between the MN A (the Funnel Beaker Culture) and MN B (the Battle Axe Culture) is worth paying attention to and discussing.

The first discovered was found at Hyllie (Malmö) and has been studied on several occasions starting at the end of the 1980s when Mac Svensson led an excavation that cut through the central sections. Much of the other sections was studied during the beginning of the 2000s. The palisade was somewhat round/oval in shape and covered an area of 4 hectares. In other words, it was a gigantic construction. The palisade was built with logs that had a dimension of between 0.2 and 0.4 metres. The height of the palisade has been estimated at between 1.5 and 3.5 metres. Four large openings have been located in the palisade. Very few finds that could be used to date the structure were found – an isolated flint axe, a hoe made from an antler and a few potsherds. Interesting however is that around the opening to a smaller space in the eastern part of the palisade, a relatively large amount of flint was discovered, which had been used for example for axe making. Both burned and unburned flint was found, without any signs of being worked. Thus, we must for the most part rely on ^{14}C-dating. These results indicate dates between 2850–2690 BC, that is, the transition between the MN A and the MN B periods (Fig. 7.7).

The next palisade construction was located at Bunkeflo (Malmö) and was situated close to the beach. Unlike at Hyllie, only parts of Bunkeflo have been excavated, but the size of the enclosure is estimated to 210 × 215 metres, which means that the enclosure had an area of about 3 ha. Like at Hyllie, there are few finds, only potsherds and flint. Chemical analyses

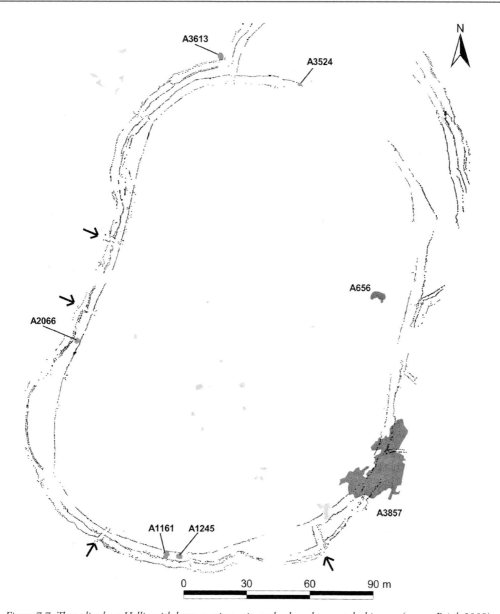

Figure 7.7. The palisade at Hyllie with large openings, pits and culture layer marked in grey (source: Brink 2009).

of the soil from the interior of the palisade enclosure do not indicate any settlement activity. However, the pits that were excavated were interesting. In addition to flint and pottery, these pits contained animal bones, which indicates that people kept pigs, sheep/goats and cattle. Hunting and fishing seem to have been only a supplement to their livelihoods.

How old is the Bunkeflo palisade then? There are remnants from older parts of both the Early Neolithic as well as the MN A, but the palisade itself can be dated to the period 2570–2500 BC, *i.e.*, somewhat younger than Hyllie and clearly datable to the MN B and the Battle Axe Culture.

The third and largest palisade enclosure is located at Bunkeflostrand (Malmö). It was excavated during the first decade of the 2000s. Kristian Brink, who led the excavation, estimated the size to be *c.* 140 × 300 metres, which meant that the palisade enclosure encompassed an area of about 5.5 ha. Inside the actual palisade, several pits of different kinds were excavated. These contained finds of fragments of flint axes and pottery, among other things. Brink prefers to see the pits, as well as the wells, as signs of settlement activity, which is a reasonable assumption. Based on ^{14}C-analyses and finds at the site, the palisade construction can be placed in the interval 2700–2600 BC, which indicates the MN B and the early Battle Axe Culture.

It is now time for us to leave the Malmö region and continue on to a place called Dösjebro, located five kilometres from the coast of the Öresund.

The site was discovered in the middle of the 1990s and excavated in 1998. The palisade construction found here comprised 500 posts that enclosed an area of *c.* 3 ha. It can be described as being almost U-shaped. Interestingly, the posts making up the palisade were freestanding and spaced about one metre apart. The discovery of burnt clay in the holes left by the posts has led the excavation leader Mac Svensson to believe that there had been a woven construction between the poles that had been caked with clay. The presence of burnt clay, soot and charcoal in the postholes indicates that the entire palisade had burned down at some time. Openings were also present in the palisade, a total of six that led into the interior of the enclosure. Similar to the other sites, finds were few and included pottery and flint. In many cases, the flint came from the manufacturing of axes. The finds discovered in a few smaller pits and postholes both inside and outside the palisade are also worth mentioning. These buried objects have a ceremonial meaning and are comprised of tightly packed pieces of discarded flint from axe making for example, as well as flint tools and an axe (Fig. 7.8).

The pottery finds and axes date Dösjebro to the later part of the Funnel Beaker Culture and the transition to the MN B (the Battle Axe Culture). This was confirmed by the ^{14}C-analyses from the postholes, which date the construction to the period 2880–2590 BC

An additional area with palisade constructions exists in Scania – Hunneberget in northeast Scania, not far from Kristianstad. At this site, archaeologists have discovered five round timber circles with a diameter that varied between *c.* 3 and 10 metres. Anders Edring, the excavator, compares these with the Brittish 'woodhenges'. They are small in comparison and preferably should be compared with the timber circles at Rispebjerg and Vasagård on Bornholm. Dating of the circles at Hunneberget is uncertain. The ^{14}C-analyses performed indicate a much later date, and they should be dated to the later part of the MN A and the transition to the MN B. This leads to a date comparable to that determined for the circles on Bornholm.

In summary, both the palisades in the Malmö region and at Dösjebro, as well as the timber circles at Hunneberget can all chronologically be placed in about the same time interval, the period between the late Funnel Beaker Culture (MN A) and the early Battle Axe Culture (MN B). In years, this covers approximately the period 2800–2500 BC

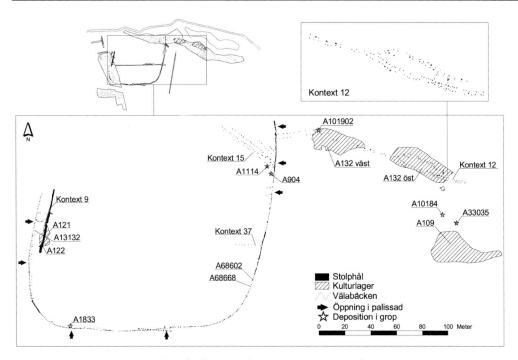

Figure 7.8. The palisade at Dösjebro in Scania (source: Andersson 2003).

Thus, there is no doubt that we see great changes in this period concerning both people and their relationship to the surrounding landscape. Here, I am referring primarily to the dealings between people and how networks were established. Changes occur in the landscape in that the large palisade enclosures are built. These will come to have great significance for different groups of people in the same way that the earlier Sarup constructions had. In times of change, people needed places where they could meet, exchange goods and perform ceremonial actions of different kinds. This could be the burying of axes, the depositing of waste from axe making or pottery.

However, we should not forget that these palisade constructions should mostly be dated to the transition between the MN A and MN B, and that they are older than the settlements and graves discussed here. It seems like the houses and graves, and their close association with one another, took over the large palisades' role as fixed points for the people of that time.

Crop growing and livestock

Knowledge about the growing of crops and raising livestock within the Battle Axe Culture is rather poor. The material that exists does however provide some fixed points. If we examine the evidence from pollen diagrams regarding vegetation and the landscape's degree of openness, it is clear that no large changes occur during the MN B. We see that the landscape started becoming more open and that the forests were used for what is usually called forest grazing farming, *i.e.*, the livestock is allowed to graze freely in the deciduous forests. It is also usually said that cultivation occurred on smaller fields, gardening farming, and that this was relatively transitory.

Regarding the significance cultivation had, we do not have enough material from the settlement to provide a detailed picture of what was cultivated and to what extent. As shown above however, it is clear that agriculture was introduced in the northern parts of Sweden during the period in question. What did they grow? Based on the studies completed, we know that barley for example and simple types of wheat such as emmer were grown. Based on knowledge from houses in the Malmö region, we can say that the majority of the cereal grain finds come from the houses.

Regarding the kinds of domesticated animals people kept during this period, dogs, cattle, pits and sheep/goats were clearly dominant. Bones from wild animals and fish also indicate that hunting and fishing occurred. From a few sites in the Malmö region, we have material indicating that fishing was quite common.

The picture painted above is generally the same for all of southern and central Sweden. Agriculture and the raising of livestock increased in significance, but it is still difficult to say anything about the extent of cultivation or about the number of livestock people kept on a farm.

Recent years' studies of ^{13}C-levels and the levels of stabile isotopes in human skeletons from graves has provided another picture that deepens our knowledge about what humans ate during this period. We have already touched on this as regards the Pitted Ware Culture and the Funnel Beaker Culture on Öland, but studies of skeletons from the Battle Axe Culture provide another picture.

Analyses of sulphur and strontium isotopes from skeletons on Öland (Resmo) show that there were people represented here who were not born on the island. It might be the case, as Elin Fornander points out, that mobility increased during the MN B. Can we see this anywhere else? Fornander has analysed skeletons from a large number of graves from the Battle Axe Culture in Scania and finds another picture.

Results from the individuals analysed clearly show that these individuals preferred a land-based diet with cereal grains and meat from land-living animals. They have obviously not consumed fish in any greater amounts. However, researchers have discovered two individuals from the Malmö region and from northeast Scania who had eaten somewhat more fish than average. The large amounts of fish bones found at one of the palisade constructions also support this conclusion.

If several of the individuals on Öland did not have local origins, it is not something that could be proved using the material from Scania. Those who had been buried in the graves examined from Malmö, Bedinge and northeast Scania obviously had local origins. From these results, we can assume that the people in Scania did not travel about much.

Now our journey continues on its last stage, which is the Late Neolithic, that is, the final part of the Stone Age.

Suggested readings

Ahlström, T. 2009. *Underjordiska dödsriken: humanosteologiska studier av neolitiska kollektivgravar.* Göteborg.

Andersson, M. 2003. *Skapa plats i landskapet. Tidig- och mellanneolitiska samhällen utmed två västskånska dalgångar.* Lund.

Berggren, Å. and Brink, K. 2010. För levande och döda – begravningsritual och social identitet i yngre stenålder. In Nilsson, B. and Rudebeck, E. (eds) *Arkeologiska och förhistoriska världar. Fält, erfarenheter och stenåldersplatser i sydvästra Skåne.* Malm: Malm Museer, Arkeologi enheten, 255–308.

Biwall, A., Hernek, R., Kihlstedt, B., Larsson, M. and Torstensdotter-Åhlin, I. 1997. In Stenålderns hyddor och hus i Syd- och Mellansverige. Larsson, M. and Olsson, E. (eds) *Regionalt och interregionalt. Stenåldersundersökningar i Syd- och Mellansverige.* Riksantikvarieämbetet. Arkeologiska Undersökningar Skrifter nr 23. Stockholm, 265–297.

Björk, N. 1998. *Fräkenrönningen – en 'by' för 5 000 år sedan.* Rapport- Länsmuseet Gävleborg 1998, 14. Gävle.

Brink, K. 2009. *I palissadernas tid: om stolphål och skärvor och sociala relationer under yngre mellanneolitikum.* Lund.

Browall, H. 2003. *Det forntida Alvastra.* Statens Historiska Museum. Stockholm.

Edenmo, R., Larsson, M., Nordqvist, B. and Olsson, E. 1997. Gropkeramikerna. Fanns de? In Larsson, M. and Olsson, E. (eds) *Regionalt och interregionalt. Stenåldersundersökningar i Syd- och Mellansverige.* Riksantikvarieämbetet. Arkeologiska Undersökningar Skrifter nr 23. Stockholm, 135–213.

Göthberg, H. (ed.) 2007. *Hus och bebyggelse i Uppland: delar av förhistoriska sammanhang.* Uppsala: Riksantikvarieämbetet. UV GAL.

Janzon, G. O. 1974. *Gotlands mellanneolitiska gravar.* Stockholm.

Janzon, G. O. and Ahlbeck, M. 2009. *The dolmen in Alvastra.* Kungl. Vitterhets historie och antikvitets akademien. Stockholm.

Larsson, L. 1982. A causewayed enclosure and a site with Valby Pottery at Stävie, Western Scania. *Meddelanden från Lunds Universitets Historiska Museum* 1981–1982, 65–114.

Larsson, L. 1985. Karlsfält. A settlement from the early and late Funnel Beaker Culture in Southern Scania, Sweden. *Acta Archaeaologica* 54, 3–71.

Larsson, L. 1992. Settlement and environment during the Middle Neolithic and Late Neolithic. In Larsson, L., Callmer, J. and Stjernquist, B. (eds) *The archaeology of the cultural landscape: field work and research in a south Swedish rural region.* Stockholm: Almqvist and Wiksell International, 91–159.

Larsson, L. 2000. Axes and fire-contacts with the gods. In Olausson, D. and Vandkilde, H. (eds) *Form, Function and Context. Material Culture studies in Scandinavian Archaeology.* Lund, 93–105.

Larsson, M. 1992. The Early and Middle Neolithic Funnel Beaker Culture in the Ystad Area (Southern Scania). Economic and Social Change, 3100–2300 BC. In Larsson, L., Callmer, J. and Stjernquist, B. (eds) *The Archaeology of the Cultural Landscape.* Acta Archaeologica Lundensia 4:19. Lund, 17–91.

Larsson, M. 2006. *A tale of a strange people. The Pitted Ware Culture in Southern Sweden.* Kalmar–Lund.

Larsson, M. 2009. The pitted ware culture in eastern middle Sweden: material culture and human agency. In Jordan, P. D. and Zvelebil, M. (eds) *Ceramics before farming: the dispersal of pottery among prehistoric Eurasian hunter-gatherers.* Walnut Creek, Left Coast Press, 395–419.

Malmer, M. P. 1975. *Stridsyxekulturen i Sverige och Norge*. Liber: Lund.

Malmer, M. P. 2002. *The Neolithic of South Sweden. FBC, GRK and STR*. Stockholm: KVHAA.

Sjögren, K.-G. 2003. *'Mångfalldige uhrminnes grafvar': megalitgravar och samhälle i Västsverige*. Göteborg.

8   Longhouses and Stone Cists

Mats Larsson

This last chapter deals with the youngest part of the Stone Age, the Late Neolithic period, and the transition to the Bronze Age. This means that we are dealing with the period *c.* 2350–1700 BC. This is also the first time in our story that we will not encounter a named culture. In older literature, we find two names used to label the period – the Age of the Stone Cists or the Age of the Dagger. Later on in the chapter, we will understand why. Like with the other chapters, we will begin with a brief background concerning research about this period. We will touch on chronology as well as look at the more significant types of tools.

Characteristic artefacts of this period are the flint daggers, which have been studied and classified for over 100 years. The foundations for the chronological division of the period were established already in 1902 by the Danish archaeologist Sophus Müller. He based his classification on the identification of five types of daggers. John-Elof Forssander revised this classification in 1936 when he differentiated between daggers and spear/lance points. His work resulted in a division of the daggers into six types.

The classification we use today is based on Ebbe Lomborg's work from 1973, which largely stems from Forssander's work. Lomborg divides the Danish daggers into sex types, with the youngest belonging to Period I of the Bronze Age. Furthermore, he considered this division to be a chronological sequence. Based on this classification, the period was divided into three groups: SN A, SN B and SN C. Based on a thorough analysis of settlements, graves and daggers, Lomborg could also see a division of Denmark into two cultural zones. The first includes North Jylland, eastern Denmark and Scania, while Zone 2 includes southern and central Jylland and North Germany. According to Lomborg, daggers were made mostly in Zone 1.

During the years following, Lomborg's classification of the Late Neolithic was the subject of several major as well as minor revisions, the latest by Helle Vandkilde, who in 1996 divided the period into two parts, SN I and SN II. The first encompasses Lomborg's periods A–B, while the second covers Period C.

It also turns out that the daggers are not an infallible or exact manner with which to date the period. Several ^{14}C-dating analyses indicate that the beginning of the SN I can be dated to *c.* 2350 BC, the transition to the SN II to *c.* 1950 BC, while the dividing line to the Bronze Age is placed at *c.* 1700 BC.

What we can say with certainty, however, is that the first daggers with lance-shaped blades were made during the SN I in the Limfjord region, with influences from the British Isles. We can also see that during the SN II, production of the daggers was moved to the eastern Danish islands. We see that influences are primarily from Central Europe during this period.

As we have done for the earlier periods, we will now examine and discuss different aspects of the Late Neolithic. We begin with the material culture, what we see as being characteristic for this period.

Daggers, sickles and arrowheads

Jan Apel indicates two possible paths for the introduction of daggers into Sweden:

- North Jylland via western Norway to the Baltic coast of Norrland
- Själland and Scania to southern and central Sweden, and to southeast Norway.

The flint dagger has often been seen as a symbol of warriors with high status and with an extensive network. Eventually, metal replaces the role of the dagger as a male status symbol.

The significant change regarding the working of flint during this period is in the technological process. Several of the characteristic objects from the late Stone Age, such as daggers, sickles and arrowheads, required extremely skilful craftsmanship, which Jan Apel sees as an apprenticeship system. The apprentice learned through training under an experienced flint worker. In plain terms, the technique is called knapping (or lithic reduction), *i.e.*, the object gets its shape through the gradual reduction of the object's surfaces. Using a more specific terminology, we call this bifacial technology, where flakes are struck from both sides of an edge or side. The technique used is soft hammer percussion, where a hammer or club of wood or antler is used as a hammer and the worker can produce thin, two-sided flint blades.

In this way, flintknappers produced the daggers described above, as well as sickles and arrowheads. The sickles were purely agricultural tools used for harvesting. We can see this through the microscopic analyses of their cutting edges. Blades of cereal grains and grasses contain silicon, which causes the edges to take on a glossy surface after use (Fig. 8.1).

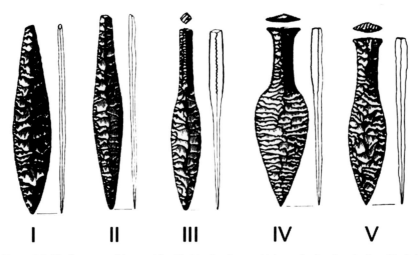

I   II   III   IV   V

Figure 8.1. The five types of daggers identified by Lomborg, which can be dated to the Late Neolithic.

Another group of objects worth mentioning are the so-called knapped flint arrowheads, which often have an emarginated base while others may be heart-shaped.

Other typical objects from the period we should mention are the single handle-hole axes, also called simple shaft-hole axes. They are generally rather small and are irregularly shaped, but there are great variations. These are probably the most common artefacts in Swedish museum collections. Attempts have been made, without success, to classify these axes into different types. Perhaps a division into two forms, rounded and square might be valid. If so, the former would belong to this period, while the latter would belong to the Bronze Age. Per Lekberg, who is the archaeologist who has most recently studied handle-hole axes, believes that the size of the axe is related to different forms of deposition. According to Lekberg, Late Neolithic people had a clear understanding regarding what was appropriate in different situations. It seems for example that axes shorter than 13 cm represented grave-goods, while axes longer than 17 cm come from depots or sacrificial deposits.

A significantly better worked variation of the shaft-hole axes are the Hagebyhöga axes, named after a discovery in a stone cist from Östergötland. They closely resemble later battle axes from the Battle Axe Culture, but with an outwards curved blade and lacking a shaft hole.

The flint axes are primarily of a kind called thick-butted axes, with outward curved blades. We should also mention another everyday object, the spoon-shaped scrapers made from flint. They are shaped in a manner that looks very much like a spoon. Another object we should note are the pendants made from shale. These are thin, up to about 10 cm long and have a hole bored through one end.

What does the pottery look like during this part of the Stone Age? Compared with earlier periods, pottery craftsmanship during this period is characterized by simple shapes and lacks ornamentation or has only simple decorations. The term 'flowerpot-like' is often used. Especially during the older part of the period, the decorations are limited to cord impressions, which in this manner and in their designs can be seen as a continuation of the late Battle Axe Culture. They are characterized by simple bead-like decorations along the mouth of the vessel.

In this context, we should not forget that metal is now beginning to come into use in Sweden. The metal came primarily from two regions: England/Ireland and Central Europe. Simple axe-blades made of copper as well as knife-blades, jewellery in the form of bracelets and rings are the most common metal objects. The influx of metals increases towards the end of the period and the transition to the Bronze Age, when we also see traces of the first local (Swedish) metal production. The finds from Pile at the outskirts of Malmö are well known, with their mixture of imported axe-blades and knife-blades from Central Europe and England/Ireland together with a smaller number of locally produced objects, mostly axes.

The site was discovered during the ploughing of a field in 1864, and the artefacts weigh almost 6 kg. The finds included axes, daggers, bracelets, rings and rods of bronze and is the oldest large discovery of metal objects in Sweden. The axes make up the largest group and the type found here is called a flanged axe. They were made from copper, with the exception of one that was made from bronze. Other objects were also made of bronze, or mixtures of bronze.

This may have been a hidden tool depot that was never dug up again, or it might have been a gift to the gods. Important to remember is that this depot can be dated to the youngest part of the Late Neolithic/transition to the Bronze Age. This is something to remember as we continue into the next section, which examines the houses and settlements during the period.

House and home

Regarding our knowledge about how houses and settlements were organised, we clearly have much more knowledge about this period compared with the previous one. From throughout Sweden, we find the characteristic longhouses and their distinctive features. This means that today, we have a significantly more detailed picture of how the people of the Stone Age lived and what their homes were like. However, it has not always been so.

The first traces of buildings identified as being houses were a number of structures found in Scania that resembled pit-houses, found at sites such as Furulund, Norrvidinge and Hagestad; however, as only smaller areas were excavated, it is difficult to formulate a more detailed picture of these. They may also be sections of a larger house. At several sites, houses with cellars and parts of the dwelling above ground have been excavated, but more about these later.

We begin with the large longhouses that appear throughout large parts of the country. The first excavations were in the Fosie IV region in Malmö between 1979 and 1983, led by Nils Björhem and Ulf Säfvestad. The longhouses from Fosie IV, which are classic today, were relatively small, with three roof-bearing posts that were also combined with regularly positioned setback roof-posts. The houses were between *c.* 13 and 17.5 metres long with a varied width between 5.8 and 6.7 metres. We can also see that the two entrances were located in the eastern part of the house, practically opposite one another. The houses are dated to the Late Neolithic, with the age for this kind of house somewhere in the period 2290–1890 BC and 2180–1780 BC The authors designated the houses as a kind of Type-house or a standardised form found in large parts of Scania (Fig. 8.2).

In addition to the above mentioned type of houses, other kinds of houses were also found at Fosie IV, for example, House 92, which had a partially dug out floor things like grindstones and stone pounding troughs were found (Fig. 8.3).

Archaeologists have also excavated Late Neolithic houses at other sites in Malmö, for example, at Svågertorp and Kv. Anten. The latter house measured *c.* 30 × 6.6–6.8 metres. However, it is quite certain that the house had been added on to and that parts of the roof-supporting structure had also been rebuilt. Together with this house, four additional longhouses of different types were excavated.

Interesting results from the site at Almhov with its long barrows, which we looked at earlier, indicate extensive settlement also from this later part of the Stone Age. All together, 38 longhouses have been excavated, which stretch in time from the Late Neolithic to the oldest part of the Bronze Age. The settlement at Almhov obviously lacks direct parallels in Scandinavia regarding the number of houses. From the archaeological excavations, we can see that the farms were scattered along a flat ridge with about 50–150 metres between them.

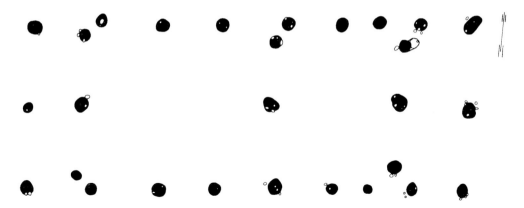

Figure 8.2. House 12 from Fosie IV in Malmö (source: Björhem and Säfvestad 1989).

Figure 8.3. Re-creation of one of the Fosie IV houses at Skånes Djurpark (Skåne's Zoo) (photograph: M. Larsson).

The size of the houses varied greatly and the longest house was about 35 metres long and between 6 and 6.5 metres wide. In other words, they were shaped slightly trapezoid. In addition to these large houses, which are among the longest found in Scania, there are also significantly smaller houses that measure only 9 metres long.

One assumes that some houses were located so close to each other that they could not have been in use at the same time, but that they had been re-built and the farms relocated a short distance away. In that they to some extent are also found in layers on top of each other, it is likely that different phases of the settlement at Almhov exist. The older phase can be dated to an earlier part of the Late Neolithic, while the larger, better-preserved houses belong to the end of this period and the beginning of the Bronze Age. Using ^{14}C-dating, one of these large houses has been dated to 1890–1680 BC

In other words, we are talking about some kind of village-like settlement at this site, at that time. This means that in many ways, we must see the late Stone Age settlements in another light. What these settlements looked like obviously varied between different areas and sites. Magnus Artursson means that considering the well-ordered, village-like settlement, the settlement at Almhov indicates a hierarchical society with the large farms belonging to the local great men.

Before we leave Scania, we should mention one additional site – Piledal, east of Ystad. At the beginning of the 1980s, a *c.* 33 metre long and 5.5 metre wide house was excavated. In addition, archaeologists have found another more fragmentary house at the site from the same period. The house had a rounded gable on the southwest side, while no gable-construction could be found on the west side. There were only a few artefacts found in the house – a characteristic arrowhead and some pottery. Based on ^{14}C-dating results, the house is dated to 1880–1760 BC, which is a late part of the period. As we can see, this type of house, called a 'Piledal house', is also found in other parts of the country, as well as at Limensgård on Bornholm.

In West Sweden, the number of houses from this period is still relatively few, but they do exist. One problem is that several of the houses are difficult to date and in general, we rely on what the houses looked like. We know of a few houses from the Halland region that are characteristic for the Late Neolithic type. One such house is from Rackabjär and was *c.* 17 metres long and 5.8 metres wide. Based on ^{14}C-dating results, the house is from the period 1885–1745 BC

From Scania and the West Coast, we will now journey northwards in order to take a closer look at what settlements in other parts of the country looked like. North of Scania, there are unfortunately too few houses to be able to form a clear picture of the layout of the settlements and how they changed over time. A longhouse from Istaby in Blekinge measuring about 30 metres strongly resembles the Piledal house mentioned above, but unfortunately, we have no definite dates for the house. It is however likely that this house is somewhat younger and should be placed in the early Bronze Age.

A few examples of Late Neolithic houses have been discovered in Östergötland. In an earlier section, we mentioned a house from the Battle Axe Culture from Kv. Paragrafen in Linköping. I wrote that this house was discovered in a layer underneath a better-preserved house from the end of the Stone Age. This house was 17 metres long and 7 metres wide, and aligned in an east-west direction. The house was nearly rectangular. Based on ^{14}C-dating results, the house is dated to 2130–1970 BC We have found additional ruins of houses in Linköping, Kv. Glasrutan, which can be dated to the Late Neolithic, but these are in such poor condition that we will not take them up here.

In connection with the extensive archaeological excavations from the beginning of the 1990s at Pryssgården in Norrköping (one of the largest excavations in the country), a large number of longhouses were discovered that span the period addressed here, *i.e.*, on through the Bronze Age and up through the Late Iron Age. The settlement is located not far from Motala Ström (River) and the well-known rock engravings at Himmelstalund. Great differences over time could for example be seen in how people dealt with their waste. During the Bronze Age, people dug large, deep pits that were gradually filled with different kinds of rubbish. We can compare this with the method used during the Iron Age for dealing with trash. No pits are dug during this period, or only very few; instead, the rubbish is left somewhere else that, based on excavations at Pryssgården we are not clear as to the location.

The oldest longhouse at Pryssgården is a house that is 32 metres long and 6 metres wide and clearly of the 'Piledal type'. Very few artefacts have been found in connection with the house and dating is thus based on ^{14}C-results, which place the house in the period 1680–1520 BC This is a late date and actually places the house in Period I of the Bronze Age, but since it points towards continuity and contact paths towards the south, I believed it was important to include it here.

North of Östergötland, the situation is worse regarding houses from the late part of the Stone Age. There are however a few, although the dating of some of these is uncertain. The most worthwhile excavations are those conducted in conjunction with the road construction on European route E4, north of Uppsala.

It is primarily the excavations at Kyrsta, a few miles north of Uppsala, that have provided us with significant information about what settlements looked like in this part of the country at the end of the Stone Age. The archaeological excavations took place during 2002, and 42 remains of houses were found. In this context, House 5 is of primary interest. House 5 was 32 metres long and 7.5 metres wide. The house was nearly rectangular and included 86 posts. There are some similarities with the houses of the 'Piledal type' mentioned above, even if the Kyrsta house is wider. One problem with the house is the determination of the age. The ^{14}C-dating analyses performed indicate a far too late age, the older Iron Age, which the appearance of the house does not support. We have not found any datable artefacts, but as I said, we rely on the house's outward appearance and consequently, the house should be dated to the Late Neolithic/older Bronze Age. We cannot come any closer than this.

It is not only from Kyrsta that we find houses of this type. Seven houses can be dated to the same period as the one at Kyrsta. However, the houses at Ryssgärdet for example are significantly smaller, 10–26 metres long. Unfortunately, we cannot reconstruct the width since the wall lines are completely lacking.

Late Neolithic dwellings – main features

As we have seen from the survey above, we generally find the same kinds of houses throughout southern and central Sweden during the last part of the Stone Age and the beginning of the Bronze Age. They do vary of course, but the similarities are striking.

We can identify the following kinds of houses:

1. pit houses
2. longhouses with dugout floors
3. longhouses with systematically placed recesses
4. long, narrow houses of the 'Piledal'-type
5. longhouses lacking systematically placed recesses.

We find some regional differences. Houses of Type 2 and 3 above are not found in Central Sweden, as far as we know. These almost seem like the houses that are most characteristic for Scania. It is also apparent that nowhere in Sweden do we find evidence that pit houses and longhouses occurred simultaneously; however, whether this indicates a chronological difference or simply a functional difference is difficult to say. What we can see however is that the houses give the impression of becoming gradually longer. Here, we can mention the very long houses found at Almhov (Malmö), Pryssgården (Norrköping) and Kyrsta (Uppsala). These houses are almost 35–36 metres long. Houses as long and from the same period, *i.e.*, *c.* 1900–1500 BC, have also been excavated in other parts of southern Scandinavia, for example on Jylland and Bornholm. These longhouses have sometimes been seen as signs of an incipient hierarchicalization of the Late Neolithic society – the emergence of a local great man elite based on large farms. We should also mention that artefacts such as axes, daggers and potsherds have been found in the postholes of several of the houses. One usually sees this as a kind of house offering meant to bring luck to those who lived there.

Regarding settlement patterns, a group of buildings based on isolated farms has been considered characteristic for almost all of southern Scandinavia; however, we should perhaps question this after what we have see in the survey above. When the classic settlements at Fosie IV (Malmö) were excavated and published at the end of the 1970s and beginning of the 1980s, the interpretation was that the farms moved around regularly within a limited area. This interpretation was the accepted one for many years and has been used for explaining Limensgård on Bornholm, St Köpinge region (Ystad) as well as in Central Sweden. Based on the large excavation at Almhov in Malmö, we can today say that at least in that part of the country we see the emergence of village-like groups of buildings, which have certainly also moved around within a limited area, but where some of the farms obviously existed at the same time. As Magnus Artursson writes, we most likely see the emergence of a few farms owned by local great men during the later part of the period and the transition to the Bronze Age. We can perhaps also see a more socially divided society, as we mentioned above. Where the basis for this change is found is something that is debated. One idea often put forth is that the people who controlled the increasingly important metal trade with copper and bronze also established the large farms. Interestingly, we find similar patterns even if we look outside of Scania, for example at Pryssgården. The oldest longhouse of the 'Piledal' type was built during the transition to the Bronze Age and then, was the only one at the site, later to be followed by several farms (Fig. 8.4).

Discoveries like the one from Pile outside of Malmö become very interesting, particularly in this context. The find can be dated to about the same time as the large farms at Almhov, and it is not located far from there. If there is a connection, it is very thought provoking.

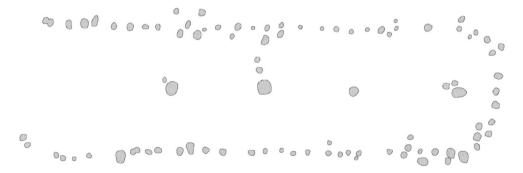

Figure 8.4. The longhouse from Piledal in Scania, which has given the name to 'Piledal' type houses (source: Larsson 1995).

Colonization phase or…?

For a long time, archaeologists have considered the Late Neolithic to be a marked time of expansion when new land areas began to be utilized and the significance of agriculture increased. These assumptions have primarily been based on two things:

- evidence from pollen diagrams
- the significant increase of stone cists in apparently new areas.

In this context, we will only be able to describe the significant elements regarding the development of the landscape, and the same is true for the changes in the economic conditions. The pollen diagrams indicate colonization in new regions such as southern Småland as well as in northern parts of Central Sweden. We see signs of clearings, even if only small, indicating an increased importance for cultivation as well as for the raising of livestock.

From the large excavations at Fosie IV in Malmö, we have a relatively large body of material indicating that people grew barley as well as bread wheat. The latter is unusual and is here interpreted as being almost a 'luxury element' in people's everyday fare. Based on the material analysed, we unfortunately cannot say anything about how the fields were constructed or how they were tended and worked.

A similar picture emerges from other parts of Sweden. The material is still much too scarce to be able to say with certainty anything regarding the extent of cultivation and the raising of livestock. From settlement sites in Central Sweden, we know that people grew various kinds of cereal grains such as barley and wheat, but as we see, the material is scanty.

Looking at finds of animal bones, we see that cattle, sheep/goats and pigs are represented at several sites in Sweden.

This assumption is supported by Kerstin Lidén's analyses of isotopes in skeletons from Närke and Östergötland. The results indicate an entirely land-based diet, probably based on a diet of meat.

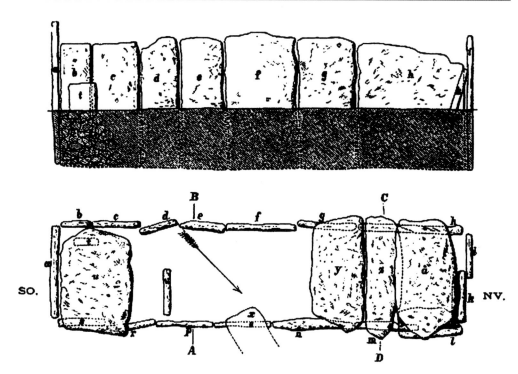

Figure 8.5. Stone cist from Västergötland.

Stone cists and earthen graves

The kinds of graves discovered from the end of the Stone Age vary greatly. Just like during the MN B, we see the return of the use of megalithic graves. One such example is the passage grave at Gillhög in Scania, where a stone cist has been constructed in the passage. Otherwise, two kinds of graves are characteristic for the period: stone cists and flat graves (earthen graves under flat ground). The burying of skeletons is most common; however, to some extent cremation also occurred. Regarding skeleton burials, we can see a strong break with the Battle Axe Culture where the dead were buried on their sides, in the Hocker-position. During the Late Neolithic, people were most often buried laid out flat on their backs (Fig. 8.5).

Stone cists, along with daggers, are probably what we primarily associate with the Late Neolithic period. We still do not know how many stone cists there are, or were, but the number preserved is estimated at about 2000. If we examine their distribution on a map, it is clear that there are two pronounced concentrations – the inner regions of Småland and Västergötland, especially the Falbygden region. Archaeologists estimate the number of stone cists in Västergötland to be about 650. This latter region is particularly interesting in that there is a large concentration of passage graves. However, the inner areas of Småland, particularly the southern parts, reveal a new picture. There are about 500 stone cists near the town of Ljungby, which is a large portion of Sweden's total number of stone cists. The northernmost known stone cists are located in Lagmansören in the region of Medelpad. This kind of grave was used during a long period, often up into the Bronze Age. There are examples that a stone cist may be the oldest grave in a Bronze Age barrow.

What is a stone cist? The majority of the cists seem to be surrounded by a mound or a flat cairn. In rare cases, they may also have a series of standing stones sporadically placed along the outer edges of the mound.

Stone cists usually have a rectangular chamber that is approximately the same width and height throughout its entire length; however, a few are more square-shaped, or wedge-shaped, where the entrance is at the narrower short side. In the older cists, there is sometimes a forum (entrance), which is then always on the outside of one of the short ends and is sometimes narrower than the chamber and sometimes the same width. In a few cases, we can see what is usually called an end-hole. In this case, two wall stones make up the short side of the stone cist, each having a half-circle shaped hole cut out, which together forms a round end-hole. Stone cists with end-holes occur in West Sweden, Närke and Östergötland, but are absent in other parts of the country. The end-hole is often interpreted as 'a spirit hole' between being alive and being dead.

It is also clear that the dead bodies in the stone cists have been moved around, but that older graves had also been cleared out. This explains why we sometimes find collections of bones outside the entrances to the stone cists.

The largest stone cist in Sweden, as well as in Scandinavia, is found at Vårgårda in Västergötland. It measures 14 × 2 metres and is located close to Södra Härene church. It was discovered when someone dug gravel from the site. The stone cist has two roof boulders, each weighing an estimated 10 tons.

Thus, what appear to be new areas are taken into use during this period, and the stone cists are good expressions of this. How do we explain the large number of stone cists in the inner parts of Småland, in Dalsland and in Värmland? Curry Heimann has discussed the stone cists in western Värmland. He has found that the cists show a large regional variation, both within and between different regions. In Värmland, it looks as though the stone cists mark where new land was taken into use and that the stone cists are not located in conjunction with agricultural land, but are placed near lakes and other watercourses. Heimann shows that Värmland had a rich and quite varied Stone Age and therefore, it would be wrong to talk about a true expansion; the conditions were already present and what we see is more like a new way of looking at the landscape.

In this context, we do not have time to discuss the stone cists in detail, so in the following, I have selected a few examples taken from different parts of the country.

We can begin our tour in Västergötland.

In 1973 in Falköping, an interesting stone cist was excavated. The stone cist was dug down into the ground and measured 5.8 metres long. It had a chamber and an antechamber, and had a vaguely trapezoid shape with a width that varied between 1.5 and 2.2 metres. The stone cist contained remains from 30 individuals who had been buried there, representing different sexes and ages. The analyses reveal that 20 of these were adults and 10 were children. As is often the case in stone cists, the finds were few, among them, a dagger, a few flint chips and amber beads. Several ^{14}C-analyses place the date at 2125–1690 BC As Eva Weiler points out,

Figure 8.6. The largest stone cist in Sweden, Vårgårda in Västergötland (photograph M. Larsson).

the grave was used over a long time. It is also interesting that some skulls show elements that indicate genetic relationships.

We will now continue on to Östergötland. In 1948, one stone cist was excavated at Svemb, near Ödeshög. It contained two rooms with a dividing wall between them. One of these had a cut out end-hole. Archaeologists found the skeletal remains of at least nineteen individuals in the stone cist, and judging from the osteological analysis, there were remains from at least eleven adult males and seven women in the grave. All but one of them had died between the ages of 30 and 60. Similarities in the shapes of their jaws and teeth indicate that these people had likely been related to one another.

In the region around Lake Mälaren, several stone cists have been excavated over the years, which has provided us with important information regarding their placement in the landscape as well as burial customs. Here we find stone cists at Dragby (Uppland), Bjurhovda (Västmanland), Annelund (Uppland), Odensala (Uppland) and Söderby (Södermanland). Their locations were not particularly monumental or prominent. They were placed on low hills and they had probably been facing towards waterways. The four that are located north of Lake Mälaren are all situated in a northwest-southeast direction, with openings towards the southeast. The stone cist in Söderby had a different orientation as it was situated in a north northeast-south southwest direction, with the opening in the southwest.

The sizes of the stone cists vary between 4.1 × 1.3 metres (Dragby) and 3 × 2 metres (Annelund). Analysable skeletal remains have only been found at Dragby and Annelund, where both bones and teeth were found. A number of ^{14}C-analyses place the five stone cists in the period 2275–1263 BC, *i.e.*, into the Bronze Age.

We will now take a closer look at the stone cist from Annelund.

The site, which is located near Enköping in Uppland, was excavated in 1987. Within the large area excavated, a significant number of structures from different prehistoric periods were discovered, but we will not deal with them here; instead, we will focus on the stone cist that was uncovered.

When the excavation began, the stone cist was completely covered by a burnt mound, *i.e.*, a mound of shattered stones and charcoal that was 0.5–0.7 metres thick and dated to the older Bronze Age. Under this, excavators found the stone cist, which was surrounded by a carefully placed cairn. The cairn measured *c.* 7 metres in diameter and was confined by a fine series of standing stones towards the south, west and north. The standing stones were made up of stones up to one metre tall. Standing stones were not found on the eastern side, and here, the cairn met up with a rock surface. The cist's capstones were partially out of place and were comprised of two, up to 1.5 metre large flat rocks. The actual cist measured *c.* 3 × 2 metres.

In the cist, archaeologists uncovered eight different layers, where layers four to eight contained skeletal remains and artefacts. It is interesting that the cist probably had a wooden ceiling that had burned, which could be determined by the signs of fire found in the first layer.

Skeletal remains were not only found in the actual cist, but also in what can be called a bone pit outside of the stone cist. The pit was *c.* 1 × 2 metres large and contained the compressed skeletal parts from about 26 individuals.

A large number of artefacts were found in the different layers of the stone cist, and among them, we should mention a flint dagger of Type III and a heart-shaped flint arrowhead. The dagger can be dated to the middle part of the Late Neolithic, which is supported by a series of ^{14}C-analyses that places the grave in the interval *c.* 2100–1400 BC, that is, into the Bronze Age.

How many people had been buried in the stone cist and what can their bones tell us about their sexes, ages and illnesses? In the bone pit, remains from about 26 individuals were found, and in the cist, remains from 42 individuals. The latter discoveries are based on teeth and remains of jawbones. Only one skeleton was found in anatomically correct condition and it was found in the upper layer. This was a man who had been about 170 cm tall. The distribution according to sex among the people buried was even, as far as could be determined, and older children and young adults were in the majority. The number of older individuals was on the other hand significantly lower. Mostly teeth have been analysed, and the examinations indicate a generally good dental health, but there were changes in the tooth enamel that reveal recurrent periods of famine. This can be compared with the examination of skeletal material from the stone cist at Dragsby, where Nils-Gustaf Gejvall saw similar changes, but in this case in the skeletons. He saw a group of stately and healthy people who every now and then were affected by periods of famine.

According to Verner Alexandersen, who conducted the examination of the material from Annelund, special morphological changes in their teeth could indicate genetic elements. We should also remember the stone cist from Svemb in Östergötland, where the teeth and the jaws also showed elements that could be hereditary.

Before we leave the stone cists behind, we should look at the previously mentioned northern stone cist at Lagmansören in the region of Medelpad. It was located on the northern riverbank along the river Indalsälven. The location is magnificent, near the mouth of the river, and can be considered very fitting for such a manifestation. Gustaf Hallström presents it as 'a North Swedish megalithic grave'. As far as we know today, the stone cist was placed under flat ground. It was small, *c.* 1.6 × 0.7 metres, and contained skeletons of a women and a child. The only grave gift was a flint scraper. The cist was situated in a northeast-southwest direction, but the southern part was already destroyed before the excavation. Interestingly, in addition to the human bones, bones (probably) from cattle and pigs as well as possibly horses and sheep/goats were found. This is interesting considering the discussion concerning places such as Bjästamon, where evidence of agriculture already exists for this period.

Cremation graves

Before our trip continues, we should discuss the use of fire in burial customs during the end of the Stone Age. We can see several examples of this in western Sweden – both from flat ground graves and from stone cists. At Årstad in central Halland, there is a cremation grave where characteristic Late Neolithic pottery has been found. The individual buried in the grave is clearly an adult, and the grave is dated to 1745–1530 BC, in other words, late in the period.

We find several examples of fire being used during burial rites in Central Sweden, for example, the stone cist at Annelund discussed above. The bones in the upper layer of the stone cist were scorched by fire, similar to some of the bones in the burnt mound. It might actually be that the use of fire in burial customs was much more common than what we realize. The bones are difficult to date and analyse, which of course makes our interpretation all the more difficult. The idea that there is continuity in burial customs from the Early Neolithic to the end of the Stone Age is not that difficult to imagine. In previous sections, we mentioned that cremation graves were common during the older parts of the Neolithic Period, at Fågelbacken and Turinge for example. As Eva Stensköld has pointed out, the houses of the dead perhaps also occurred during the Late Stone Age. She believes that the houses of the dead, or skeletonization sites, which have been identified, are likely composed of posts that probably held up a wall-less roof. In addition, pits or dugout areas can be found in trenches on the outside. In these, we usually find burnt or un-burnt bones, pottery, soot and charcoal. Stensköld identifies several such constructions, such as from Skogs-Tibble in Upland for example, where a house-like structure, 5.67 × 1.8 metres, was excavated during the 1990s. The house was comprised of eight posts that formed a rectangle. Human bones were found in four hidden graves in the house. A number of ^{14}C-analyses place the construction in the period 2900–2300 BC In her survey, Stensköld discusses several similar buildings, as well as others having other shapes and constructions. She sees the houses of the dead and the skeletonization sites as a 'no man's land' where the dead are separated from the living by posts, stones, *etc.* This is the dangerous phase, and here there are taboos and ideas about how one should behave. When the body had decayed, people returned to the site. Sometimes they burned the dead and the bones were sorted, or the individual was taken to a grave that might have been a stone cist or a flat ground grave. As Stensköld also points out, the dead were sometimes placed directly in the grave without having been previously placed in a house of the dead.

Flat ground graves

After discussing stone cists and providing some examples regarding how these could be constructed and what they could contain, it is now time to look at the other large group of graves, namely, the flat ground graves.

These kinds of graves can seem very different from one another. For example, the dead can be buried in wooden cists, some covered with stones and some not, they can be buried in stone cists or not have any visible markings at all. They often form large or small grave fields, which we will look closer at in this section. We can often also see a clear continuance of the Battle Axe Culture's grave fields, such as at Bedinge and Löderup in Scania. Today, we are familiar with this kind of grave from many parts of the country; however, very few have been found in Central Sweden. It is thus appropriate that we begin here.

Before we continue, we should mention that graves of a completely different kind also occur during this period. Sites that have been interpreted as being mass graves have been found at two places in western Östergötland. The first is from Rogslösa and was excavated in 1927 by Bengt Cnattingius. He found 18 skeletons lying on a bed of cobblestones and smaller limestone paving stones. Underneath the skeletons, a significant number of artefacts were uncovered that had clear Late Neolithic features, such as daggers. At the Svanshals Svanegård estate in 1864, several human skeletons were discovered lying in three rows on flat limestone rocks. Several Late Neolithic artefacts such as daggers and handle-hole axes were found under the skeletons.

The flat ground graves so common in southern Sweden are uncommon in the eastern part of Central Sweden; however, in connection with excavations at Borg, near Norrköping, archaeologists uncovered what is believed to be a flat ground grave. Characteristic finds of pottery support this. Excavations at Tyskeryd in Väversunda, Western Östergötland, resulted in the discovery of three flat ground graves with skeletons stretched out on their backs. In one of the graves, excavators found three skeletons that were placed head to foot. One of the teeth from one of the skeletons has been ^{14}C-dated to the Late Neolithic, 2080–1730 BC

Flat ground graves are common in South Sweden with a concentration in Scania, but recently, such graves have, for example, also been found on Öland.

In recent years, a significant number of flat ground graves have been excavated in the Malmö region, which can be connected with the extensive Late Neolithic settlements found here. The preservation conditions for bone are not always favourable, which means that our knowledge regarding the individuals buried here is not always satisfactory.

There are exceptions however, and one such example is Kv. Tannhäuser (Fosie) in Malmö. In 1966, a large grave field was excavated here. Eleven graves were examined containing thirteen individuals, which meant that two of the graves were double graves. In four of the graves, traces of wooden structures were found and it is likely that all of the graves had had some kind of wooden structure. Five of the graves had no grave gifts and when they did occur, the gifts included daggers of an early type, slate pendants, spear points and smaller piece of a dagger.

One of the double graves (A1) was covered by a large amount of stone packing measuring *c.* 6 × 3 metres. Also found in the grave was a stone hearth that has been determined to be contemporary with the grave due to the discovery of a spoon-shaped scraper and a few small pieces of pottery. The dead had been placed in the grave head to foot, and unfortunately, no skeletal parts remained except for the teeth.

The occurrence of a hearth in the grave has led Eva Stensköld to see this as a part of the actual death rite, which is perhaps a good interpretation.

Late Neolithic trends

Now that we have reached the Late Neolithic, we have also reached the end of our long journey, which has both taken us back in time as well as on a geographically long voyage. We have seen great changes in the landscape, in buildings, in settlements, in sources of livelihood and especially in people themselves. During the end of the Stone Age, changes in living conditions and new contacts created a society that had little in common with the Late Mesolithic…or did it? We can in fact see that the changes actually began already 6,500 years ago with new paths of contact and impulses that changed the hunters' society for good. What then is characteristic of the youngest part of the Stone Age?

Nils Björhem and Björn Magnusson Staaf write in a newly published synthesis of the most recent archaeological excavations in the Malmö region that:

> the open Late Neolithic landscape where forest coverage increasingly receded was likely caused by an increase in grazing, a process that continued into the older Bronze Age.

This is a probable picture for how the landscape changed, at least in South Scania, but is it true for other parts of the country? Historical studies of vegetation status in other parts of the country seem to support this pattern, but it is probably mostly true for the fertile flatlands in Scania, Halland, the Kalmar region, Västergötland, Östergötland, Närke and the Uppsala plains.

In these areas, it is clear that the landscape opens up and that this is likely due to the increase in livestock-raising, which afterwards, brings with it a clearing of the forests. It is also true that during this period, we can also see more permanent farming practices. We can also see that it is primarily in these areas that we find the large farms so characteristic of the period, with their long main buildings. The buildings give the impression of having followed different paths, and in some cases, for example at Almhov in Malmö, we can see an almost village-like concentration, while we mostly see isolated farms in other parts of the country. Even if in the case of Almhow we can talk about villages, we should assume that the isolated farm is still the primary production unit.

That the longhouse structures are now strongly established in large areas is a clear break with the previous Battle Axe Culture. However, we should remember that several of their grave fields are still being used. The Late Neolithic flat ground burial custom is also something that indicates affiliation. Here, we can see a continuation of place and a historical perspective, which indicates that people looked back even then, and that the sites of their ancestors were important. This is something that is obvious regarding the burials in the megalithic graves we find at several sites.

The stone cists also point towards both the future and the past. Certain elements of design, such as the usual rectangular chamber with its entrance chamber, can be seen as indicating the architecture of the passage graves. We can also see the stone cist as a depiction of that time's longhouse, and in this way, it could represent the individual household. The analyses of the skeletons and teeth that have been completed and which indicate genetic relationships between those buried in the cists support this idea.

There are also similarities in the collective burial customs and perhaps in the treatment of the dead as well. Here, we can point out the houses of the dead that existed during the Funnel Beaker Culture as well as during the Late Neolithic.

Regarding the material culture, significant changes take place where the replacement of the dagger with the battle axe as the male status symbol is the most conspicuous. Flint craftsmanship also reaches its apex during this period and the making of daggers seems to have been centralized, first to northern Jylland and later to East Denmark, including Scania. The flintknappers had to compete with an increase in the import of metals in the form of copper, bronze and to a lesser extent, gold. This altered the social relationships as well as interactions between people during this period. Those who controlled the metal had more power and greater influence. What we see is an increasingly hierarchical society, which is also seen in the increasingly larger farms during the youngest part of the period and the transition to the Bronze Age, *c.* 1600 BC The very large houses of the so-called 'Piledal-type' are dated to this period and have been excavated at several sites throughout the country. In most cases, these are the oldest longhouses at the sites, such as at Pryssgården in Östergötland. This first large farm is followed by several more during the following centuries of the Bronze Age.

Before our long journey comes to an end, we should return to the events in North Sweden one last time. Evert Baudou considers the changes in Norrland around 2000 BC as significant and central, mostly due to the great increase in contacts towards the east. Certainly, these contacts existed before this (Lillberget, for example), but what we now see is a completely new world of design – especially flat-knapped spearheads and arrowheads made of quartzite. A few of these have even been found in the Mälardalen Valley region. We can directly compare these with the southern Scandinavian flint designs such as the surface knapped arrowheads. A significant number of surface knapped objects made of flint also come from areas in Russia.

Evert Baudou summarizes the development and innovations in the following manner: the large semi-subterranean houses (crushed stone houses) in the inland regions were replaced by numerous small, round collections of huts. This indicates changes in group structures. The terrain near the mountains is worked more intensively, most likely for hunting reindeer and mining quartzite. Quartzite arrowheads are prestigious objects and replace some of those made from shale. Importantly, elk looses its symbolic value (though not its economic value), and is replaced by weapons (the spear).

In summary, we can say that the Late Neolithic is a very exciting period that reveals great variation in both building structures and in burial customs, but where we can still see development towards more standardised designs, both in the appearance of houses and in the material culture.

Suggested readings

Apel, J. 2001. *Daggers, knowledge and power.* Uppsala.
Artursson, M. 2009. *Bebyggelse och samhällsstruktur: södra och mellersta Skandinavien under senneolitikum och bronsålder 2300–500 f.Kr.* Göteborg.
Baudou, E. 1995. *Norrlands forntid – ett historiskt perspektiv.* Umeå.
Biwall, A., Hernek, R., Kihlstedt, B., Larsson, M. and Torstensdotter-Åhlin, I. 1997. In Stenålderns hyddor och hus i Syd- och Mellansverige. Larsson, M. and Olsson, E. (eds) *Regionalt och interregionalt. Stenåldersundersökningar i Syd- och Mellansverige.* Riksantikvarieämbetet. Arkeologiska Undersökningar Skrifter nr 23. Stockholm, 265–297.
Björhem, N. and Säfvestad, U. 1989. *Fosie IV.* Malmö: Malmömuseer.
Björhem, N. and Magnusson Staaf, B. 2006. *Långhuslandskapet: en studie av bebyggelse och samhälle från stenålder till järnålder.* Malmö: Malmö kulturmiljö.
Borna Ahlkvist, H. 2002. *Hällristarnas hem: gårdsbebyggelse och struktur i Pryssgården under bronsålder.* Lund.
Hamilton, J. Karlenby, L. and Fagerlund, D. (eds). 1995. *Arkeologi på väg: undersökningar för E18. Annelund: enhällkista och bebyggelse från senneolitikum och bronsålder: RAÄ 17 och 84, Stenvreten 8:22 och 8:3, Enköpings stad, Uppland.* Stockholm: Avd. För arkeologiska undersökningar (UV), Riksantikvarieämbetet.
Jensen, J. 2001. *Danmarks Oldtid. Stenalder 13,000–2,000 f.Kr.* Gyldendahl: Köpenhamn.
Lekberg, P. 2002. *Yxors liv, människors landskap: en studie av kulturlandskap och samhälle i Mellansveriges senneolitikum.* Uppsala.
Ryberg, E. 2004. *Hällkistornas landskap: en guide till hällkistorna i Göteryd socken.* Atremi: Mjölby.
Ryberg, E. 2005. The attractive force: gallery-graves in the landscape. In Artelius, T. and Svanberg, F. (eds) *Dealing with the Dead: Archaeological perspectives on prehistoric Scandinavian burial ritual.* Riksantikvarieämbetet. Stockholm, 187–200.
Stensköld, E. 2004. *Att berätta en senneolitisk historia: sten och metall i södra Sverige 2350–1700 f.Kr.* Stockholm.
Vandkilde, H. 1996. *From Stone to Bronze: The metalwork of the late Neolithic and earliest Bronze Age in Denmark.* Århus.

Epilogue

Mats Larsson

We have now come to the end of our long journey. Our travels have taken us from the end of the Mesolithic to the dawn of the Bronze Age, during which time metals have forever changed human's view of themselves and their surrounding world.

During the approximately 6,500 years that I have covered in this book, we have also seen how the climate, and thus the landscape have changed. The relationship between land and water influenced people's lives in many ways, for example through changes in areas of settlements and the variable availability of food from the sea. During some periods, the changes were so rapid that it is quite possible that people experienced them close up and during their own life times. How this affected people is something about which we can only speculate, but it is quite clear that they were affected.

Neither should we forget that people during this long era were not at all isolated, and that they did not lack contacts or networks. Already during the Late Mesolithic we see how foreign objects appeared in the southern parts of the country, for example in the form of axes made from unfamiliar kinds of stones. Early on, metal became a part of people's everyday lives, even if in the beginning it was only in small quantities and only in the form of axe blades or jewellery. Even in the northern parts of the country, the population established networks, which we see in the occurrence of Russian flint, copper and asbestos pottery at settlements in the far north.

The establishment of networks within Sweden is also something we have seen in the finds of flint axes from Bjurselet.

Innovations spread rapidly throughout the country, as we see with the example of agriculture. It does not take many years until the objects so characteristic for the Funnel Beaker Culture – collared flasks, battle axes, cereal grains and domestic livestock – to appear in the central parts of the country. In the same way, we see how people began building longhouses almost 6,000 years ago that were largely of the same type in many parts of the country. However, we should also remember that certain expressions, for example the building of dolmens and passage graves, do not have the same extensive distribution. We are still missing clear signs of these in Central Sweden, with the exception of Östergötland. It is obviously so that some expressions were accepted, while others were not. Why this is the case is something for which it is difficult to provide a clear-cut explanation. One suggestion is that these monuments did not ideologically or socially fit into the prevailing ideology in this part of the country.

It is also the case that certain expressions of the material culture had a strong impact. Such is the case for example with certain aspects of the Pitted Ware Culture's forms of expression, like certain pottery decorations. We can see that these are taken up in the late southern Swedish Funnel Beaker Culture, and the emergence of regional groups during the end of the MN A and beginning of the MN B can be seen as a step in the ideological and social changes that lead to what we today call the Battle Axe Culture, with its individualistic forms of expression. In many ways, this continues on through the end of the Stone Age, but we do see how the battle axe is replaced by the dagger as a symbol of the male warrior. During this period, a more stable society emerges in many parts of the country, concentrated around the large farms with their longhouses. Much evidence indicates that it is now that agriculture and the raising of livestock gain a firm hold on people, and the landscape opens up in a more permanent manner.

References

Adamsen, C. and Ebbesen, K. (eds) 1986. *Stridsøksetid i Sydskandinavien: beretning fra et symposium 28.–30.X.1985 i Vejle*. Köpenhamn: Forhistorisk arkœologisk institut.

Albrethsen, S. E. and Petersen, E. B. 1977. Excavations of a Mesolithic cemetery at Vedbæk, Denmark. *Acta Archaeologica* 47, 1–28.

Alexandersson, K. 2001. Möre i centrum: mesolitikum i sydöstra Kalmar län. In Magnusson, G. and Selling S. (eds) *Möre*. Kalmar: Kalmar läns museum, 111–128.

Almered Olsson, G. 1990. Naturvetenskap och bebyggclsehistoria. *Bebyggelsehistorisk tidskrift* 19.

Almgren, O. 1906. Uppländska stenåldersboplatser. *Fornvännen* 1, 1–19.

Ahlström, T. 2009. *Underjordiska dödsriken: humanosteologiska studier av neolitiska kollektivgravar*. Göteborg: Göteborg University.

Andréasson, P.-G. (ed.) 2006. *Geobiosfären – en introduktion*. Lund: Studentlitteratur.

Andersen, N. H. 1989. *Sarup: befæstede kultpladser fra bondestenalderen*. Jutland Archaeological Society. Aarhus: Aarhus Universitetsforlag.

Andersen, N. H. 1997. *Sarup. Vol. 1, The Sarup Enclosures: The Funnel Beaker Culture of the Sarup site including two causewayed camps compared to the contemporary settlements in the area and other European enclosures*. Aarhus: Aarhus University Press

Andersen, S. H. 1975. Ringkloster, en jysk inlandsboplads med Ertebøllekultur. *KUML* 1973/74, 11–94.

Andersen, S. H. 1979. Aggersund. En Ertebølleboplads ved Limfjorden. *KUML* 1978, 7–50.

Andersen, S. H. 1991. Norsminde. A 'Kökkenmödding' with Late Mesolithic and Early Neolithic Occupation. *Journal of Danish Archaeology* 8, 1989, 13–41.

Andersen, S. H. 1993. Björnsholm. A stratified Kökkenmödding on the Central Limfjord, North Jutland. *Journal of Danish Archaeology* 10, 1991, 59–96.

Andersen, S. H. 2001. Danske kökkenmöddinger anno 2000. In O. L. Jensen, Sörensen, S. and Hansen, K. M. (eds). *Danmarks jægerstenalder-status og perspektiver*. Hörsholm: Hörsholms Egns Museum, 21–43.

Andersen, S. H. and Johansen, E. 1992. An Early Neolithic grave at Björnsholm, North Jutland. *Journal of Danish Archaeology*, 1990, 38–58.

Andersson, A.-K. 2011. Tracing the future in the past: the introduction of the Neolithic in eastern Scania: tracking change in a local perspective. In *The Dynamics of Neolithisation in Europe: Studies in honour of Andrew Sherratt*, 353–363.

Andersson, B. 1999. *Människan i Norrland under mesolitikum: en bearbetning av tre boplatser med hjälp av sammanfogning av avslag och bruksskadeanalys*. Umeå: Umeå University

Andersson, M. 2003. *Skapa plats i landskapet. Tidig- och mellanneolitiska samhällen utmed två västskånska dalgångar*. Lund: Almqvist and Wiksell International

Andersson, M. 2004. *Making Place in the Landscape*. Riksantikvarieämbetet.

Andersson, M. and Nilsson, B. 2008. Döserygg: den skånska myllan gömde sex långdösar. *Populär arkeologi*. 2008(26), 1, 16–17.

Andersson, M. and Nilsson, B. 2009a. Döserygg och Skegriedösarna – Megalitgravarna på Söderslätt i ny belysning. *Ale* Nr 4, 1–16.

Andersson, M. 2009b (ed). *Dödens väg. E 6 och arkeologi på Söderslätt*. Riksantikvarieämbetet. UV Syd. Lund: Riksantikvarieämbetet.

Andersson, M. and Wallebom, B. 2010. *Döserygg. Grav och samlingsplats från början av yngre stenålder*. Skåne, Håslöv socken. Väg E6, Trelleborg-Vellinge. UV Syd Rapport 2010: 30. Lund: Riksantikvarieämbetet.

Apel, J., Hadevik, C. and Sundström, L. 1997. Burning down the house: the transformational use of fire and other aspects of an early Neolithic TRB site in eastern central Sweden. *Tor* 27, 5–47.

Apel, J. 2001. *Daggers, knowledge and power*. Uppsala: Uppsala University.

Artursson, M. 1995. *Bollbacken: En sen gropkeramisk boplats och ett gravfält från äldre järnålder*. RAÄ 258, Tortuna socken, Västmanland. Rapporter från Arkeologikonsult.

Artursson, M. 2005. *Byggnadstradition och bebyggelsestruktur under senneolitikum och bronsålder: västra Skåne i ett skandinaviskt perspektiv*. UV Syd, Lund: Avdelningen för arkeologiska undersökningar, Riksantikvarieämbetet.

Artursson, M. 2009. *Bebyggelse och samhällsstruktur: södra och mellersta Skandinavien under senneolitikum och bronsålder 2300–500 f. Kr.* Göteborg: Göteborg University.

Axelsson, T. 2010. *Landskap. Visuella and rumsliga relationer i Falbygdens neolitikum*. Göteborg: Göteborg University.

Bagge, A. 1938. Stenåldersboplatsen vid Fagervik i Krokeks sn, Östergötland. Ett preliminärt meddelande. *Meddelanden från Östergötlands Fornminnesförening* 1937–1938, 1–9.

Bagge A. 1951. Fagervik. *Acta Archaeologica* XXII, 57–118.

Bagge, A. and Kjellmark, K. 1939. *Stenåldersboplatserna vid Siretorp*. Stockholm: KVHAA.

Bartholin, T. S. 1978. Alvastra pile dwelling: Tree studies. The dating and the landscape. *Fornvännen* 73, 213–219.

Baudou, E. 1995. *Norrlands forntid-ett historiskt perspektiv*. Umeå: CEWE förlaget.

Becker, C. J. 1947. Mosefundne lerkar. *Aarböger for Nordisk Oldkyndighed og Historie*. Köpenhamn: Det kgl. Nordiske Oldskriftselskab.

Becker, C. J. 1954. Die mittelneolitischen Kulturen in Südskandinavien. *Acta Archaeologica* XXV, 49–150.

Bell, M. and Walker, M. J. C. 2005. *Late Quaternary Environmental Change – Physical and Human Perspectives*. London: Pearson Education Ltd.

Berggren, Å. 2007. *Till och från ett kärr: den arkeologiska undersökningen av Hindbygården*. Malmö: Malmö Kulturmiljö.

Berggren, Å. 2010. *Med kärret som källa: om begreppen offer och ritual inom arkeologin*. Lund: Lund University.

Berggren, Å. and Brink, K. 2010. För levande och döda-begravningsritual och social identitet i yngre stenålder. In Nilsson, B. and Rudebeck, E. (eds) *Arkeologiska och förhistoriska världar. Fält, erfarenheter och stenåldersplatser i sydvästra Skåne*. Malmö: Malmö Museer, Arkeologi enheten, 255–308.

Berglund, B. E. 1986. *Early agriculture in Scandinavia: research problems related to pollen-analytical studies*. Lund: Department of Geology, University of Lund.

Bergman, I. 1995. *Från Döudden till Varghalsen*. Umeå: Umeå University.

Bergsvik, K. A. 2003. Mesolithic Ethnicity: Too hard to handle? In Larsson, L., Kindgren, H., Knutson, K., Loeffler, D. and Åkerlund, A. (eds) *Mesolithic on the Move. Papers presented at the Sixth International Conference on the Mesolithic in Europe, Stockholm 2000*. Oxford: Oxbow Books, 290–301.

Biwall, A., Hernek, R., Kihlstedt, B., Larsson, M. and Torstensdotter-Åhlin, I. 1997. Stenålderns hyddor och hus i Syd- och Mellansverige. In Larsson, M. and Olsson, E. (eds) *Regionalt och interregionalt. Stenåldersundersökningar i Syd- och Mellansverige*. Riksantikvarieämbetet. Arkeologiska Undersökningar Skrifter nr. 23. Stockholm, 265–297.

Bjurling, O., Salomonsson, B., Tomner, L. and Bager, E. (eds) 1971. *Malmö stads historia. Del. 1.* Malmö: Malmö stad.

Björhem, N. and Säfvestad, U. 1989. *Fosie IV*. Malmö: Malmö museer.

Björhem, N. and Magnusson Staaf, B. 2006. *Långhuslandskapet: en studie av bebyggelse och samhälle från stenålder till järnålder*. Malmö: Malmö kulturmiljö.

Björck, N. 1998. *Fräkenrönningen- en 'by' för 5,000 år sedan*. Rapport – Länsmuseet Gävleborg 1998, 14. Gävle: Länsmuseet.

Björck, N. and Hjärtner-Holdar, E. (eds) 2008. *Mellan hav och skog. Högmossen, en stenåldersmiljö vid en skimrande strand i norra Uppland*. Volym 6. Arkeologi E4 Uppland-studier. Riksantikvarieämbetet/ UV Gal.

Bogucki, P. 1988. *Forest Farmers and Stockherders. Early Agriculture and its Consequences in North-Central Europe*. Cambridge: Cambridge University Press.

Bolin, H. and Edenmo, R. 2001. *Övre Grundsjön, Vojmsjön och Lilla Mark*. Rapport över arkeologiska undersökningar. Stockholm: Riksantikvarieämbetet.

Borna Ahlkvist, H. 2002. *Hällristarnas hem: gårdsbebyggelse och struktur i Pryssgården under bronsålder*. Lund: Riksantikvarieämbetet.

Bradley, R. 1998. *The significance of monuments: on the shaping of human experience in Neolithic and Bronze Age Europe*. London: Routledge.

Bradley, R. 2005. *Ritual and Domestic Life in Prehistoric Europe*. London: Routledge.

Brink, K. 2004. The palisade enclosure at Hyllie, SW Scania. *Journal of Nordic Archaeological Science*, 14. Stockholm, 35–43.

Brink, K. 2009. *I palissadernas tid: om stolphål och skärvor och sociala relationer under yngre mellanneolitikum*. Malmö: Malmö Museer, Arkeologienheten, Malmöfynd nr 21.

Browall, H. 1986. Alvastra pålbyggnad – social och ekonomisk bas. *Theses and Papers in North-European Archaeology* 15.

Browall, H. 2003. *Det forntida Alvastra*. Statens Historiska Museum. Stockholm: Statens Historiska Museer.

Browall, H. 2011. *Alvastra Pålbyggnad. 1909–1930 års utgrävningar*. Stockholm: KVHAA.

Burenhult, G. 1973. *En långdös vid Hindby mosse, Malmö: anl. 1, kv. Bronsyxan, Fosie sn.* Malmö: Malmö museum.

Burenhult, G. (ed.) 1997. *Remote sensing: applied techniques for the study of cultural resources and the localization, identification and documentation of sub-surface prehistoric remains in Swedish archaeology.* Vol. 1. Stockholm: Stockholm University.

Burenhult, G. and Brandt, B. (eds) 2002. *Remote sensing: applied techniques for the study of cultural resources and the localization, identification and documentation of sub-surface prehistoric remains in Swedish archaeology.* Vol. 2, Archaeological investigations, remote sensing case studies and osteo-anthropological studies. Stockholm: Stockholm University.

Carlsson, A. 1998. *Tolkande arkeologi och svensk forntidshistoria. Stenåldern.* Stockholm Studies in Archaeology 17. Stockholm.

Carlsson, A. 2001. *Tolkande arkeologi och svensk forntidshistoria. Bronsåldern (med senneolitikum och förromersk järnålder).* Stockholm Studies in Archaeology 22. Stockholm.

Carlsson, T. 2004. Neolitisk närvaro. En nästan fyndlös tidigneolitisk gård vid Bleckenstad i Ekeby socken, Östergötland. *Fornvännen* 99, 1–8.

Carlsson, T. 2007. *Mesolitiska möten: Strandvägen, en senmesolitisk boplats vid Motala ström.* Lund: Riksantikvarieämbetet.

Cederlund, C. O. 1961. Yxor av Hagebyhögatyp. *Fornvännen* 56, 65–79.

Cnattingius, B. 1934. Stenåldersgraven vid Bårstad i Rogslösa, Östergötland. In Larsen H., Odencrantz R. and Olsen, P. (eds) *Studier tillägnade Gunnar Ekholm.* Uppsala.

Cronberg, C. 2001. Husesyn. In Karsten, P. and Knarrström, B. (eds) *Tågerup specialstudier,* Skånska spår-arkeologi längs Västkustbanan. Stockholm: Riksantikvarieämbetet, 82–154.

Cullberg, C. 1963. *Megalitgraven i Rössberga: utgrävningsrapport.* Stockholm: Riksantikvarieämbetet.

Damell, D. and Nilsson, C. 1973. En östgötsk hällkista. *Tor* 1972–1973.

Davidsen, K. 1978. *The final TRB culture in Denmark: a settlement study.* Köpenhamn: Akademisk Forlag.

During, E. 1986. *The fauna of Alvastra: an osteological analysis of animal bones from a Neolithic pile dwelling.* Stockholm: Stockholm University.

Ebbesen, K. 1975. *Die jüngere Trichterbecherkultur auf den dänischen Inseln.* Köpenhamn: Attika.

Ebbesen, K. 2006. *The Battle Axe period.* Köpenhamn: Attika.

Ebbesen, K. 2007. *Danske dysser.* Köpenhamn: Attika.

Ebbesen, K. 2009. *Danske jættestuer.* Vordingborg: Attika.

Edenmo, R., Larsson, M., Nordqvist, B. and Olsson, E. 1997. Gropkeramikerna. Fanns de? In Larsson, M. and Olsson, E. (eds) *Regionalt och interregionalt. Stenåldersundersökningar i Syd- och Mellansverige.* Riksantikvarieämbetet. Arkeologiska Undersökningar Skrifter nr. 23. Stockholm, 135–213.

Edenmo, R. 2008. *Prestigeekonomi under yngre stenåldern: gåvoutbyten och regionala identiteter i den svenska båtyxekulturen.* Uppsala: Uppsala University.

Engström, T. and Thomasson, H. 1932. Nya stenåldersboplatser inom Kolmården. *KVHAA* del 37, 2–5.

Eriksen, P. and Madsen, T. 1984. Hanstedgård. A settlement site from the Funnel beaker culture. *Journal of Danish Archaeology* 3, 63–83.

Eriksson, G. 2004. Part time farmers or hard-core sealers? Västerbjers studied by means of stable isotope analysis. *Journal of Anthropological Archaeology* 23, 135–162.

Eriksson, G., Linderholm, A., Fornander, E., Kanstrup, M., Shoultz, P., Olofsson, H. and Lidén, K. 2008. Same island, different diet: Cultural evolution of food practice on Öland, Sweden, from the Mesolithic to the Roman Period. *Journal of Anthropological Archaeology* 27, 520–543.

Evans, J. A., Chenery, C. A. and Fitzpatrick, A. P. 2006. Bronze age childhood migration of individuals near Stonehenge, revealed by strontium and oxygen isotope tooth enamel analysis. *Archaeometry* 48, 309–321.

Fischer, A. 1982. Trade in danubian Shaft-hole Axes and the Introduction of Neolithic Economy. *Journal of Danish Archaeology* 1, 7–12.

Fischer, A. 2001. Food for feasting? An evaluation of explanations of the neolihisation of Denmark and southern Sweden. In Fischer, A. and Kristiansen, K. (eds) *The Neolihisation of Denmark. 150 year debate.* Sheffield: Sheffield University Press, 343–393.

Florin, S. 1948. *Kustförskjutningen och bebyggelseutvecklingen i östra Mellansverige under senkvartär tid.* Stockholm: Stockholm University.

Florin, S., Florin, M.-B. and Schiemann, E. 1958. *Vråkulturen: stenåldersboplatserna vid Mogetorp, Östra Vrå och Brokvarn.* Stockholm: Almqvist and Wiksell.

Fornander, E. 2010. *Arkeologisk undersökning av RAÄ 447 i Korsnäs, Grödinge socken, Södermanland.* Rapporter från Arkeologiska Forskningslaboratoriet nr. 15. Stockholm.

Fornander, E. 2011. *Consuming and communicating identities: dietary diversity and interaction in Middle Neolithic Sweden.* Stockholm: Stockholm University.

Forsberg, L. 1985. *Site variability and settlement patterns: an analysis of the hunter-gatherer settlement system in the Lule River Valley, 1500 BC–BC/AD.* Umeå: Umeå University.

Forssander, J.-E. 1933. *Die schwedische Bootaxtkultur und ihre kontinentaleuropäischen Voraussetzungen.* Lund: Borelius.

Fredsjö, Å.1953. *Studier i Västsveriges äldre stenålder.* Lund: Göteborg University.

Gidlöf, K., Hammarstrand-Dehnman, K. and Johansson, T. (eds) 2006. *Almhov-delområde 1.* Rapport över arkeologisk slutundersökning. Malmö: Rapport no. 39, Malmö Kulturmiljö.

Gill, A. 2003. *Stenålder i Mälardalen.* Stockholm: Stockholm University.

Greisman, A. 2009. The role of fire and human impact in Holocene forest and landscape dynamics of the bore-nemoral zone of southern Sweden – a multiproxy study of two sites in the province of Småland. *University of Kalmar, Faculty of Natural Sciences Dissertation Series* No. 62.

Greisman, A. and Gaillard, M.-J. 2009. The role of climate variability and fire in early and mid Holocene forest dynamics of southern Sweden. *Journal of Quaternary Science* 24, 593–611.

Grygiel, R. 1986. The Household Cluster as a fundamental social unit of the Lengyel Culture in the polish lowlands. *Prace i Materialy* 31, 1984.

Gurstad-Nilsson, H. 2001. En neolitisering – två förlopp: tankar kring jordbrukskulturens etablering i Kalmarsundsområdet. In Magnusson, G. and Selling, S. (eds) *Möre.* Kalmar: Kalmar läns museum, 129–164.

Gustafsson, P. and Spång, L. G. (eds) 2007. *Stenålderns stationer: arkeologi i Botniabanans spår.* Stockholm: Riksantikvarieämbetet.

Gustafsson, S. 1995. *Fosie IV. Jordbrukets förändring och utveckling från senneolitikum till yngre järnålder.* Malmö Museer Rapport nr 5. Malmö: Malmö Museer.

Göransson, H. 1987. Neolithic Man and the forest environment around Alvastra Pile Dwelling. *Theses and Papers in North-European Archaeology* 20.

Göransson, H 1995. *Alvastra pile dwelling: paleoethnobotanical studies.* Lund: Lund University Press.

Göransson, H. 2002. Alvastra pile dwelling – a 5000-year old byre? In Nordic Archaeobotany – NAG 2000 in Umeå, Viklund, K. (ed.) *Nordic Archaeobotany and Environment* 15, 67–84.

Göthberg, H., Kyhlberg, O. and Vinberg, A. (eds) *Hus och Gård.* Katalogdel. Riksantikvarieämbetet.

Göthberg, H. (ed.) 2007. *Hus och bebyggelse i Uppland: delar av förhistoriska sammanhang.* Volym 3. Arkeologi E4 Uppland-studier Riksantikvarieämbetet/UV GAL.

Götherström, A., Anderung, C., Hellborg, L., Elburg, R., Smith, C., Bradley, D. G. and Ellegren, H. 2005. Cattle domestication in the Near east was followed by hybridatioon with aurochs bulls in Europe. *Proceedings of the Royal Society series* B 272, 2345–2350.

Hackwitz, K. von. 2009. *Längs med Hjälmarens stränder och förbi: relationen mellan den gropkeramiska kulturen och båtyxekulturen.* Stockholm: Stockholm University.

Halén, O. 1994. *Sedentariness during the Stone Age of Northern Sweden: in the light of the Alträsket site, c. 5000 BC, and the Comb Ware site Lillberget, c. 3900 BC: source critical problems of representativity in archaeology.* Lund: Lund University.

Hallgren, F., Bergström, Å. and Larsson, Å. 1995. *Pärlängsberget: en kustboplats från övergången mellan senmesolitikum och tidigneolitikum*: Raä 143, Ene 4:92, Överjärna sn, Södermanland. Upplands Väsby: Arkeologikonsult.

Hallgren, F. (ed.) 1997. Skogsmossen, an early neolithic settlement site and sacrificia fen in the northern borderland of the funnel-beaker culture. *Tor* 29, 49–111.

Hallgren, F. 2004. The introduction of ceramic technology around the Baltic Sea in the 6th Millennium. In Knutsson, H. (ed.) *Coast to Coast. Arrival.* Coast to coast books no. 10. Uppsala: Uppsala University, 123–143.

Hallgren, F. 2008. *Identitet i praktik. Lokala, regionala och överregionala sociala sammanhang inom nordlig trattbägarkultur.* Uppsala: Uppsala University.

Hamilton, J., Karlenby, L. and Fagerlund, D. (eds) 1995. *Arkeologi på väg: undersökningar för E18. Annelund: en hällkista och bebyggelse från senneolitikum och bronsålder: RAÄ 17 och 84, Stenvreten 8:22 och 8:3, Enköpings stad, Uppland.* Stockholm: Avd. för arkeologiska undersökningar (UV), Riksantikvarieämbet.

Hartz, S., Lübke, H. and Terberger, T. 2007. From fish and seal to sheep and cattle: New research into the process of neolithisation in northern Germany. In Whittle, A. and Cummings, V. (eds) *Going Over. The Mesolithic–Neolithic Transition in North-West Europe.* Proceedings of the British Academy 144. Oxford: Oxford University Press, 567–594.

Heidenstam, V. von. 1915. *Svenskarna och deras hövdingar: berättelser för unga och gamla.* Stockholm: Bonnier.

Heimann, C. 2005. *Förflutna rum: landskapets neolitisering i sydvästra Värmland.* Göteborg: Göteborg University.

Hellerström, S. 2007. *Tidigneolitikum vid Dalby:* Skåne, Dalby socken, Dalby 63:105, RAÄ 56, Lunds kommun: arkeologisk förundersökning. Lund: Avdelningen för arkeologiska undersökningar, Riks-antikvarieämbet.

Hernek, R. 1989. Den spetsnackiga yxan av flinta. *Fornvännen* 83 (1988), 216–223.

Hodder, I. 1990. *The Domestication of Europe.* Cambridge: Blackwell.

Holm, L. 2006. *Stenålderskust i norr: bosättning, försörjning och kontakter i södra Norrland.* Umeå: Umeå University.

Hårdh, B. 1986. *Ceramic decoration and social organization: regional variations seen in material from south Swedish passage-graves.* Malmö: LiberFörlag/Gleerup.

Hårdh, B. 1990. *Patterns of deposition and settlement: studies on the megalithic tombs of West Scania.* Stockholm: Almqvist and Wiksell International.

Jacomet, S., Leuzinger, U. and Schibler, J. 2004. Die jungsteinzeitliche Seeufersiedlung Arbon Bleiche 3. Umwelt und *Wirtschaft. Archäologie im Thurgau* Band 12.

Janik, L. 2003. Changing paradigms: food as a metaphor for cultural identity. In Parker-Pearson, M. (ed.) *Food, Culture and Identity in the Neolithic and Early Bronze Age.* BAR 1117. Oxford: Archaeopress, 113–125.

Janzon, G. O. 1974. *Gotlands mellanneolitiska gravar.* Stockholm: Stockholm University.

Janzon, G. O. and Ahlbeck, M. 2009. *The dolmen in Alvastra.* Kungl. Vitterhets historie och antikvitets akademien. Stockholm: Kungl. *etc.*

Jennbert, K. 1984. *Den produktiva gåvan.* Acta Archaeologica Lundensia 4, 16. Lund: Lund University.

Jennbert, K. 1985. Neolithisation – A Scanian Perspective. *Journal of Danish Archaeology* 4 (1986), 196–198.

Jensen, J. 2001. *Danmarks Oldtid. Stenalder 13.000–2.000 f.Kr.* Gyldendahl. Köpenhamn: Gyldendahl.

Johansson B. O. H. 1961. Stenåldershällkistor från svensk-norska gränslandskap. *Tor* 7, 54–75.

Jones, M. and Brown, T. 2000. Agricultural origins: the evidence of modern and ancient DNA. *Holocene* 10, 769–776.

Jones, S. 1997. *An Archaeology of Ethnicity. Constructing identities in the past and present.* London: Routledge.

Jordan, P. D. and Zvelebil, M. (eds) 2009. *Ceramics before farming: the dispersal of pottery among prehistoric Eurasian hunter-gatherers.* Walnut Creek: Left Coast Press.

Juel-Jensen, H. 1994. *Flint tools and plant working. Hidden traces of stone age technology.* Aarhus: Aarhus University Press.

Karlén, W. and Kuylenstierna, J. 1996. On solar forcing of Holocene climate evidence from Scandinavia. *The Holocene* 6, 359–65.

Karsten, P. 1994. *Att kasta yxan i sjön. En studie över rituell tradition och förändring utifrån skånska neolitiska offerfynd.* Lund: Lund University.

Karsten, P. 2001. *Dansarna från Bökeberg.* Stockholm: Riksantikvarieämbetet.

Kaul, F., Nielsen, F. O. and Nielsen, P. O. 2002. Vasagård og Rispebjerg. To indhegnede bopladser fra yngre stenalder på Bronholm. *Nationalmuseets Arbejdsmark*, 119–138.

Kempfner-Jörgensen, L. and Watt, M. 1985. Settlement sites with Middle Neolithic houses at Grödby, Bornholm. *Journal of Danish Archaeology* 4, 97–101.

Kihlstedt, B. 2006. *Boplats och gravar från tidigneolitikum vid Östra Vrå, Södermanland.* UV Mitt, rapport 2007:7. Stockholm: Riksantikavrieämbetet.

Kihlstedt, B., Larsson, M. and Nordqvist, B. 1997. Neolitiserngen i Syd-Väst- och Mellansverige-social och ideologisk förändring. In Larsson, M. and Olsson, E. (eds) *Regionalt och interregionalt. Stenåldersundersökningar i Syd- och Mellansverige.* Riksantikvarieämbetet. Arkeologiska Undersökningar Skrifter nr. 23. Stockholm: Riksantikvarieämbetet, 135–213.

Klassen, L. 2004. *Jade und Kupfer. Untersuchungen zum Neolithisierungsprozess im westlichen Osteseeraum undter besonderes Berucksichtung der Kulturentwicklung Europas 5500–3500 BC.* Aarhus: Jutland Archaeological Society. Moesgårds Museum.

Knutsson, H. 1995. *Slutvandrat? Aspekter på övergången från rörlig till bofast tillvaro.* Uppsala: Uppsala University.

Knutsson, K. and Christiansson, H. (eds) 1989. *The Bjurselet settlement III: finds and features.* Vol. 1. Uppsala: Societas archaeologica Upsaliensis.

Knutsson, K. and Christiansson, H. (eds) 1989. *The Bjurselet settlement III: finds and features.* Vol. 2. Uppsala: Societas archaeologica Upsaliensis.

Knutsson, K. and Christiansson, H. (eds) 1989. *The Bjurselet settlement III: finds and features: excavation report for 1962 to 1968.* Uppsala: Societas archaeologica Upsaliensis.

Koch, E. 1998. Neolithic bog pots from Zealand, Mön, Lolland and Falster. Köpenhamn: Nordiske Fortidsminder Serie B, vol. 16.

Kraft, S. and Damell, D. (eds) 1976. *Linköpings historia. 1, Från äldsta tid till 1567.* Linköping: Linköpings Stad.

Kyhlberg, O., Göthberg, H. and Vinberg, A. (eds) 1995. *Hus and gård i det förurbana samhället 1–2.* Stockholm: Avd. för arkeologiska undersökningar, Riksantikvarieämbetet.

Lagergren-Olsson, A. 2003. En skånsk keramikhistoria. In Svensson, M. (ed.) *I det neolitiska rummet.* Riksantikvarieämbetet. Lund: Riksantikvarieämbetet, 172–212.

Lalueza-Fox, C., Rompler, H., Caramelli, D., Stauberg, C., Catalano, G., Hughes, D., Rohland, N., Pilli, E., Longo, L., Condemi, S., de la Rasilla, M., Fortea, J., Rosas, A., Stoneking, M., Schoneberg, T., Bertranpetit, J. and Hofreiter, M. 2007. A melanocortin 1 receptor allele suggests varying pigmentation among Neanderthal. *Science* 318, 1453–1455.

Larson, G. 2011. Genetics and Domestication. Important questions for new answers. *Current Anthropology* 52, S485–S495.

Larsson, L. 1982. A causewayed enclosure and a site with Valby Pottery at Stävie, Western Scania. *Meddelanden från Lunds Universitets Historiska Museum* 1981–1982, 65–114.

Larsson, L. 1983. *Ageröd V. An Atlantic bog site in Central Scania.* Acta Archaeologica Lundensia Series in 8°. No. 12.

Larsson, L. 1985. Karlsfält. A settlement from the early and late Funnel Beaker Culture in Southern Scania, Sweden. *Acta Archaeaologica* 54, 1983, 3–71.

Larsson, L. 1988. *Ett fångstsamhälle för 7000 år sedan. Boplatser och gravar i Skateholm.* Kristianstad: Signum.

Larsson, L. (ed.) 1989a. *Stridsyxekultur i Sydskandinavien: rapport från det andra nordiska symposiet om stridsyxetid i Sydskandinavien,* 31.X–2.XI 1988. Lund: Arkeologiska inst.

Larsson, L. 1989b. Boplatser, bebyggelse och bygder. Stridsyxekultur i södra Skåne. In Larsson, L. (ed.) *Stridsyxekultur i Sydskandinavien.* Lund: Lund University, 53–77.

Larsson, L. 1992. Settlement and environment during the Middle Neolithic and Late Neolithic. In Larsson, L., Callmer, J. and Stjernquist, B. (eds) *The Archaeology of the Cultural Landscape: Fieldwork and research in a south Swedish rural region.* Stockholm: Almqvist and Wiksell International, 91–159.

Larsson, L. 2000. Axes and fire: contacts with the gods. In Olausson, D. and Vandkilde, H. (eds) *Form, Function and Context. Material Culture studies in Scandinavian Archaeology.* Lund: Almqvist and Wiksell International, 93–105

Larsson, L. 2002a. Undersökningen av Jättegraven. In Larsson, L. (ed.) *Monumentala gravformer i det äldsta bondesamhället.* Lund: Lund University, 7–33.

Larsson, L. 2002b. Aspekter på Jättegraven. In Larsson, L. (ed.) *Monumentala gravformer i det äldsta bondesamhället.* Lund: Lund University, 35–46.

Larsson, L. 2004. The Mesolithic period in Southern Scandinavia: with special reference to burials and cemeteries. In Saville, A. (ed.) *Mesolithic Scotland and its neighbours: the early Holocene prehistory of Scotland, its British and Irish context, and some Northern European perspective,* 371–392.

Larsson, L. 2007a. Mistrust traditions, consider inovations? The Mesolithic-Neolithic transition in southern Scandinavia. In Whittle, A. and Cummings, V. (eds) *Going Over. The Mesolithic–Neolithic Transition in North-West Europe.* Proceedings of the British Academy 144. Oxford: Oxford University Press, 597–617.

Larsson, L. 2007b. Regional development or external influences? The Battle Axe period in Southwestern Scandinavia. In Larsson, M. and Parker-Pearson, M. (eds) *From Stonehenge to the Baltic: Living with cultural diversity in the third millennium BC.* BAR International Series 1692S. Oxford: Archaeopress, 11–16.

Larsson, L. and Broström, S.-G. 2010. Samlingsplats för tidiga bönder. *Populär arkeologi.* 2010(28), 2: 4–7

Larsson, M. 1980. An Early Neolithic grave from Malmö. *Meddelanden från Lunds Universitets Historiska Museum 1979–1980,* 23–28.

Larsson, M. 1984. *Tidigneolitikum i Sydvästskåne. Kronologi och bosättningsmönster.* Acta Archaeologica Lundensia 4, 17. Malmö.

Larsson, M. 1985. *The Early Neolithic Funnel Beaker Culture in South-West Scania, Sweden.* BAR International Series 264. Oxford: Archaeopress.

Larsson, M. 1986. Bredasten-An Early Ertebølle Site with Dwelling Structure in South Scania. *Meddelanden från Lunds universitets historiska museum* 1985–1986, 5–25.

Larsson, M. 1987. Neolithisation in Scania. A Funnel Beaker Perspective. *Journal of Danish Archaeology* 5 1986, 244–246.

Larsson, M. 1992. The Early and Middle Neolithic Funnel Beaker Culture in the Ystad Area (Southern Scania). Economic and Social Change, 3100–2300 BC. In Larsson, L., Callmer, J. and Stjernquist, B. (eds) *The Archaeology of the Cultural Landscape.* Acta Archaeologica Lundensia 4:19. Lund: Almqvist and Wiksell International, 17–91.

Larsson, M. 1994. *Sten- och järnåldershus vid Brunneby:* arkeologisk undersökning: RAÄ 42 och 128, Brunneby socken, Motala kommun, Östergötland. Linköping: Byrån för arkeologiska undersökningar, Riksantikvarieämbetet.

Larsson, M. 1995. Förhistoriska och tidigmedeltida hus i södra Sverige. In Kyhlberg, O., Göthberg, H. and Vinberg, A. (eds) 1995. *Hus and gård i det förurbana samhället 1 artiklar.* Stockholm: Avd. för arkeologiska undersökningar, Riksantikvarieämbetet.

Larsson, M. 1996. *Skedet-Tyskeryd: arkeologisk utredning: Väversunda socken, Vadstena kommun, Östergötland.* Linköping: Avd. för arkeologiska undersökningar, Riksantikvarieämbetet.

Larsson, M. 1997. Stenåldersjägare vid Siljan, en atlantisk boplats vid Leksand. *Fornvännnen* 89, 237–250.

Larsson, M. 1999. Den gropkeramiska kulturens 'mikrorum'. Kring boplatsen Åby i Östergötland. *Forskaren i Fält.* En vänbok till Kristina Lamm. Riksantikvarieämbetet. Arkeologiska Undersökningar Skrifter nr. 27. Stockholm: Riksantikvarieämbetet, 43–58.

Larsson, M. 2003. People and Sherds. The Pitted Ware Site Åby in Östergötland, Eastern Sweden. In Samuelsson, C. and Ytterberg, N. (eds) *Uniting Sea.* Uppsala: Uppsala University, 117–131.

Larsson M. 2004. Living in cultural diversity. The Pitted Ware Culture and its relatives. *JONAS, Journal of Nordic Archaeological science* 14, 61–69.

Larsson, M. 2006. *A tale of a strange people. The Pitted Ware Culture in Southern Sweden.* Kalmar-Lund: Kalmar Studies in Archaeology 2, University of Kalmar.

Larsson, M. 2007a. I was walking through the wood the other day. Man and landscape during the late Mesolithic and early Neolithic in Scania, southern Sweden. In Hårdh, B., Jennbert, K. and Olausson, D. (eds) *On the road. Studies in honour of Lars Larsson.* Stockholm: Almqvist and Wiksell International, 212–217.

Larsson, M. 2007b. The guardians and protectors of mind: ritual structures in the Middle Neolithic of Southern Sweden. In Larsson, M. and Parker-Pearson, M. (eds) *From Stonehenge to the Baltic: Living with cultural diversity in the third millennium BC.* BAR International Series 1692. Oxford: Archaeopress, 17–23.

Larsson, M. 2009. The pitted ware culture in eastern middle Sweden: material culture and human agency. In Jordan, P. D. and Zvelebil, M. (eds) *Ceramics before Farming: The dispersal of pottery among prehistoric Eurasian hunter-gatherers.* Walnut Creek: Left Coast Press, 395–419.

Larsson, M. and Rzepecki, S. 2005. Pottery, houses and graves: the early Funnel Beaker Culture in Southern Sweden and Central Poland. *Lund Archaeological Review 2002/2003,* 1–21.

Larsson, M. and Olsson, E. (eds) 1997. *Regionalt och interregionalt. Stenåldersundersökningar i Syd- och*

Mellansverige. Riksantikvarieämbetet. Arkeologiska Undersökningar. Skrifter nr 23. Stockholm: Riksantikvarieämbetet.

Larsson, Å. M. 2009. *Breaking and Making Bodies and Pots: Material and ritual practices in Sweden in the third millennium BC*. Uppsala: Uppsala University.

Larsson, Å. M. 2009. *Pots, pits and people: hunter-gatherer pottery traditions in Neolithic Sweden. Early farmers, late foragers, and ceramic traditions: on the beginning of pottery in the Near East and Europe*. Canbridge: Cambridge Scholars, 239–270.

Lass Jensen, O., Sørensen, S. A. and Møller Hansen, K. (eds) 2001. *Danmarks jægerstenalder – status og perspektiver*: beretning fra symposiet 'status og perspektiver inden for dansk mesolitikum' afholdt i Vordingborg, september 1998. Hørsholm: Hørsholm Egns Museum.

Lekberg, P. 2002. *Yxors liv, människors landskap: en studie av kulturlandskap och samhälle i Mellansveriges senneolitikum*. Uppsala: Uppsala University.

Lidén, K. 1995. *Prehistoric diet transitions: an archaeological perspective*. Stockholm: Stockholm University.

Lindahl, A. and Gejvall N.-G. 1950. Hällkistan vid Svemb i Ödeshögs socken. *Östergötlands och Linköpings stads museum*. Meddelanden 1948–1950. Linköping.

Lindahl, A and Gejvall, N.-G. 1973. *Båtyxegraven från Bergsvägen i Linköping*: En vägledning från Länsmuseet i Linköping. Linköping: Länsmuseet.

Lindeblad, K. and Nielsen, A. L. 1997. Kungens gods i Borg. *Om utgrävningarna vid Borgs säteri i Östergötland*. Riksantikvarieämbetet. Avdelningen för arkeologiska undersökningar. Rapport UV Linköping 1997:12. Linköping.

Linderholm, A. 2008. *Migration in Prehistory: DNA and stable isotope analyses of Swedish skeletal material*. Stockholm: Stockholm University.

Linderholm, A., Fornander, E., Eriksson, G., Mörth, C. M. and Lidén, K. 2010. Increasing mobility at the Neolithic/Bronze Age transition – sulphur isotope evidence from Öland, Sweden. In Elin Fornander: *Consuming and communicating identities Dietary diversity and interaction in Middle Neolithic Sweden*. PhD Thesis. Stockholm: Stockholm University.

Lindström, J. 1994. Gläntan – Dödshuset från stridsyxetid. *Sörmlandsbygden (Nyköping)* 63, 59–70.

Liversage, D. 1992. *Barkaer: long barrows and settlements*. Köpenhamn: Akademisk Forlag.

Lomborg, E. 1973. *Die Flintdolche Dänemarks: Studien über Chronologie und Kulturbeziehungen des südskandinavischen Spätneolithikums*. Köpenhamn: Det kgl. Nordiske Oldskriftselskab.

Lukes, A. and Zvelebil, M. (eds) 2004. *LBK dialogues: studies in the formation of the linear pottery culture*. BAR S-1304. Oxford: Archaeopress.

Lundberg, Å. 1997. *Vinterbyar: ett bandsamhälles territorier i Norrlands inland, 4500–2500 f. Kr.* Umeå: Umeå University.

Löfstrand, L. 1974. *Yngre stenålderns kustboplatser. Undersökningarna vid Äs och studier i den gropkeramiska kulturens kronologi och ekologi*. Uppsala: Uppsala University.

Madsen, T. 1979. Earthen Long Barrows and Timber Structures: Aspects of the Early Neolithic Mortuary Practice in Denmark. *Proceedings of the Prehistoric Society* 45, 301–320.

Madsen, T. 1982. Settlement Systems of Early Agricultural Societies in East Jutland: A regional study of change. *Journal of Anthropological Archaeology* 1, 197–236.

Madsen, T. 1986. Where did all the hunters go? *Journal of Danish Archaeology* 5, 229–237.

Madsen, T. and Jensen, H. J. 1982. Settlement and land use in the Early Neolithic Denmark. *Analecta Prehistorica Leidensia* XV, 63–87.

Madsen, T. and Petersen, J. E. 1984. Tidligneolitiske anlaeg ved Mosegården, Östjylland. Regionale og kronologiske forskele i dansk tidligneolitikum. *Kuml* 1982/1983, 61–111.

Malmer, M. P. 1962. *Jungneolithische Studien.* Lund: Gleerups/Habelt Lund/Bonn.

Malmer, M. P. 1969. *Gropkeramikboplatsen Jonstorp RÄ.* Antikvariskt Arkiv. Stockholm.

Malmer, M. P. 1975. *Stridsyxekulturen i Sverige och Norge.* Lund: Liber.

Malmer, M. P. 2002. *The Neolithic of South Sweden. FBC, GRK and STR.* Stockholm: KVHAA.

Malmström, H. 2007. *Ancient DNA as a means to investigate the European Neolithic.* Uppsala: Uppsala University.

Malmström, H., Linderholm, A., Liden, K., Storå, J., Molnar, P., Holmlund, G. Jakobsson, M. and Götherström, A. 2010. High frequency of lactose intolerance in prehistoric hunter-gatherer population in northern Europe. *BMC Evolutionary Biology* 10, DOI: 101186/1471–2148–10–89.

Malmström, H., Gilbert, M. T. P., Thomas, M. G., Brändström, M., Stora, J., Molnar, P., Andersen, P. K., Bendixen, C., Holmlund, G., Götherström, A. and Willerslev, E. 2009. Ancient DNA Reveals Lack of Continuity between Neolithic Hunter-Gatherers and Contemporary Scandinavians. *Current Biology* 19, 1758–1762.

Meurers-Balke, J. 1983. *Siggeneben-Sud. Ein Fundplatz der fruhen Trichterbecherkultur an der holsteinischen Ostseekuste.* Offa-Bücher 50. Neumünster: Karl Wachholtz.

Midgley, M. 1992. *TRB Culture. The First Farmers of the North European Plain.* Edinburgh: Edinburgh University Press.

Midgley, M. 2005. *The monumental cemeteries of prehistoric Europe.* Stroud: Tempus.

Montelius O. 1905. Östergötland under hednatiden *2. Svenska Fornminnesföreningens Tidskrift* 12, 3, 249–313.

Nerman, B. 1911. Östergötlands stenålder. *Meddelanden från Östergötlands fornminnesförening*: 1–39.

Nielsen, P.-O. 2001. *Oldtiden i Danmark. Bondestenalderen.* Copenhagen: Sesam.

Nielsen, P.-O. 1999. Limensgård and Grødbygård. Settlements with house remains from the Early, Middle and Late Neolithic on Bornholm. In Fabech, C. and Ringtved, J. (eds) *Settlement and Landscape.* Aarhus: Aarhus University Press.

Nordqvist, B. 2000. *Coastal adaptations in the Mesolithic: a study of coastal sites with organic remains from the Boreal and Atlantic periods in Western Sweden.* Göteborg: Göteborg University.

Oldeberg, A. 1952. *Studien über die schwedische Bootaxtkultur.* Stockholm: Wahlström och Widstrand.

Olsson, F. and Lemdahl, G. 2009. A continuous Holocene beetle record from the site Stavsåkra, southern Sweden: implications for the last 10,600 years of forest and land use history. *Journal of Quaternary Science* 24, 612–626.

Olsson, F., Gaillard, M.-J., Lemdahl, G., Greisman, A., Lanos, P., Marguerie, D., Marcoux, N., Skoglund, P. and Wäglind, J. 2010. A continuous record of fire covering the last 10,500 calendar years from southern Sweden. The role of climate and human activities. *Palaeogeography, Palaeoclimatology, Palaeoecology* 291, 128–141.

Papmehl-Dufay, L. 2006. *Shaping an Identity: Pitted ware pottery and potters in south-east Sweden.* Stockholm: Stockholm University.

Papmehl-Dufay, L. 2008. *Ölands äldsta grav?*: kulturlager och gravar från stenålder och järnålder: arkeologisk förundersökning, Tings Ene 1:1, Köping socken, Öland. Kalmar: Kalmar läns museum.

Papmehl-Dufay, L. 2009. *En trattbägarlokal i Resmo.* Kalmar Läns museum. Rapport 2009, 29.

Papmehl-Dufay, L. 2010a. Stenåldersgravar i Köpingsvik. In Alexandersson, K., Papmehl-Dufay, L. and Wikell, R. (eds) *Forntid längs Ostkusten* 1. Kalmar: Kalmar läns museum, 40–53.

Papmehl-Dufay, L. 2010b. Runsbäck. En trattbägarboplats på Öland. In Alexandersson, K., Papmehl-Dufay, L. and Wikell, R. (eds) *Forntid längs Ostkusten* 1. Kalmar: Kalmar läns museum, 64–81.

Persson, P. 1999. *Neolitikums början. Undersökningar kring jordbrukets introduktion i Nordeuropa.* Göteborg: Göteborg University.

Persson, P. and Sjögren, K.-G. (eds) 2001. *Falbygdens gånggrifter. [D. 1], Undersökningar 1985–1998.* Göteborg: Göteborg University.

Petersen-Vang, P. 1984. Chronological and regional variation in the Late Mesolithic. *Journal of Danish Archaeology* 3, 21–45.

Possnert, G. 1995. ^{14}C-mätaren, arkeologernas ur, moderniserad till oigenkännelighet. *Populär Arkeologi* 13(1), 20–23.

Price, T. D. (ed.) 2000. *Europe's first farmers.* Cambridge: Cambridge University Press.

Price, T. D. and Gebauer, A. B. (eds) 2005. *Smakkerup Huse a late Mesolithic coastal site in northwest Zealand, Denmark.* Aarhus: Aarhus University Press.

Price, D. T., Ambrose, S. H., Bennike, P., Heinemeier, J., Noe-Nygaard, N., Petersen, E. B., Vang Petersen, P. and Richards, M. P. 2007. New information on the Stone Age graves at Dragsholm, Denmark. *Acta Archaeologica* 78:2, 193–219.

Pruvost, M., Bellone, R., Benecke, N., Sandoval-Castellanos, E., Cieslak, M., Kuznetsova, T., Morales-Muniz, A., O'Connor, T., Reissmann, M., Hofreiter, M. and Ludwig, A. 2011. Genotypes of predomestic horses match phenotypes painted in Paleolithic works of cave art. *Proceedings of the National Academy of Sciences USA* 108, 18626–18630.

Richter, J. and Noe-Nygaard, N. 2003 A late mesolithic hunting station at Agernæs, Fyn, Denmark: differentiation and specialisation in the late Ertebølle culture-heralding introduction of agriculture? *Acta Archaeologica* 74, 1–64.

Roberts, N. 1998. *The Holocene: An environmental history.* Oxford: Blackwell.

Rowley-Conwy, P. 2004. How the west was lost: a reconsideration of agricultural origins in Britain, Ireland, and Southern Scandinavia. *Current anthropology* 45, Suppl. Aug–Oct 2004, 83–113.

Rudebeck, E. and Ödman, C. 2000. *Kristineberg. En gravplats under 4500 år.* Stadsantikvariska avdelningen: Kultur Malmö.

Rudebeck, E. 2010. I trästodernas skugga- monumentala möten I neolitiseringens tid. In Nilsson, B. and Rudebeck, E. (eds) *Arkeologiska och förhistoriska världar. Fält, erfarenheter och stenåldersplatser i sydvästra Skåne.* Malmö: Malmö Museer, Arkeologi enheten, 83–253.

Ryberg, E. 2004. *Hällkistornas landskap: en guide till hällkistorna i Göteryd socken.* Atremi: Mjölby.

Salomonsson, B. 1970. Die Värby Funde. *Acta Archaeologica* 41, 55–95.

Sandén, U., Brink, K., Högberg, A, Nilsson, L. and Skoglund, P. 2010. Fester och festande vid Hyllie. Nya tolkningar av mellanneolitiska plaster och bebyggelsemönster i Sydvästra Skåne. *Fornvännen* 105, 169–186.

Sarauw, G. and Alin, J. 1923. *Götaälvsområdets fornminnen.* Göteborg: Göteborgs Stad.

Segerberg, A. 1999. *Bälinge Mossar. Kustbor i Uppland under yngre stenåldern.* Uppsala: Uppsala University.

Sherratt, A. 1981. Plough and Pastoralism. Aspects of the secondary products revolution. In Hodder, I., Isaac, G. and Hammond, N. (eds) *Pattern of the past.* Cambridge: Cambridge University Press, 261–307.

Sjögren, K.-G. 2003. '*Mångfalldige uhrminnes grafvar': megalitgravar och samhälle i Västsverige.* Göteborg: Göteborg University.

Skaarup, J. 1975. *Stengade: ein langeländischer Wohnplatz mit Hausresten aus der fruhhneolithischen Zeit.* Rudkøbing: Langelands museum.

Skoglund, P. 2005. *Vardagens landskap: lokala perspektiv på bronsålderns materiella kultur.* Stockholm: Almquist and Wiksell International.

Stenbäck, N. 2003. *Människorna vid havet. Platser och keramik på ålandsöarna perioden 3500–2000 f Kr.* Stockholm: Stockholm University.

Stenbäck, N. (ed.) 2007. *Stenåldern I Uppland. Uppdragsarkeologi och eftertanke.* Volym 1. Arkeologi E4 Uppland-studier. Riksantikvarieämbetet/UV Gal.

Stenvall, J. 2007. *En Vråboplats i Kimstad.* UV Öst Raport 2007:45. Linköping: Riksantikvarieämbetet.

Stilborg, O. 2003. Keramikhantverket i Välabäcksdalen. In Svensson, M. (ed.) *I det neolitiska rummet.* Riksantikvarieämbctet.

Stensköld, E. 2004. *Att berätta en senneolitisk historia: sten och metall i södra Sverige 2350–1700 f. Kr.* Stockholm: Stockholm University.

Storå, J. 2001. *Reading Bones: Stone Age hunters and seals in the Baltic.* Stockholm: Stockholm University.

Strassburg, J. 2000. *Shamanic Shadows.* Stockholm: Stockholm University.

Strinnholm, A. 2000. *Bland säljägare och fårfarmare.* Uppsala: Uppsala University.

Strömberg, M. 1968. *Der Dolmen Trollasten in St. Köping, Schonen.* Lund: Gleerups/Habelt Lund/Bonn.

Strömberg, M. 1971. *Die Megalithgräber von Hagestad: zur Problematik von Grabbauten und Grabriten.* Lund/Bonn: Gleerups/Habelt Lund/Bonn.

Strömberg, M. 1975. *Studien zu einem Gräberfeld in Löderup: Jungneolithikum bis römische Kaiserzeit: Grabsitte, Kontinuität, Sozialstruktur.* Lund/Bonn: Gleerups/Habelt Lund/Bonn.

Strömberg, M. 1982. *Ingelstorp: zur Siedlungsentwicklung eines südschwedischen Dorfes.* Lund/Bonn: Gleerups/Habelt Lund/Bonn.

Strömberg, M. 1992. A Concentration of Houses from the Late Neolithic/Early Bronze Age at Hagestad. *Meddelanden från Lunds universitets historiska museum* 9, 1991–1992, 57–89..

Sugita, S. 2007a. Theory of quantitative reconstruction of vegetation. I. Pollen from large sites REVEALS regional vegetation composition. *The Holocene* 17, 229–241.

Sugita, S. 2007b. Theory of quantitative reconstruction of vegetation. II. All you need is LOVE. *The Holocene* 17, 243–257.

Sundström, L. 2003. *Det hotade kollektivet.Neolitiseringsprocessen ur ett östmellansvenskt perspektiv.* Uppsala: Uppsala University.

Svensson, M. 1986. Trattbägarboplatsen 'Hindby Mosse': aspekter på dess struktur och funktion. *Elbogen* 3, 97–125.

Svensson, M. 2002. Palisade enclosures – the second generation of enclosed sites in the Neolithic of Northern Europe. In Gibson, A. (ed.) *Behind Wooden Walls: Neolithic Enclosures in Europe.* BAR International Series 1013. Oxford: Archaeopress, 26–59.

Svensson, M. 2003. I det neolitiska rummet. *Skånska spår-arkeologi längs Västkustbanan.* Lund: Riksantikvarieämbetet.

Sörensen. S. 1995. Lollikhuse. A dwelling site under a kitchen midden. *Journal of Danish Archaeology* 11, 1992–93, 19–29.

Taffinder, J. 1998. *The Allure of the Exotic: The social use of non-local raw materials during the Stone Age in Sweden.* Uppsala: Uppsala University.

Tesch, S. 1993. *Houses, Farmsteads, and Long-term Change: A regional study of prehistoric settlements in the Köpinge area, in Scania, southern Sweden.* Uppsala: Uppsala University.

Thomas, J. 1991. *Rethinking the Neolithic.* Cambridge: Cambridge University Press.

Thomas, J. 1999. *Understanding the Neolithic.* London: Routledge.

Tilley, C. 1982. *An Assessment of the Scanian Battle-Axe Tradition: Towards a social perspective.* Lund: Scripta Minora Lund University.

Tilley, C. 1996. *Ethnography of the Neolithic. Early Prehistoric societies in Southern Scandinavia.* Cambridge: Cambridge University Press.

Troels-Smith, J. 1953. Ertebøllekultur – bondekultur: resultater af de sidste 10 aars undersøgelser i Aamosen, Vestsjælland. *Aarbøger for nordisk oldkyndighed og historie*, 5–62.

Troels-Smith, J. 1967. *The Ertebølle culture and its background*. Groningen: Wolters.

Tuominen, K., Johansson, T. and Gruber, A. 2008. *Svågertorps industriområde Delområde J and L, Bunkeflo socken i Malmö kommun Skåne län*. Malmö Kulturmiljö Enheten för Arkeologi Rapport 2008, 079.

Vandkilde, H. 1996. *From stone to bronze: the metalwork of the late Neolithic and earliest Bronze Age in Denmark*. Århus: Aarhus University Press.

Weiler, E. and Iregren, E. 1977. *Fornlämning 5, hällkista Åttagårdsområdet, Fredriksberg, Falköping, Västergötland*: arkeologisk undersökning 1973. Stockholm: Riksantikvarieämbetet.

Weiler, E. 1994. *Innovationsmiljöer i bronsålderns samhälle och idévärld: kring ny teknologi och begravningsritual i Västergötland*. Umeå: Umeå University.

Welinder, S. 1971. Överåda. A Pitted Ware Culture site in Eastern Sweden. *Meddelanden från Lunds Universitets Historiska Museum* 1969–1970, 5–98.

Welinder, S. 1975. *Prehistoric agriculture in eastern middle Sweden: a model for food production, population growth, agricultural innovations, and ecological limitations in prehistoric eastern middle Sweden 4000 BC–AD 1000*. Lund: Lund University.

Welinder, S. 1977. *The Mesolithic stone age of eastern middle Sweden*. Stockholm: Almqvist and Wiksell international.

Welinder, S. 1998. Del 1. Neolitikum-bronsålder 3900–500 f.Kr. *Det svenska jordbrukets historia*. Stockholm: Natur och Kultur.

Welinder, S. 2009. *Sveriges Historia* 13000 f.kr–600 e. Kr. Stockholm: Norstedts.

Westergaard, B. 1995. Neolitiska hus – problem och möjligheter med exempel från Halland. *Utskrift* 4 (Halmstad), 4–13.

Westergaard, B. 1998. Slottsmöllan – en västsvensk tidigneolitisk kustboplats. *In situ* (Göteborg), 27–40.

Westergaard, B. 2008. *Trattbägare i O-bygd*. UV Väst, Rapport 2008:40. Riksantikvarieänbetet.

Westergaard, B. 2009. *Klockbägare i N-bygd?*: senneolitiska hus i mellersta Halland: Halland, Skrea socken, Gödastorp 3:11, del av RAÄ 223: arkeologisk undersökning. Mölndal: UV Väst, Avdelningen för arkeologiska undersökningar, Riksantikvarieämbet.

Winge, G. 1976. *Gravfältet vid Kastanjegården*. Malmö: Malmö museum.

Wyszormirska, B. 1984. *Figurplastik och gravskick hos nord- och österuropas fångstkulturer*. Lund: Lund University.

Wyszomirska, B. and Larsson, L. (eds) 1989. *Arkeologi och religion: rapport från arkeologidagarna 16–18 januari 1989*. Lund: Arkeologiska Institute, Lund University.

Zvelebil, M. (ed.) 1986. *Hunters in transition: mesolithic societies of temperate Eurasia and their transition to farming*. Cambridge: Cambridge University Press.

Zvelebil, M., Dennell, R. and Domanska, L. (eds) 1998. *Harvesting the sea, farming the forest: the emergence of Neolithic societies in the Baltic region*. Sheffield: Sheffield Academic Press.